THE

NAKED
CONSTITUTION

THE
NAKED
CONSTITUTION

What the Founders Said and Why It Still Matters

ADAM FREEDMAN

BROADSIDE BOOKS
An Imprint of HarperCollinsPublishers
www.broadsidebooks.net

HarperCollins books may be purchased for educational, business, or sales promotional use. For information, please write: Special Markets Department, HarperCollins Publishers, 10 East 53rd Street, New York, NY 10022.

Broadside Books™ and the Broadside logo are trademarks of HarperCollins Publishers.

FIRST EDITION

Designed by William Ruoto

Library of Congress Cataloging-in-Publication Data

Freedman, Adam.
The naked Constitution : what the Founders said and why it still matters / by Adam Freedman.
      p.   cm.
ISBN 978-0-06-209463-6
1. Constitutional law—United States—Interpretation and construction. 2. Federal government—United States. 3. United States. Constitution. 10th Amendment. I. Title.
KF4550.F74   2012
342.7302'9—dc23   2012019498

12 13 14 15 16   OV/RRD   10 9 8 7 6 5 4 3 2 1

For Cecilia and Fiona

CONTENTS

THE
NAKED
CONSTITUTION

CHAPTER ONE

IS HOMEWORK CONSTITUTIONAL?

The Living Constitution vs. the Naked Constitution

Are you serious?

—Former House Speaker Nancy Pelosi

In the spring of 2004, a high school math teacher in Milwaukee named Aaron Bieniek gave his students three precalculus assignments that had to be completed over the summer vacation. Like students the world over, the kids in Bieniek's classroom moaned and groaned about having to do work over vacation. But this was America, and so it was perhaps inevitable that one of the students would declare the assignments to be downright unconstitutional.

Seventeen-year-old Peer Larson had a summer job lined up and couldn't squeeze homework into his busy schedule. He turned the assignments in late and, as a result, got a lower grade than he would have otherwise. Outraged by the reduction in grade, Peer and his father sued everyone in sight—Bieniek, the high school, the principal, the superintendent, and several others—for violating their constitutional rights. They argued that the math

assignments violated both the Fourth and Fourteenth Amendments to the Constitution. The father-son team pushed their
claim up to the Wisconsin Court of Appeals, which tossed out
the lawsuit, explaining that even under the broadest reading of
the Constitution, one could not derive a "fundamental right
to . . . homework-free summers." The court scolded the Larsons
for making a "frivolous" argument and held them liable for court
costs and attorneys' fees.

Personally, I think the court was too harsh on Peer and
his dad. Who can blame ordinary citizens like the Larsons for
trying to stretch the Constitution when America's elites have
been playing the same game for decades? It's called the "Living
Constitution"—a theory that invites judges and politicians to rewrite the Founding Fathers' words. You might think it's absurd
to say that the Constitution prohibits summer homework; but
then, is that any more absurd than saying that the Constitution
forbids the Pledge of Allegiance, or the death penalty, or voter
identification laws? Under the Living Constitution, judges have
sought to prohibit all those things.

The Living Constitution requires all sorts of policies that
are not mentioned anywhere in the constitutional text: abortion
on demand, gay marriage, school busing, and so on. Nothing,
in fact, is more common than the spectacle of courts inventing
"constitutional" rights that are not in the text, while disregarding
those that are. The real Constitution is passé; the Living Constitution reigns supreme.

Politicians may swear to uphold the Constitution, but most
of them don't seem inclined to read it. Doing so would only re-
mind them that the federal government was meant to be one of
strictly limited powers rather than the Leviathan we've ended
up with. There is virtually no aspect of our lives, no matter how

picayune, that isn't covered by some federal department, be it the Regional Fishery Management Council, the Indian Arts and Crafts Board, or the Marine Mammal Commission. Want to give a name to that creek in your backyard? Better run it past the U.S. Board on Geographic Names.

Liberals are not solely to blame for the growth of the federal machine; big-government conservatives have been willing collaborators. But with the election of Barack Obama and a strongly Democratic Congress (until 2010), the trend toward ever more centralized power went into high gear. In 2011 the federal government ran a budget deficit of about $1.3 trillion, or 8.5 percent of gross domestic product (GDP), as compared to the forty-year average of 2.8 percent. At the end of 2008, the national debt had reached an already-scandalous 40 percent of GDP. By the end of 2011, it had gone up to *67 percent* of GDP, or about $15 trillion, give or take a billion.

America's broke, but the federal government is living high on the hog. Hundreds of billions of dollars have been sucked out of the private economy and redirected to the federal government, to be doled out for purposes that are politically expedient but flatly unconstitutional. As of December 2011, the richest, fastest-growing city in the United States was Washington, DC. That city also led the nation in economic confidence. What's not to be confident about?

The 2010 health care law (the Affordable Care Act) represents the perfect storm of the Obama era, bringing together the accumulation of federal power and the degradation of individual liberty. Supporters of the law, no doubt, would argue that it fulfills the Constitution's promise to "secure the blessings of liberty to ourselves and our posterity"—it just happens to do so by threatening Americans with fines and imprisonment if they fail to buy federally approved health insurance. When asked about the constitutionality of that mandate, former House Speaker Nancy Pelosi replied with an incredulous "Are you serious?" Well, yes, actually, we are.

Where has the Supreme Court been? For the most part, rubber-stamping the excesses of big government. To be sure, each one of the nine justices knows the Constitution backward and forward; a few of them even venerate the document. But that doesn't mean they're going to get all fanatical and Tea Partyish about it. Take Justice Stephen Breyer, who has argued that the Supreme Court should be free to ignore the Constitution's literal "text" whenever a majority of justices dislike the "consequences" of adhering to it. Justice Elena Kagan, in her confirmation hearings, made it clear that she would not vote to strike down a hypothetical law requiring Americans to eat their vegetables. In June 2012, Kagan would join the Court's majority in holding that the government can force you to buy health insurance.

IN DEFENSE OF ORIGINAL MEANING

This book is an attack on the mainstream notion that the Constitution is nothing more than a decorative parchment; a nifty relic that never gets in the way of politicians' grand designs. It is also an argument in favor of *originalism*—that is, adhering to the original meaning of the Constitution—a concept derided by establishment figures such as former Justice David Souter ("simplistic," he says), University of Chicago professor David Strauss ("wrongheaded"), and, well, virtually every opinion-maker you can shake a stick at.

Notwithstanding the barbs from the chattering classes, I

aim to keep things cheerful. Our task is not an easy one, but it is relatively straightforward. The originalist approach I advocate builds on the following premises:

1. The Constitution is the law.
2. Like any law, it should be followed in both letter and spirit.
3. If a particular provision of the Constitution is not clear, we should look to the meaning that its words would have conveyed to those who ratified it, and the people they represented. In other words, the main text of the Constitution should bear the meaning it had when it was ratified in 1789; the Bill of Rights, when it was ratified in 1791; the Fourteenth Amendment, when it was ratified in 1868, and so on.

I know what you're thinking: it can't be that simple. Alas, Americans have been badgered into thinking that fidelity to the written Constitution is a sign of mental weakness. In October 2010, for example, *Newsweek*'s Andrew Romano lashed out at "constitutional fundamentalists" in the Tea Party who "seek refuge from the complexity and confusion of modern life in the comforting embrace of an authoritarian scripture." Those poor deluded Tea Partiers. They *think* they support the Constitution because it's "the supreme law of the land" (Article VI); in reality, they're just angry because they can't figure out how to use Skype.

At America's law schools, students are taught to regard the Constitution as an enigmatic puzzle accessible only to tenured faculty and enlightened judges. Entire academic careers have been built upon the proposition that the Constitution cannot possibly mean what it says. To get a sense of the bogus mystery surrounding the Constitution, just take a look at some of the titles at your local law school library: *Our Elusive Constitution*, *Our Unsettled Constitution*, *Our Unknown Constitution*, *The Invisible Constitution*, *The Dynamic Constitution*, and *The Unpredictable Constitution*.

Get a grip. We're not talking about the Dead Sea Scrolls or the Prophecies of Nostradamus. We're talking about a document of 4,300 words; 7,500 if you throw in all the amendments. The average *New Yorker* essayist is just getting warmed up at 7,500 words. The Constitution is not simple, but it's not that complicated, either. Moreover, most of the controversies in constitutional law revolve around four or five key passages of the document.

Why all the hocus-pocus? It's not because the Constitution is obscure, but rather because it is all too clear, and it stands for things that politicians, judges, and academics can't abide. It gives states the freedom to allow—or not—things like abortion and gay marriage. It provides for unfettered freedom of speech that doesn't leave room for politically correct "speech codes." It embraces robust property and contract rights that are anathema to politicians bent on regulating the private sector to within an inch of its life.

IT'S ALIVE!

In order to get around the written Constitution, judges, politicians, and academics routinely extol the virtues of a Living Constitution. The underlying theory is that the Constitution is literally capable of changing meaning over time, without the mess and inconvenience of formal amendments. Like an awkward teenager, the Living Constitution can wake up on any given morning to discover that it's sprouted some new powers or had an outbreak of new rights.

It's not a new idea. The theory has its roots in the "progressive" philosophy expounded by Woodrow Wilson in the years before he became president. Wilson criticized the Founders' checks and balances as an unnecessary drag on the efficiency of government. In his landmark speech "What Is Progress?" Wilson declared the Constitution to be a "living thing," and he urged that it be interpreted according to "the Darwinian principle." That is, the Constitution must evolve.

Two decades later, the Constitution started evolving like crazy to accommodate Franklin Roosevelt's New Deal, a rash of programs that did not fit the Founders' design. In 1934 Edward Corwin, a political scientist who served in FDR's administration, declared that "the first requirement of the Constitution of a progressive society is that it keep pace with that society." The way that the Constitution "keeps pace" with society—according to Corwin and his heirs—is not by amendment but by creative interpretation. According to this view, judges can, and should, rewrite the Constitution according to the prevailing zeitgeist. And the Founders' words? They should play "at most, a ceremonial role," according to the 2010 book *The Living Constitution* by Professor David Strauss.

Cast aside any thought of finding common ground with the Living Constitution crowd. It is impossible to make even the most rudimentary statement about the Constitution without incurring their disapproval.

Is the Constitution *law*? Experts disagree. At prestigious law schools across the United States, professors have been arguing for years about whether the Constitution is actually a binding law. In 1980 Paul Brest, then the dean of Stanford Law School,

denounced the Constitution as being of "questionable authority." The Constitution does not bind us, according to Brest and
others, because it's so infernally old. Professor Strauss neatly
summarizes this objection when he asks: "Why should we be required to follow decisions made hundreds of years ago by people
who are no longer alive?" Besides, argues Strauss, if judges stuck
to original meaning, they'd have to abandon precedents like
Roe v. Wade and *Brown v. Board of Education*—two opinions,
incidentally, written by "people who are no longer alive."

If the Constitution is so badly out of date, why not amend
it? The document contains an entire section, Article V, that lays
out the mechanisms for amending the text. Living Constitution
theorists, however, deny that formal amendments are a viable option. The Article V process is "cumbersome," argues Strauss, and
"too difficult to be a realistic means of change and adaptation."
So difficult, in fact, that the document has been successfully
amended twenty-seven times.

In the world of the Living Constitution, change comes not
by amendment, but by the brute force of federal legislation and
Supreme Court diktat. As long ago as 1978, Oxford professor
Lord Beloff marveled at the "widespread belief" in America that
the Supreme Court "is entitled to act as a continuing constitutional convention." Yale law professor Bruce Ackerman famously
described American constitutional history as a series of "constitutional moments" when one or more branches of the federal
government assert the power to change the Constitution without
amendment. For his academic achievement, Ackerman would go
on to receive the Order of Merit—from France.

But surely, even left-wing professors must agree that original meaning is a useful tool for understanding the Constitution,
right? Nope. Professor Strauss objects to originalism for the same

reason he objects to the Article V amendment process: it's just too difficult. In the first place, figuring out the original understanding of a constitutional provision is a "task of historians" that can be "brutally hard," says Strauss. And after that, there is the further task—do these labors never cease?—of "translating those understandings so that they address today's problems."

Professor Strauss is not the only academic to recoil from the hard work of originalism. Two leading Harvard scholars, Laurence Tribe and Michael Dorf, wrote that any attempt to interpret the Constitution is doomed because its words are so "malleable" that they can be twisted to support "meanings at opposite ends of virtually any legal, political, or ideological spectrum." One of their colleagues, Mark Tushnet, argues that judges should not be expected to abide by the Constitution's text because it is "opaque."

There is a particle of truth here. In some cases, it does require a little digging to get at the original meaning of a constitutional provision. But that hardly means that the truth is undiscoverable. To the contrary, an abundance of materials is freely available to anyone interested in learning what the words of the Constitution meant to the ratifying public. The Constitution did not appear out of nowhere; it grew out of institutions that Americans had been living with for generations. By 1787, written constitutions were old hat for Americans. Beginning with Virginia's first charter in 1606, Americans had been reading, writing, and debating different plans of government for two hundred years. Colonial charters, state constitutions, and various plans for united colonies or states: all of them had dealt with the same issues that confronted the delegates at Philadelphia.

As the political scientist Sydney George Fisher observed in *The Evolution of the Constitution*, "at the time the Constitution was framed, in 1787, our people had had a vast experience in constitution-making—greater and more varied . . . than any other people in the world." Much of that experience was relatively recent. In 1775 the Continental Congress had passed a resolution calling on each colony to replace its colonial government with a constitution suited for independence. That decree set off a flurry of constitution-drafting, with the result that each new state had an opportunity—at the moment of independence—to review its traditions and take a crack at framing a government.

The "delegates came to the Convention of 1787 with all this experience in their minds," according to Fisher. Thus, when they provided for things like the regulation of commerce, or a presidential veto, or Senate advice and consent, they were echoing familiar phrases in American public life. No detailed explanations were thought necessary. Behind every word of the Constitution lie nearly two centuries of experience in self-government *before* 1787. Original meaning requires us to look for that deeper historical meaning. Yes, sometimes that involves hard work and long hours, but not always.

THE FOUNDERS AND THE LIVING CONSTITUTION

To all their arguments against originalism, liberals have added one more, and it's a howler: the Founding Fathers themselves believed in a Living Constitution. Justice Breyer, for example, "argues that the Founding Fathers did want a living Constitution," according to a September 10, 2010, report by National Public Radio's legal analyst Nina Tottenberg. Such assertions are usually based on the framers' decision to keep the notes of the Philadelphia convention secret, along with James Madison's statement that neither he nor the other framers should be given "oracular" authority in construing the Constitution.

Madison wasn't arguing for a Living Constitution but establishing an important principle: constitutional law is not an exercise in trying to guess at the secret intentions of the framers. Indeed, originalists should not attempt to channel the Founding Fathers. Instead, as I've noted, originalists should seek to understand what the Constitution meant to those who ratified the document, and the people they represented. With that proposition, Madison heartily agreed. In 1796 he declared—on the floor of the House of Representatives—that when searching for the meaning of the Constitution, "we must look for it . . . in the State Conventions, which accepted and ratified [it]." That's why this school of thought is sometimes referred to as "original *public* meaning." For all I know, James Madison privately thought that the Constitution was a recipe for fruitcake. It doesn't matter; it wouldn't change the public meaning of the document one iota.

Besides, if the Founding Fathers really subscribed to the Living Constitution philosophy, why did they create a new document at all? Clearly the Founders were dissatisfied with the existing charter, the Articles of Confederation. Why didn't they simply profess their belief in a "Living Articles of Confederation" and then proceed to "interpret" the document to suit their needs?

And finally, one might expect Justice Breyer and his allies to produce *some* evidence that the Founding Fathers wanted future generations to treat their document as a sort of loose framework, without getting hung up on the text. Good luck with that one. If history teaches us anything, it is that the Founders cared deeply about every word in the Constitution.

For one thing, they spent an awfully long time producing such a short document. The delegates to the Philadelphia convention—including Ben Franklin, George Washington, and dozens of other leading citizens—gathered at Independence Hall in Philadelphia in mid-May 1787 and did not finally adjourn until four months later. These were men who did not blanch at the prospect of summer homework.

Day after day, the delegates hammered out the wording of various resolutions until the "Committee of Detail," chaired by John Rutledge of South Carolina, produced a preliminary draft—which was then subjected to weeks of further debate. In the stifling heat, the delegates summoned up the energy to fight over virtually every syllable in the draft. The word *president*, for example, was the subject of a protracted debate. Most delegates perceived *governor* to be a much stronger title than *president*, the latter term suggesting one who merely presides. Early drafts of the Constitution called for a federal "governor," but this was changed to "president" in the final draft, probably as a symbolic concession to those concerned about the degree of power granted to the chief executive. Years later, John Adams would still grumble about the inadequacy of the title, arguing that "there were presidents of fire companies and of a cricket club."

After the delegates had agreed to the basic draft of the Constitution, they appointed a five-man "Committee of Stile" to further refine the language of the document. Does any of this sound like the work of men who did not expect their exact words to carry the force of law? Did the most important men in America spend four months locked up in a hot, airless chamber (the delegates kept the windows closed to maintain secrecy) for the sake of a document that would play a mere "ceremonial" role in the law?

THE NAKED CONSTITUTION

The late constitutional scholar Raoul Berger argued that the measure of constitutional law ought to be "the Constitution itself, stripped of judicial encrustations." To which I would add: stripped of academic encrustations, too.

That is what the Naked Constitution is all about. It's what you get when you peel away the accumulated nonsense with which judges, politicians, and professors have obscured the Constitution's true meaning. As the nineteenth-century abolitionist Lysander Spooner declared, courts ought to be guided exclusively by "the naked language" of the Constitution. Had they done so, Spooner wrote in 1845, slavery would never have been allowed in the first place.

The Naked Constitution is essential to the rule of law—that is, the principle that the law represents fixed rules that can restrain the ambitions of men. If the Constitution is "alive," then its meaning is not fixed; rather, it means whatever a majority of Congress or a majority of the Supreme Court says it means.

The Living Constitution is a recipe for tyranny, whether it be the tyranny of Congress or the tyranny of five Supreme Court justices. It is ironic that adherents of the Living Constitution claim to be "progressives." There is nothing progressive about rendering legal documents meaningless. In 1799 Albert Gallatin, an important political figure of the founding era, reminded his countrymen that their liberties "are only protected by a parchment—by words. They may be destroyed whenever it shall be admitted that the strict and common sense of words may be construed away." More than ever, America needs a political system that respects—and doesn't merely pay lip service to—the "strict and common sense" of the words of the Constitution.

In the chapters that follow, I will focus on the crucial words of the Constitution, the Bill of Rights, and other key amendments. I'll explore what those words originally meant, and how they have been twisted over the years to erode individual liberties and expand government power beyond the wildest nightmares of the Founding Fathers.* In the final chapter, I argue that the best way to restore the spirit of the Naked Constitution is for the people to demand a national convention, as provided for in Article V. To keep things interactive, you'll want to leaf through the Constitution yourself to savor the framers' language firsthand. Consider that your homework assignment.

---

* A quick note on terminology. When I refer to the "framers," I mean the people who wrote the Constitution: the fifty-five delegates to the Philadelphia convention, and the authors of the various amendments. By "ratifiers," I mean all those who approved the Constitution in the state ratifying conventions as well as the state and federal politicians who approved the amendments. "Founders" and "Founding Fathers" refer generally to everyone who played a significant role in the adoption of the Constitution and Bill of Rights.

CHAPTER TWO

WE THE PEOPLE

*Was the Constitution Really Written to Protect Terrorists,
Illegal Aliens, and Chimpanzees?*

WE THE PEOPLE of the United States, in Order to form
a more perfect Union, establish Justice, insure domestic
Tranquility, provide for the common defence, promote
the general Welfare, and secure the Blessings of Liberty to
ourselves and our Posterity, do ordain and establish this
CONSTITUTION for the United States of America.

—PREAMBLE

ON OCTOBER 26, 2011, a San Diego corporation was sued for
violating the Thirteenth Amendment, which forbids slavery. The
plaintiffs alleged that the corporation had kept them in "bond-
age" for years—in some cases, decades—against their will. They
were being held in large water tanks, but that was the good part.
The plaintiffs were five killer whales—acting through People for
the Ethical Treatment of Animals (PETA)—and the defendant
was SeaWorld.

There is, to put it mildly, some confusion about exactly to
whom the Constitution applies. Under the Living Constitution,
it isn't just U.S. citizens and lawful residents who enjoy the bless-

ings of liberty, but illegal aliens, terrorists, and, evidently, large dolphins. Is there any support for these outlandish theories in the actual text of the Constitution?

Here's a clue. According to the Preamble, it is "the People" who "ordain and establish this Constitution." And the very last sentence of the Bill of Rights grants "the people" all powers not delegated to the federal or state governments. Call me literal-minded, but these passages suggest to me human beings rather than orcas. More important, they show that the concept of "the people" was an important one for the Founding Fathers' generation. The Constitution, for example, envisions that "the people" will elect their congressmen (Article I), petition the government (First Amendment), and serve in the militia (Second Amendment).

Now, let's see. Who can do things like voting and approving a new Constitution? Who retains the powers not granted to government? Citizens, of course. In a pinch, one might also include lawful permanent residents among "the people"—there is evidence to support such a reading. But even if you go that far, don't expect to be congratulated on your liberality. Unless you concede that the people include enemy combatants in Guantánamo Bay and every guy who sneaks across the border, you'll be branded as a reactionary by the Living Constitution crowd. Just ask former U.S. district court judge Paul Cassell.

WE, THE FUGITIVES

On October 27, 2002, Officer Tracey Cook drove up to a house in the Salt Lake City suburb of West Jordan, Utah, to investigate a domestic dispute. Two sisters had been arguing loudly—so loudly that the neighbors had called in a complaint.

One sister had thrown a brick at the car of the other sister's boyfriend, a man named Jorge. Officer Cook interviewed Jorge to confirm the story. Something about Jorge made her suspicious: she demanded to see his identification and, after checking with a dispatch officer, discovered that Jorge was an illegal alien who had previously been convicted of cocaine possession and deported. Moreover, there was an outstanding warrant for his arrest. Officer Cook arrested Jorge—whose full name is Jorge Esparza-Mendoza—for illegally reentering the United States.

The case of *U.S. v. Esparza-Mendoza* went to federal court, where Jorge argued that Officer Cook's request to see his identification violated his constitutional right to be free from "unreasonable searches and seizures." That's a right guaranteed by the Fourth Amendment, which states:

> The right of *the people* to be secure in their persons, houses, papers, and effects, against unreasonable searches and seizures, shall not be violated [emphasis added].

Let's assume that a mere request for identification is an "unreasonable search and seizure." Does the Fourth Amendment apply? No, because the Fourth Amendment exists for the protection of "the people," not for illegal aliens fleeing from the law. That's the conclusion that Judge Cassell reached. After a lengthy examination of the constitutional text, as well as other founding-era documents, Cassell concluded that a previously deported illegal alien felon "is not one of 'the People' the Amendment protects."

In return for his faithful reading of the original meaning of the Fourth Amendment, Judge Cassell was subjected to a blistering attack from the professional Left. Penn State law professor Victor Romero, for example, attacked Cassell in his 2005 book

Alienated for issuing a ruling that "perpetuates the stereotype of the 'illegal alien.'" It's true: Cassell did buy into the crazy notion that people who sneak into the country after having been deported are, in some sense, "illegal." Of course, given his hatred of stereotypes, Romero goes on to explain that the *Esparza-Mendoza* decision is "unsurprising" in light of Cassell's background as an Idaho native and a conservative. Heck, that sort of person is bound to rule against the Mexican guy! Romero's critique goes on for pages sprinkled with words like *antiessentialism* and *antisubordination*, yet the professor devotes not a single word to the original meaning of the Fourth Amendment.

In a similar vein, the ACLU issued a press release lambasting the judge for "inviting police to make snap judgments . . . based on appearance, ethnicity, or race"—presumably on the theory that your average cop is just waiting for any excuse to frisk the guy with the funny accent (talk about stereotypes). In reality, a person's ethnicity does not reveal whether he is a previously deported illegal alien felon, which is the only category of alien excluded from the Fourth Amendment under Cassell's decision. Not exactly the stuff of snap judgments. Moreover, as Cassell himself pointed out in his ruling, even alien felons are guaranteed due process under the Fifth and Fourteenth Amendments, which apply to all "persons" rather than "the people." But parsing the text is hard work. Much easier to pick the result you want and savage those who disagree.

THE FOUNDERS' PEEPS

The fact that Judge Cassell's decision in *Esparza-Mendoza* was even controversial speaks volumes about the fate of the Constitution under political correctness. In reaching his decision, Cassell asked exactly the right question: What did "the people" mean to those who read and ratified the Constitution and Bill of Rights?

At the time of ratification, the word *people* conveyed the concept of "citizens" and, possibly, lawful permanent residents. Consider how the word is used in the Constitution. Article I creates a House of Representatives to be chosen by "the people," the First Amendment protects the right of "the people" to assemble "and to petition the Government," and the Second Amendment guarantees the right of "the people" to bear arms. That right is not conditioned on militia service (see chapter 8), but the wording of the Second Amendment obviously assumes that the people, or a subset of the people, can be called up to serve in the state militias.

Voting, petitioning, and military service: these were the classic hallmarks of citizenship. It seems unlikely, to say the least, that it is sheer coincidence that the framers reserved these particular rights and duties to "the people" rather than using the broader terms *persons* or *inhabitants*, which appear elsewhere in the Constitution. "The People," observed Chief Justice Thomas Cooley of the Michigan Supreme Court in 1883, "must be understood to be those who, by the existing Constitution, are crowned with political rights."

The framers' use of the word *people* reflects the vocabulary of social contract theory—the concept that government involves an ongoing agreement among the governed. This is the philosophy made famous by the English philosopher John Locke, who in the seventeenth century argued that governments should be made by the "Consent of the People." The same spirit animated virtually all American political documents in the revolutionary era. The Declaration of Independence, for example, rests on the somewhat startling (to British eyes) assumption that King George's power derived from the consent of the colonists. The time had come, said the Declaration, "for one *people* to dissolve the political bands which have connected them with another" (emphasis added). The king took a different view and promptly dispatched twenty thousand troops to patch up the social contract. In any event, the Declaration reflects the Founders' vision of a "people" with the capacity to form and dissolve governments.

The Massachusetts Constitution of 1780 spells out this theory in unambiguous detail—it was written by future president John Adams, a man who was nothing if not thorough. "The body politic," declares Adams's constitution, "is formed by a voluntary association of individuals: it is a social compact, by which the whole *people* covenants with each citizen, and each citizen with the whole *people*" (emphasis added). The preamble to Pennsylvania's 1776 constitution similarly declares that government is founded on the authority of "the people" and that "the people" have the inherent right to change governments. In the same year, the Virginia Declaration of Rights refers to legislatures as "representatives of the people," by which they mean "all men with permanent common interest with, and attachment to, the community." In the early years following ratification of the Constitution, its nature as a social contract was often acknowledged. In 1793 Chief Justice John Jay described the Constitution as "a compact made by the people of the United States to govern themselves" (*Chisholm v. Georgia*).

Even in commercial law, the definition of "people" mirrored social contract theory. In 1792, a British court held that the word *people* in an insurance contract referred to "the ruling power of the country." In case you're wondering, the question arose because a shipowner was trying to collect on a policy of insurance that covered certain acts by "all kings, princes, and people of what nation, condition or quality soever." The ship in question had been attacked by a mob in Elly Harbor, Ireland. Clearly, that mob was not a king or a prince, but weren't they "people"? No, said the court, a mob does not constitute "people"; rather, "people" refers to those who collectively constitute "the supreme power" of a nation.

GIVE US YOUR TIRED, YOUR POOR . . .

By using "the people" to describe a political community, the framers did not necessarily intend to exclude *lawful* resident aliens. Evidence suggests that in early America, legal immigrants enjoyed many of the incidents of citizenship—even voting. In colonial America and the early United States some aliens actually were allowed to vote. This was the position of the Dutch and Swedes in New York, and the French Huguenots in colonial South Carolina. Even after independence, legal historians argue that there was no explicit prohibition against alien suffrage, only a common-law bias against it. It was not until the nineteenth century that aliens were systematically excluded from the franchise.

The same cannot, however, be said for illegal aliens, particularly illegal alien *felons*, like Jorge Esparza-Mendoza. The Founders had a particular aversion to immigration by alien criminals, since the colonies had been used as a dumping ground for British convicts. It is stretching the word *people* far beyond its eighteenth-century meaning to include those who would not be in the country except for a violation of federal law.

Once upon a time, the Supreme Court understood the distinction between legal and illegal immigrants. In 1904 the Court rejected an appeal by John Turner, a British anarchist who had entered the United States illegally and who fought deportation on the basis of the First Amendment. Turner argued that the immigration law excluding anarchists violated his rights under the First Amendment, which, as you'll recall, protects the right of "the people" to assemble and petition the government. In other words, Turner argued that by merely showing up at the U.S. border, anyone on the planet would be admitted to the rights of the American people, regardless of whether he had a legal right to enter the country in the first place. "We are at a loss," declared the Court with suitable bewilderment: by attempting to enter the United States illegally, Turner "does not become one of the people to whom these things [i.e., speech, assembly] are secured by the Constitution."

And again, in 1953, the Supreme Court declared that the Bill of Rights is "a futile authority" for an alien seeking admission to the United States. An alien becomes invested with constitutional rights, said the Court, only after he "*lawfully* enters and resides in this country" (emphasis added).

As late as 1976, Justice John Paul Stevens—one of the Court's leading liberals—considered it uncontroversial to state that aliens have fewer rights than citizens. In *Mathews v. Diaz*, Stevens declared that no alien—whether tourist, resident diplomat, or "illegal entrant"—can advance "even a colorable constitutional claim to share in the bounty that a conscientious sovereign makes available to its own citizens and some of its guests."

But by the time Stevens made that remark, the Living Constitution was already beginning to "evolve." The idea of limiting constitutional rights to certain classes of persons came to be seen as unfashionable, if not downright hard-hearted. Left-wing pressure groups advocated the broadest possible application of the Bill of

Rights. Rather than trying to achieve their goals through constitutional amendment, liberals simply found activist judges willing to ignore the Constitution's original meaning. In 1971, for example, the Court of Appeals for the District of Columbia declared that illegal aliens in the United States "are sheltered by the Fourth Amendment." The court offered no reasoning, no textual analysis, no explanation as to why an amendment that expressly protects "the people" should apply to illegal aliens who, by any measure, are not part of the American body politic. By 1984 the Supreme Court jumped on the bandwagon in *INS v. Lopez-Mendoza*, in which the Court assumed—again, without any analysis—that illegal aliens fall under the Fourth Amendment.

DOWN MEXICO WAY

Now that rights were being bestowed on illegal aliens within the United States, why not nonresident aliens? That was the conclusion reached by the ultraliberal Ninth Circuit Court of Appeals in *United States v. Verdugo-Urquidez*. In that case, a Mexican drug kingpin—whose only connection to the United States was that he had been shipping drugs there for years—argued that his Fourth Amendment rights had been violated by an "unreasonable search." The search in question was conducted by Mexican police (with DEA assistance) at the drug lord's house in Mexicali.

The Ninth Circuit Court of Appeals swallowed this argument, holding that the Fourth Amendment protects Verdugo-Urquidez from a search conducted *by Mexican police in Mexico*. The decision was unprecedented and, in the words of the sole dissenting judge, "startling." In reaching its conclusion, the court quoted from various founding-era documents to demonstrate that the Founding Fathers believed in certain "natural rights" with universal application. Such evidence of the framers' "intent" (as the court called it) is utterly irrelevant if the text doesn't bear it out. The framers might have believed in natural rights; they might have believed in the Tooth Fairy, for all we care. The question is: What did they say? On that issue, the Ninth Circuit briefly cited a number of cases interpreting the word *person* under the Constitution. The court then conceded that *people* is a different word from *person*, but then concluded—without any analysis—that "we do not read ['people'] as restricting the application of the fourth amendment."

The government appealed *Verdugo-Urquidez* to the Supreme Court, where the ACLU filed an amicus (friend of the court) brief urging the Court to uphold the Ninth Circuit's decision. Instead, and almost miraculously, the Court reversed. In the majority opinion, Chief Justice William Rehnquist observed—as though stumbling across some long-forgotten artifact—that "'the People' seems to have been a term of art employed in select parts of the Constitution." As we've seen, that is exactly the case: "the people" are linked by such concepts as voting, militia service, political speech, and assembly.

Although it has been blasted by liberals, the Supreme Court's decision in *Verdugo-Urquidez* does not go nearly far enough. While Rehnquist was clear that a nonresident alien is not one of "the people," his reasoning does not apply to illegal aliens who live in the United States. In fact, his decision leaves the door open for virtually every illegal immigrant to be considered one of "the people." According to Rehnquist, "the people" refers to "a class of persons who are part of a national community or who have otherwise developed sufficient connection with this country to be considered part of that community."

Beg pardon? Why not just say that "the people" are U.S. citizens and lawful permanent residents? That, at least, would be a coherent way to translate the framers' words into modern reality. Rehnquist attempted to clarify his "sufficient connection" test by stating that it favored only those who have "accepted some societal obligations," as though aliens who don't just take a penny but occasionally leave a penny magically become part of the body politic.

BORDERLINE LAW

Because illegal immigrants are, by definition, resident in the United States, *Verdugo-Urquidez* presents no obstacle to the relentless promotion of illegal immigrant rights. Even Judge Cassell's excellent analysis in *Esparza-Mendoza* reached a dead end on appeal. Although the Tenth Circuit Court of Appeals upheld Judge Cassell's order, it did so on different grounds—that Officer Cook's "search" was reasonable and, therefore, could not have violated the Fourth Amendment. The appellate court refused to endorse the original meaning of "the people."

In 2007, students in the Yale Law School legal clinic succeeded in persuading an immigration judge to toss out evidence against a group of illegal immigrants who complained of a warrantless search. The judge berated the government for its "egregious" disregard of the immigrants' constitutional rights. And even though the government had every right to deport the individuals, it opted to let them stay long enough to sue Uncle Sam for violating their rights. In fact, U.S. Immigration and Customs Enforcement (ICE) announced a policy of not deporting anyone who is engaged in a "legitimate" effort to protect their "civil rights or civil liberties." In the meantime, Yale's hometown of

New Haven, Connecticut, became the first city in the nation to issue municipal identification cards to illegal aliens so that they can enjoy local services.

THE BATTLE CONTINUES

Not all is lost in the battle over immigrant rights. In fact, the revival of the Second Amendment opens up a whole new front. In *Heller v. District of Columbia* the Supreme Court affirmed the plain meaning of the Second Amendment, that "the people" have a right to keep and bear arms (see chapter 8). In *Heller*, the plaintiffs were U.S. citizens, so there was no disagreement about whether they were part of "the people." But in the subsequent case of *United States v. Portillo-Munoz*, an undocumented Mexican resident challenged the constitutionality of a federal law that forbids illegal immigrants from having guns. Relying largely on *Verdugo-Urquidez*, the Fifth Circuit Court of Appeals held that the phrase "the people" in the Second Amendment does not include illegal immigrants. Judge James Dennis, a Clinton appointee, dissented, making the predictable argument that under *Verdugo-Urquidez*, the plaintiff satisfied the "sufficient connection" test because he had held a job for six months, paid rent, and had a girlfriend. Under Judge Dennis's standard, if you ever had a pen pal in a foreign land, he is probably one of "the people," too.

FRENEMY COMBATANTS

Illegal immigrants are no longer the most sought-after beneficiaries of the Living Constitution. That honor goes to foreign terrorists. Ever since the September 11 attacks, the goal of every fashionable lawyer in New York and D.C. has been to represent a Guantánamo Bay detainee. As the *Wall Street Journal*'s Bill McGurn noted in a December 16, 2008, column, "Every lawyer wants his own detainee." It's the ultimate radical chic accessory. The elite lawyers who flocked to the defense of terrorists even have an informal club: the "Guantánamo Bay Bar Association."

They don't defend terrorists for the money, of course; it's all done strictly pro bono—short for *pro bono publico*, "for the public good." And for the sake of the public good, these spirited lawyers have asserted every constitutional right under the sun. Everybody deserves to have a lawyer, I know, but I'd hate to see what these guys do for the public *bad*.

Until the Gitmo Bar Association took an interest in the matter, the Supreme Court had never held that enemy combatants possessed *any* constitutional rights, unless they were detained on U.S. soil. And even on U.S. soil, presumed enemies of the United States had never been granted the full rights of U.S. citizens. In 1798—just seven years after the Bill of Rights was ratified—Congress passed the Alien Enemies Act, which empowered the president to deport any alien whom he suspects to be involved in any machinations against the United States. Yes, that law was part of President Adams's notorious Alien and Sedition Acts, but it wasn't the controversial part. In fact, although Adams's successor, Thomas Jefferson, set out to repeal the bits about sedition (libel), he did not seek repeal of the Alien Enemies Act. Nor did any later president; in fact, the law survives to this day. Under the current U.S. Code, citizens of hostile nations are "liable to be apprehended, restrained, secured, and removed as alien enemies" at the president's command, anytime, and without due process. If enemy aliens were covered by the Fifth Amendment, this law would be unthinkable. I don't mean to suggest that it is invariably good policy for the president to round up potentially hostile foreigners every time there's a war. But it isn't unconstitutional.

When it comes to enemy combatants *outside* the United States, the law was well settled before September 11, 2001. In 1950, the Supreme Court held that a group of German World War II POWs, captured and held outside the United States, had no constitutional right to file a habeas corpus motion (which puts the burden on the government to justify the detention). Among other things, the POWs argued that the Fifth Amendment's guarantee of due process applies to all "persons," and therefore it must apply to them, bringing with it the related right to habeas corpus. The problem with that interpretation, as the Supreme Court immediately recognized, is that it gives enemy combatants a decided advantage over American soldiers. That's because the Fifth Amendment, by its own terms, does not fully apply to U.S. soldiers serving in "time of War or public danger." In other words, as the Court explained, "American citizens conscripted into the military service are . . . stripped of their Fifth Amendment rights." But there's no equivalent exemption for enemy soldiers. The only rational explanation, as the Supreme Court concluded, is that nobody reading the Fifth Amendment in 1791 would have interpreted the term "any person" to include "those in arms against us" (*Johnson v. Eisentrager*).

For sixty years, the Supreme Court stood by its decision in *Eisentrager*. How could the Constitution be read to give enemy fighters the full panoply of due process rights while denying the same rights to American soldiers? Indeed, the *Eisentrager* Court noted that if POWs could haul the U.S. government into court on habeas corpus motions, they could also sue Uncle Sam for any other alleged violation of constitutional rights. The resulting litigation would, the Court said, "bring aid and comfort to the enemy." Those words were chosen deliberately: they come from the Constitution's definition of treason (Article III, Section 3).

A single Washington law firm, Wilmer Hale, devoted over 35,000 hours of attorney time to helping enemy fighters get around *Eisentrager*. In round figures, that's about $17 million worth of aid and comfort. The lawyers finally succeeded with the Supreme Court's 2008 decision in *Boumediene v. Bush*. In *Boumediene*, the Court held that enemy combatants held overseas—at Guantánamo Bay—enjoy exactly the same habeas corpus rights as U.S. citizens under Article I, Section 9. As Justice Antonin Scalia stated in his scathing dissent, the majority's opinion in *Boumediene* "warps our Constitution" and "will almost certainly cause more Americans to be killed."

The majority in *Boumediene* said that its decision would apply "only" to the extraterritorial reach of habeas corpus. Enemy combatants would not be afforded any other constitutional rights. Never. Promise. Somehow, the Guantánamo Bay Bar Association missed that part of the ruling. Within months, a group of four Guantánamo detainees were in federal court arguing that *Boumediene* had effectively overturned *Eisentrager* and *Verdugo-Urquidez*, meaning that nonresident aliens can be "people" and "persons" under the Constitution. Why not? If a Mexican drug lord can be part of the people, why not Islamic extremists bent on killing Americans? If killer whales, why not plain old killers? Fortunately, the detainees lost against the Obama administration, which found itself suddenly enthusiastic about *Eisentrager*, *Verdugo-Urquidez*, and all the other precedents that the Left detests.

But the Gitmo lawyers are nothing if not persistent. In 2011 they were busy trying to win freedom for Osama Bin Laden's former propaganda director, Ali Hamza al-Bahlul, who is serving a life sentence for his role in producing terrorist recruiting videos for al-Qaeda. Supported by a bevy of pro bono lawyers, al-Bahlul, a Yemeni citizen, argued that the videos that he produced while working *for* al-Qaeda *in* Afghanistan were protected by the First Amendment. This is tantamount to a foreign spy arguing that the reports he makes to his home government are "free speech." That argument was shot down by the Military Commission Review Court, which again cited *Eisentrager* and *Verdugo-Urquidez*.

YASSER, THAT'S MY (AMERICAN) BABY

A handful of enemy combatants are actually U.S. citizens. Take Yasser Esam Hamdi, a Saudi who was captured while fighting for the Taliban against U.S. forces in Afghanistan. It turned out that Hamdi had a claim to U.S. citizenship, which allowed him to mount a serious challenge to his detention—serious enough to go all the way to the Supreme Court.

Why did Hamdi have a claim to citizenship? Because he had been born in Louisiana while his parents (both Saudi citizens) were temporarily living there, due to his father's work. The family returned to Saudi Arabia when Yasser was a toddler, after which he lost all connection to the United States—until he decided to wage war against her. Under the doctrine of "birthright citizenship," however, that brief sojourn in the United States was enough to make Hamdi an automatic citizen. The doctrine works equally well for the millions of children born to illegal immigrants.

Birthright citizenship is supposedly based on the Fourteenth Amendment, which states that "all persons born or naturalized in the United States, and *subject to the jurisdiction thereof,* are citizens of the United States" (emphasis added). Notice the words in italics: "subject to the jurisdiction thereof." Those words have been edited out of the Living version of the Fourteenth Amendment, so that what remains is "all persons born . . . in the United States . . . are citizens."

But if the framers of the Fourteenth Amendment simply meant to say that birth was sufficient to confer citizenship, why would they add those extra words? As it happens, Senator Jacob Howard of Michigan—the original author of the clause—answered that question on the floor of Congress. He said that the bit about jurisdiction was meant to exclude "persons born in the United States who are foreigners, aliens, who belong to families of ambassadors or foreign ministers." Howard went on to explain that "jurisdiction" meant "full and complete jurisdiction," such as the United States enjoys over its current citizens. Other senators chimed in with agreement.

The opinion of Senator Howard and his colleagues was no secret. The post–Civil War amendments to the Constitution (the Thirteenth, Fourteenth, and Fifteenth) were the top stories of the day. As one of the chief sponsors of the Fourteenth Amendment, Howard's speeches were "extensively" reported in newspapers and magazines, as Justice Clarence Thomas pointed out (in a different context) in his concurring opinion in *McDonald v. Chicago*. The men who went on to ratify those amendments in the states would have been well aware of Senator Howard's interpretation of the jurisdiction clause; that *was* the original meaning of the clause. In 1873, just five years after ratification of the amendment, the U.S. Attorney General issued a legal opinion affirming that the word *jurisdiction* meant "absolute and complete jurisdiction" so as to exclude aliens, even aliens born on American soil.

The birthright clause, then, requires more than physical

presence in the United States; the requirement of "absolute" jurisdiction excludes any children who might owe allegiance to another sovereign, such as "children of subjects of any foreign government," as the Supreme Court explained in 1884. In fact, the requirement of political allegiance was so important that the Court originally held that the children of American Indians do not qualify for automatic citizenship because they owe "immediate allegiance" to their tribe, not the United States. In the words of John Eastman, dean of the Chapman University Law School, "The notion that the framers of the Fourteenth Amendment, when seeking to guarantee the right of citizenship to the former slaves, also sought to guarantee citizenship to the children of enemies of the United States who were in our territory illegally, is simply too absurd to be a credible interpretation of the Citizenship Clause."

In a bizarre twist, the jurisdictional requirement—so crucial to the framers of the amendment—was abruptly jettisoned in 1898. This came about in the case of *United States v. Wong Kim Ark*, decided by the same august Supreme Court that two years earlier had blessed the "separate but equal" doctrine in *Plessy v. Ferguson*. In *Wong Kim Ark*, the Court held that the Fourteenth Amendment guaranteed citizenship to any child born in the United States of foreign parents, so long as the parents have a "permanent" residence in the United States. The Court allowed only a narrow exception to that rule for the children of foreign diplomats.

The legacy of *Wong Kim Ark* is a federal immigration law that makes no distinction between the children of legal and illegal immigrants—they all get automatic citizenship. In effect, the United States is "encouraging foreigners to come to the United States solely to enable them to confer U.S. citizenship on their future children," according to Richard Posner, a federal appellate judge. Of the 5 million children living with their illegal immigrant parents in 2008, 79 percent were born in America, according to the Pew Hispanic Center. Pew estimates that 340,000 of the 4.3 million babies born in the United States in 2008 were the offspring of unauthorized immigrants. There is a "huge and growing industry in Asia that arranges tourist visas for pregnant women so they can fly to the United States and give birth to an American," according to a 2002 article in the *Washington Times*, citing immigration expert Craig Nelson.

If all of this were merely the consequence of a faithful reading of the Fourteenth Amendment, the only solution would be to amend the amendment. But as we've seen, the birthright citizenship doctrine is not remotely faithful to the original meaning. Not even *Wong Kim Ark*, which mangled the amendment, requires citizenship for the children of illegal aliens, since the parents in that case were legal residents. America's anchor babies are the result of a flawed reading of a flawed precedent.

In 2011 Senators Rand Paul and Richard Vitter proposed a constitutional amendment that would limit birthright citizenship to those who have at least one parent who is either in the United States legally or is an active member of the armed forces. When Republicans in Congress began floating this proposal the year before, Democratic Senate majority leader Harry Reid declared, "They've either taken leave of their senses or their principles." Granted, Reid is something of an authority on abandoning principles: in 1993, the Nevada Democrat introduced his own bill to limit birthright citizenship to those children born to mothers who are themselves citizens or lawful permanent residents. Reid's stated purpose was "to curb criminal activity, to defend against acts of international terrorism, to protect American workers from

unfair labor competition, and to relieve pressure on public services."

The birthright clause needs to be fixed. It is not entirely clear
that it has to be done by constitutional amendment, since the
Fourteenth Amendment itself empowers Congress to pass "appropriate legislation" to enforce its provisions. Reid's proposal,
for example, was an ordinary statute. But for the avoidance of
doubt, the Paul/Vitter approach of an amendment is the better
route. That's why I include their idea among the proposals that
an Article V convention should consider (see chapter 12).

When Yasser Hamdi's case reached the Supreme Court in
2004, Justice Scalia referred to him as not a citizen but "a presumed American citizen," underscoring the dubious merit of his
birthright claim. Nonetheless, using that presumed citizenship as
his basis, Scalia argued that Hamdi could not be held indefinitely
without charges, unless Congress suspends habeas corpus (Article
I, Section 9), which it had not done. Membership has its privileges: an American citizen is entitled to know on what charges
he or she is being held. If somebody like Hamdi insists on being
deemed a U.S. citizen, then the charge ought to be treason, for
which the traditional punishment is death (see chapter 10).

But Scalia's opinion in *Hamdi* was a dissenting one. The
majority of the Court held that an American citizen held on U.S.
soil—Hamdi had been transferred to a brig in Virginia—had no
right to habeas corpus. (For more on *Hamdi*, see chapter 4.) Although that was a terrible decision, it was soon supplanted by an
even worse one. In 2008 the Supreme Court went to the opposite
extreme, holding in *Boumediene* that *non*citizens held *outside* the
United States enjoy the very rights that Yasser Hamdi had been
denied just four years earlier. Say what you like about the Living
Constitution, it keeps things interesting.

"DRED SCOTT REPUBLICANS"

The liberal rejoinder to all this talk about birthright citizenship is to accuse Republicans of trying to revive the Supreme Court's most infamous decision: *Dred Scott v. Sandford* (1857), which held that only whites could be citizens. The phrase "Dred Scott Republicans"—common in the blogosphere circa 2010—is the intellectual and rhetorical equivalent of comparing one's opponent to Adolf Hitler. Still, it's worth taking a look at *Dred Scott* to show not only why the liberal argument is nonsense, but also why *Dred Scott* was not an originalist decision.

Here's what happened. A slave named Dred Scott sued his owner, John Sandford, to gain his freedom. The lawsuit was based on the fact that Scott's previous owner, an army physician, had taken him to live in Illinois and in the territory of Upper Louisiana, both of which prohibited slavery. Having been legally free in those places, the argument went, Scott could not be forced back to his former status.

The Court's opinion was written by Chief Justice Roger Taney, a member of the Maryland elite who freed his own slaves, but who resented northern efforts to force the issue. Taney's opinion actually starts off on the right foot, correctly observing that

> the words "people of the United States" and "citizens" are synonymous terms. . . . They both describe the political body who . . . form the sovereignty, and who hold the power and conduct the Government through their representatives.

This much, as we've seen, is an accurate reading of the Constitution's original meaning. A similar view was articulated by law professors Akhil Amar and Alan Hirsch in their 1998 book *For the People*: " 'The People' in the Constitution is linked to the concept of citizenship, *i.e.*, 'who retains ownership over and responsibility for governance.' " But to say that Taney got one thing right is not to endorse his entire opinion.

Where Taney goes wrong is his assertion that an emancipated slave cannot become one of the people. According to Taney's logic, only whites could become citizens because only whites had been citizens in 1789. The Constitution, he declared, "was formed by [whites], and for them and their posterity, but for no one else." But there is nothing in the Constitution's text that requires such a racial test for citizenship, as the abolitionist Lysander Spooner had pointed out a decade earlier in *The Unconstitutionality of Slavery*. Taney argued that the framers could not have considered blacks to be human. If they had, the Declaration of Independence's statement that "all men are created equal"—written as it was by slaveholder Thomas Jefferson—would have been sheer hypocrisy. And Taney would be shocked (shocked!) to discover that any of the Founders were susceptible to such a weakness. *Dred Scott*, then, is just an early example of a judge superimposing his own views on the framers' words. Taney relied not on the public's original understanding of the Constitution but on what he assumed to be the secret, undisclosed intent of its framers.

Abolishing universal birthright citizenship would not restore *Dred Scott*. To the contrary, it would restore the original meaning of the Fourteenth Amendment, which was expressly intended to overturn *Dred Scott*. With liberals so hopelessly confused about the citizenship clause, it's no wonder Harry Reid keeps changing his position.

EVIL CORPORATIONS

Notwithstanding their warm embrace of terrorists, illegal aliens, and killer whales, liberals would not extend constitutional personhood to all comers. Corporations, for example, are out of luck. So are the unborn.

Abolishing corporate personhood was one of the great motivators of the Occupy Wall Street movement of 2011; that is, assuming "motivated" is the right term to describe people who spend their days lazing around public parks. The citizens of Boulder, Colorado, even passed a symbolic resolution rejecting corporate personhood. In this context, "corporate personhood" is merely a code term for the Supreme Court's *Citizens United* decision (see chapter 6), holding that the First Amendment protects political speech made by corporations. *Citizens United* also protects speech by labor unions, but oddly enough, the OWS crowd appears to be untroubled by "union personhood."

Citizens United does not, however, depend upon defining corporations as constitutional "persons." For one thing, the freedom of speech clause of the First Amendment is not limited to "people" or "persons." It simply declares that "Congress shall make no law . . . abridging the freedom of speech." That freedom applies to Americans individually and collectively, no matter how they choose to organize themselves. As the Cato Institute's Ilya Shapiro notes, "Corporations are merely one of the ways in which rights-bearing individuals associate to better engage in a whole host of constitutionally-protected activity." If the First Amendment did not allow people to speak through corporations, that would be bad news for the Sierra Club and the *New York Times*—both corporations.

The irony is that if liberals would stop obsessing about *Citi-*

zens United, they would actually find themselves in possession of something resembling a valid point. There is a line of cases holding corporations to be "persons" under the Fourteenth Amendment, and those cases do depart from original meaning. There is no evidence that anyone who read or ratified the Fourteenth Amendment in 1868 would have understood the word "person" to include corporations. In *Santa Clara v. Southern Pacific Railroad Co.* (1886), however, the Supreme Court announced the rule that corporations are "persons" for purposes of the equal protection clause of the Fourteenth Amendment. That clause forbids the states from "deny[ing] to any person within its jurisdiction the equal protection of the laws."

The result of the *Santa Clara* rule of corporate personhood was a flood of cases in which railroads and other businesses successfully challenged regulations and taxes that applied "unequally" to corporations and human beings. Those cases largely came to an end in the New Deal; however, there is a continuing legacy of precedents holding corporations to be constitutional persons under various provisions of the Bill of Rights. This was the reasoning of the Supreme Court's 1978 decision in *First National Bank of Boston v. Bellotti*. The corporate personhood cases are not the result of a Wall Street conspiracy; they're just poorly reasoned. The issue is not whether the Constitution endows corporations with stand-alone rights; rather, it is whether individuals must sacrifice their constitutional rights when they associate in a corporate form. Justice Scalia made this point in his concurring opinion in *Citizens United*, but to no avail. The tone for the Left's reaction was set by Justice Stevens, who dissented on the nonsensical basis that "corporations have no consciences, no beliefs, no feelings, no thoughts, no desires." And they also have no ability to speak— except through the *human beings* who own them.

THE UNBORN

The Supreme Court's 1973 decision in *Roe v. Wade* turned abortion—which had been a matter of state law—into a matter of federal constitutional law. As we'll see in chapter 5, the "right" to abortion on demand represented the height of judicial activism. With absolutely no support in the Constitution itself, the Court's majority invented a right based on the "penumbra" (shadows) of other rights.

Among other things, the *Roe* Court held that fetuses are not "persons" within the meaning of the Fourteenth Amendment. Justice Harry Blackmun, in his majority opinion. conceded that if the unborn counted as constitutional persons, the concept of a right to abortion would "collapse." Thus, one response to *Roe* was the almost immediate proposal of a constitutional amendment—the Hogan Amendment—to recognize the personhood of all human life from the moment of conception. The proposed amendment failed, but pro-life supporters have continued to introduce similar legislation, generally known as "human life amendments." As of 2011, over three hundred such proposals have been introduced in Congress, according to the National Committee for a Human Life Amendment. Most of them never made it out of committee, and only one came to a formal floor vote on the floor of the Senate, where it was defeated.

Why would conservatives go to the trouble of trying—against all odds—to amend the Constitution in this manner? Why not adopt the liberal tactic, and simply argue that judges should "interpret" the word *person* in the Fifth and Fourteenth Amendments to include the unborn? Because they know that such an interpretation would violate original meaning. When the Bill of Rights was ratified, the law extended few protections to the unborn before "quickening," the traditional term for the point at which the mother can feel the fetus's movements. Even after quickening, abortion was not murder or manslaughter, although it was "a very heinous misdemeanor," according to Sir William Blackstone's *Commentaries on the Laws of England* (1765–69)—the most influential lawbook in America during the founding era. The law was the same at the time the Fourteenth Amendment was ratified.

Of course, if one took the Living Constitution approach, it would be a short day's work to "update" the meaning of *person*. Consider all the developments in biology, genetics, and neonatal technology since the ratification of the Fourteenth Amendment in 1868. Isn't it silly to adhere blindly to a nineteenth-century view of when life begins? And yet liberal legal scholars suddenly become ardent originalists when confronted with the possibility of reinterpreting the Fourteenth Amendment. Yale law professor Jack Balkin, for example, cites Blackstonian common law to argue that it "would make little sense" to interpret the Fourteenth Amendment as conferring personhood from the moment of conception. In fact, Balkin insists that the word *person* be read to mean exactly "what it meant in 1868." Similarly, left-wing professor Ronald Dworkin has argued that the Constitution forbids states from extending personhood to the unborn because a fetus is "not part of the constitutional population."

Despite paying lip service to original meaning, these scholars continue to heartily approve of the notion that the Constitution guarantees the right to perform a procedure—abortion—that was considered "a very heinous misdemeanor" both in 1791 and 1868. Following the twists and turns of liberal logic, such as it is, brings us to the strange land of American jurisprudence, where the Constitution is considered a "living organism," while a six-month-old fetus is a mere clump of cells.

ABOUT THOSE ORCAS

Animals are another story. The PETA lawsuit I mentioned at the beginning of the chapter was not the first time the Thirteenth Amendment has been invoked on behalf of animals. In 2000 Laurence Tribe, a celebrity Harvard professor once considered a short-list candidate for Supreme Court justice, argued that a chimpanzee used for medical research had been "enslaved," contrary to the Constitution.

Cruelty to animals is, of course, a very bad thing. But to turn animal rights into a constitutional issue is yet another example of the Living Constitution as a vehicle to advance every goal in the liberal agenda. Is it bad? Then the Constitution must prohibit it! Is it good? Then the Constitution must guarantee it!

Organizations such as the Nonhuman Rights Project (NhRP) are fighting to establish the constitutional personhood of animals. There is not, of course, a shred of evidence in the text or history of the Constitution to support that conclusion. Nonetheless, in the PETA lawsuit the NhRP dutifully submitted an amicus brief on behalf of the orcas, arguing that the court must recognize animals as persons. The judge disagreed: on February 8, 2012, he dismissed the lawsuit, going out on a limb to conclude that the Thirteenth Amendment does not actually guarantee freedom for killer whales.

The president of NhRP is Steven M. Wise, a law professor whose attempts to turn the Constitution into a charter for animal rights veer into self-parody—even PETA tried to block NhRP from filing its brief. In his book *Rattling the Cage*, Wise writes that "being human is an overly specific criterion for legal rights and not an essential element of legal personhood." Those who disagree are labeled as "unreasonable." And by page 87, Wise has compared those who oppose legal personhood for chimpanzees to Hitler, Eichmann, and the Confederate slave owners.

The book has its lighter moments, too. Wise recounts the story of John Quincy Adams, sixth president of the United States, who in 1837 presented a petition to Congress on behalf of twenty-two slaves. A South Carolina congressman, Henry Laurens Pinckney, remarked that Adams might as well present a petition from an animal. Adams replied: "Sir . . . if a horse or a dog had the power of speech and of writing, and he should send [me] a petition, [I] would present it to the House." Today, Adams would probably be faulted for his insensitivity to illiterate animals.

CHAPTER THREE

CONGRESS

Who Killed Our Government of Limited Powers?

The Congress shall have Power to lay and collect Taxes, Duties, Imposts and Excises, to pay the Debts and provide for the common Defence and general Welfare of the United States; . . . To regulate Commerce with foreign Nations, and among the several States. . . . And [t]o make all Laws which shall be necessary and proper for carrying into Execution the foregoing Powers.

—ARTICLE I, SECTION 8

"THE ERA OF BIG GOVERNMENT is over." So said President Bill Clinton in January 1996. He was right, big government *was* history. The era of gargantuan government had begun.

The federal government had been bulking up for many decades before 1996. Still, Clinton, with his vast appetites—personal and political—aptly symbolized a central government that had overrun all constitutional boundaries. After Clinton, we saw a Republican administration and a Republican Congress, and the size of government . . . grew some more.

But even after the epic spending of the Clinton and Bush years, President Obama made his predecessors look like penny-pinchers. Determined not to let a "good crisis" go to waste, as his chief of staff said at the height of the 2008–9 financial crisis, Obama and his congressional allies unleashed an orgy of government programs. The federal government would take over or remake banks, insurers, car companies, the health care industry, and even student loans. There would be lavish subsidies for dodgy start-ups eager to sell windmills and solar panels, while established businesses would have to purchase "pollution permits" before they did anything rash like manufacturing things. New government agencies were born, and existing ones would get bizarrely expanded mandates. NASA, for example, was told to get busy improving U.S. relations with the Muslim world. In its spare time, the space agency could figure out how to get to Mars.

There's a quaint theory making the rounds that Washington has bitten off more than it can chew, constitutionally speaking. There are even those who say that the federal government is— stop me if you've heard this one—a government of limited powers. Well, actually, the Founders came right out and said it. James Madison, the "father of the Constitution," said in 1791 that the "essential characteristic" of the new federal government is that it is "composed of limited and enumerated powers."

Madison was referring to Article I of the Constitution, which states that Congress shall exercise only the powers "herein granted." Those specific powers are then listed, or "enumerated," in Article I, Section 8. Lest anyone think that the enumerated powers were mere examples of an open-ended grant of power to the federal government, the framers inserted the Tenth Amendment, which provides that "the powers not delegated to the [federal government] by the Constitution . . . are reserved to the States . . . or to the people." The text is clear that Congress may exercise only its enumerated powers; the rest belongs to the states or the people.

THE CLAUSE THAT ATE PHILADELPHIA

If Congress actually stuck to the powers granted in the Constitution, the federal government would be less than half its current size. According to David Walker, the former comptroller general of the United States, only 40 percent of the federal budget in fiscal years 2008–11 was devoted to the functions expressly delegated to the federal government. The other 60 percent consists of programs that, while near and dear to congressmen as vote-getters, go well beyond any good-faith reading of Congress's powers. Take the Department of Education. You'll search in vain for a constitutional clause authorizing a federal education bureaucracy, but now that we've got one, what politician wants to be "against education"?

When forced to defend the constitutionality of Washington's metastasizing agencies and programs, politicians usually point to some combination of the commerce clause, the necessary and proper clause, and the general welfare clause, all of which are found in Article I, Section 8. The commerce clause is the most popular; it grants Congress power "to regulate Commerce with foreign Nations, and among the several States, and with the Indian tribes." Yes, that is one of the enumerated powers, but its scope depends upon how one defines the key terms: "commerce," and "among the several States." Originally, those words had relatively narrow meanings, as we will see. Under the Living Constitution, however, "commerce" has been defined to include such disparate activities as payment of child support, racial discrimination, loan sharking, and transporting liquor for one's own consumption.

Law professors, judges, and politicians have generally been reluctant to concede that the commerce clause has been mangled beyond recognition. This is no doubt because the clause is seen as an essential tool of "progressives," empowering Congress to enact New Deal reforms, civil rights legislation, and health and safety regulations. But then, during the presidency of George W. Bush (*cue Storm Trooper music*), the commerce clause was invoked so frequently and controversially that even some liberals had their doubts about its scope.

SCORE ONE FOR THE WAR ON DRUGS?

Diane Monson was a forty-something accountant suffering from a degenerative spinal disease that causes chronic pain and debilitating muscle spasms. After conventional pharmaceuticals failed to control her symptoms, Monson's doctor had prescribed cannabis—a legal option under California's medical marijuana law. It worked, so Monson began growing marijuana for her own medicinal use.

On August 15, 2002, agents of the U.S. Drug Enforcement Agency raided Monson's house in Oroville, California, demanding that she turn over the plants. When the local sheriff arrived, he tried to persuade the DEA agents that Monson was within her rights to grow marijuana, but to no avail. After a three-hour standoff, the feds seized and ultimately destroyed Monson's plants.

Monson and another medical marijuana user named Angel Raich sued then–attorney general John Ashcroft for exceeding his constitutional authority. The Supreme Court, however, ruled against Monson and Raich, saying that the DEA had simply been exercising the federal government's power—you guessed it—"to regulate Commerce . . . among the several States." The commerce clause, you see, was the legal basis for the Controlled Substances Act, under which the feds raided Monson's home (*Gonzales v. Raich*).

One might well wonder how mere possession of marijuana could constitute "commerce," or how growing a plant *in California* for use *in California* could be something that takes place "among the several States." The majority opinion in *Raich* neatly sidestepped those questions, instead declaring that Monson's pot-growing was an "economic" activity, relying on *Webster's Third New International Dictionary* for the definition of "economics"— "the production, distribution, and consumption of commodities." In his dissenting opinion, Justice Clarence Thomas took a slightly different tack: he discussed the meaning of the word that actually appears in the Constitution: *commerce*. Moreover, Thomas cited dictionaries from the founding era—since the framers and ratifiers of Article I did not have access to *Webster's Third New International Dictionary*—conclusively showing that *commerce* was not meant to encompass things like homegrown crops. Antics like this explain why Thomas is regularly branded as "outside the mainstream."

TRADE AND TRAFFICK

The Monson/Raich case shows just how far Congress and the Courts have strayed from the framers' commerce clause. There's no excuse for this lack of fidelity on the part of Congress—it's not as though *commerce* had been an esoteric term in 1787. To the contrary, the regulation of commerce was the very issue that brought the delegates to Philadelphia in the first place. In the years following the Revolution, the states had erected so many protectionist barriers against each other that the Republic's economy was in jeopardy. Under the Articles of Confederation, however, Congress was powerless to intervene.

In 1786 delegates from five states—New York, New Jersey, Delaware, Pennsylvania, and Virginia—met in Annapolis to consider the problem. After a brief session, they passed a resolution calling for a new convention the following May in Philadelphia, with the express purpose of devising a uniform system of "commercial regulations" throughout the states. As the eminent political scientist Sydney George Fisher put it, there was "no more important clause" in the whole Constitution "than that which gives Congress power to 'regulate commerce with foreign nations and among the several States, and with the Indian tribes.'"

What did *commerce* mean in 1787? The word derives from the Latin *commercium*, which is a mixture of *com* (with) and *merci* (merchandise); thus, it literally means "with merchandise." It had been widely used in English since the sixteenth century. Samuel Johnson's *Dictionary of the English Language* (1755)—the preeminent lexicon on both sides of the Atlantic during the founding era—defines *commerce* as including "exchange of one thing for another; interchange of any thing; trade; traffick." Other dictionaries of the period similarly defined *commerce* as "trade or traffick."

Similarly, in legal documents of the era, "commerce" referred to trade. Sir William Blackstone, for example, repeatedly uses the word in its mercantile sense ("money is the medium of commerce") in his *Commentaries on the Laws of England*. The leading English law dictionary of the day—that of Giles Jacobs—defined "commerce" as "Traffick, Trade or Merchandise in Buying and Selling of Goods." Not surprisingly, when Americans referred to "commerce" in the eighteenth century, they were talking about trade;

particularly, international trade. In 1765, for example, the Continental Congress called on the British Parliament to repeal various laws that restricted "American commerce," by which they meant laws that inhibited American trade with the mother country.

The innovative part of the commerce clause was the power to regulate not only foreign and Indian commerce but also commerce "among the several States"—a power that the Congress lacked under the Articles of Confederation. The other parts of the clause—regulation of trade with foreign nations and Indian tribes—existed in earlier documents. The Articles of Confederation, for example, gave Congress the exclusive power "of regulating the trade . . . with the Indians." And the plans of union proposed by Ben Franklin (1754), Thomas Hutchinson (1754), and William Henry Drayton (1778) all provided for a Congress with power to regulate trade with the Indians. The draft constitution proposed by Charles Pinckney in 1787 substituted "commerce" for "trade," a change that occasioned exactly no comment whatsoever from the delegates at Philadelphia who ultimately adopted Pinckney's language.

The delegates at the state conventions that ratified the Constitution would have understood "commerce" as referring to trade—that is, buying, selling, and bartering—as well as to "traffick"—that is, exporting or marketing goods, a sense that survives in such phrases as "trafficking in stolen goods." Trade and traffick could also include shipping, an important point, since the young republic was already earning considerable revenue transporting foreign goods in American ships, or "bottoms," as they were sometimes called. That usage will help explain Alexander Hamilton's thought-provoking remark that the federal Constitution would help Americans to maintain "an active commerce in our own bottoms."

"Commerce" was not understood to be a breezy reference to all economic activity, *pace* the Supreme Court. In fact, at the Philadelphia convention, the delegates decisively rejected a proposal that would have given Congress the power "to establish public institutions, rewards, and immunities for the promotion of agriculture, commerce, trades, and manufactures." Not only does the wording show that the framers distinguished "commerce" from "manufactures," but the defeat of the proposal also reflects the general consensus of the convention that Congress should not have power over the general economy.

THE PROBLEM WITH INTERCOURSE

The Court's first crack at interpreting the commerce clause came in 1824 in *Gibbons v. Ogden,* a lawsuit between two men who operated competing steamboat routes between New York and New Jersey. Gibbons got his "coasting" license from the federal government; Ogden got his from New York State. Naturally, Ogden argued that the federal government had no business regulating steamboats and, therefore, Gibbons's license was invalid. Gibbons countered that the power to license steamboats flowed from the commerce clause—and the Supreme Court agreed.

There was nothing especially startling about the result in *Gibbons*: it was reasonable to conclude that steamboats ferrying people and goods from one state to another are part of interstate commerce, even under a narrow reading of "commerce." But the author of *Gibbons*, Chief Justice John Marshall, took the opportunity to engage in a meandering discussion of the potential breadth of the commerce clause. He pointedly criticized Ogden's lawyer for defining *commerce* as merely "traffic." "Commerce, undoubtedly, is traffic," said Marshall, "but it is something more: it is intercourse." At the time of Gibbons, "intercourse" had a potentially broad meaning, including trade but also social interactions. What Marshall meant by "intercourse," however, is anybody's guess. The Chief Justice hedged his bets splendidly, concluding that commerce isn't *all* forms of intercourse, just "commercial intercourse." Defining *commerce* as "commercial intercourse" is about as helpful as defining *alcohol* as an "alcoholic beverage." If you didn't understand the noun, you're unlikely to understand the adjective.

Marshall then turned his analytical skills to the second part of the commerce clause—"among the several States"—which, up until that time, had been pretty clear. As Georgetown University law professor Randy Barnett has pointed out, "among the several States" was originally understood to mean "between people of different states." That is, the framers gave Congress the power to regulate, say, the importation of buggy whips from one state to another. In Federalist No. 42—one of the celebrated Federalist Papers originally written to persuade New Yorkers to ratify the Constitution—Madison described the commerce power as extending to trade "between State and State."

Marshall, however, defined *among* as "intermingled with," which at first blush seems to be a distinction without a difference: commerce among the states must involve two or more states; in other words, *interstate* commerce. But Marshall planted another time bomb in his famous opinion: he noted that Congress could regulate a state's internal commerce whenever that commerce might "*affect* other States" (emphasis added). Marshall's statement was completely irrelevant to the issue in *Gibbons*. That case *did* involve commerce between two states, namely New York and

New Jersey, so there was no reason to consider Congress's ability to regulate intrastate activity that might merely "affect" another state.

In cases like *Gibbons*, Marshall set the standard for later generations of activist judges (see chapter 5). His description of the commerce clause was dictated not by the text or by logic but by his desire to achieve a result. That result—as historian Thomas DiLorenzo argues in *Hamilton's Curse*—was the imposition of the "Hamiltonian interpretation of the Constitution," that is, an interpretation that maximizes the power of the central government. During the Washington administration, Hamilton had aggressively stretched the Constitution to argue for federal involvement in areas like manufacturing and banking that are nowhere mentioned in the text. In 1791, for example, Hamilton successfully pushed legislation for a federally chartered bank on the specious theory that such a bank was "necessary and proper" to execute Congress's enumerated power "to borrow money." Madison had disdainfully, and correctly, pointed out that it was hardly necessary to create a bank in order to borrow money. But Hamilton had the votes in Congress, so the legislation went through.

Hamilton's ambitions were cut short by his ill-fated duel with Aaron Burr, but Marshall, a like-minded Federalist who "revered Hamilton" (in the words of biographer Ron Chernow), used his position to continue Hamilton's program. Serving as chief justice from 1801 until his death in 1835, Marshall consistently reached decisions that just happened to aggrandize the federal government at the expense of the states. His treatment of "commerce" is classic; rather than offering a succinct definition, Marshall created ambiguities that Congress could exploit at opportune moments.

WHAT COMMERCE CLAUSE?

Ever since *Gibbons*, the meaning of the commerce clause has been all intercoursed up. With Marshall's vague formulation in the background, "commerce" could mean anything a politician desired. In the early twentieth century, for example, the commerce clause was used to justify federal regulation of lotteries, white slavery, and other species of "moral" legislation. The Supreme Court did, however, set some boundaries to the federal commerce power. In the 1895 *Sugar Trust Cases*, for example, the Court held that the commerce clause did not authorize Congress to regulate manufacturing activities, since such activities are distinct from commerce.

The Supreme Court also developed the doctrine that Congress could regulate *intrastate* activities only when such activities have a "direct" effect on interstate commerce. When Franklin Roosevelt's New Deal took shape, the Court found that most of FDR's legislation was too "indirectly" related to commerce to pass constitutional muster. The justices killed off the Railroad Retirement Act in 1935. They went on to invalidate the National Industrial Recovery Act, the Bituminous Coal Conservation Act, and the Agricultural Adjustment Act, all important planks of the New Deal. At that point, FDR introduced legislation that would have packed the Court with six additional pro–New Deal judges, effectively silencing recalcitrant justices.

FDR's imperious court-packing scheme put extreme pressure on Justice Owen Roberts, who had been the swing vote in each of the New Deal cases decided by the Court. In the face of this unprecedented institutional challenge, Roberts puffed out his chest and roared: *Commerce clause? What commerce clause?* In 1937 Roberts switched sides and decided that Article I gave Congress power to regulate purely intrastate labor practices in the name of "protecting" commerce (*NLRB v. Jones & Laughlin Steel Corp.*). In fact, he joined the Court's opinion that *no* field of regulation was "forbidden" to Congress as long as there was some connection to commerce. As for the definition of *commerce*, well, it is "a practical conception," mused the Court, which must be construed according to "actual experience." Actual experience presumably includes things like presidential threats.

With Justice Roberts's surrender, and the retirement of conservative Justice Willis Van Devanter, the Supreme Court went on to reverse its earlier New Deal decisions, now upholding every federal program that FDR could dream up. Not that the justices were making up law from scratch; to the contrary, they had an old ally: John Marshall. In the 1941 case of *United States v. Darby*, the Court cited *Gibbons v. Ogden* to justify the federal takeover of employment law, something that had previously been the province of the states.

In 1942 the Court cited *Gibbons*'s definition of commerce—"with a breadth never yet exceeded"—as the basis for Congress's power to dictate how much food citizens can grow for their own consumption. The case of *Wickard v. Filburn* involved an Ohio farmer (Filburn) who cultivated eleven acres of wheat more than the federal government had allowed under the Agricultural Adjustment Act. Mr. Filburn did not sell the excess wheat; rather, he used it on his own farm, to feed livestock and make flour for his family. Applying "the principles first enunciated by Chief Justice Marshall in *Gibbons v. Ogden*," the Court held that the commerce power "is not confined in its exercise to the regulation of commerce among the States." Funny, I could have sworn the clause was precisely "confined" to the power "to regulate Commerce . . . among the several States."

What makes *Wickard* such a landmark is that it combines

Marshall's expansive definition of commerce with the "necessary and proper" clause of Article I, Section 8. The latter provision empowers Congress to "make all laws which shall be *necessary and proper* for carrying into Execution the [enumerated] Powers" (emphasis added). The assumption in cases like *Wickard*—and now the conventional wisdom—is that the necessary and proper clause "is an enlargement . . . of the powers expressly granted to Congress," to quote a Web site devoted to continuing legal education. Justice Antonin Scalia has referred to the necessary and proper clause as "the last, best hope" of those who defend unconstitutional congressional action. The potent combination of commerce power and the necessary and proper clause has given Congress "powers undreamed of by the Framers," according to Professor Jethro Lieberman of New York Law School.

The vast edifice of congressional power, however, is based on a misunderstanding of the phrase "necessary and proper." At the time of the nation's founding, "necessary and proper" was a boilerplate phrase found in powers of attorney and similar instruments. A power of attorney is a form by which a "principal" grants certain powers to his "agent" to act on his or her behalf. Although it may seem quaint to modern eyes, the founding generation commonly thought of government as the "agent" of the people, and thus, just like any other agent, it ought to be bound by a fiduciary duty to respect the wishes of its principal. The law assumed that every agent possessed certain additional, "incidental" powers; that is, powers that were indispensable, or at least reasonably necessary, to carry out the expressly granted powers. Far from being a license to expand its jurisdiction indefinitely, the "necessary and proper" language was actually a command to Congress to adopt only those measures that were *necessary* to carry out its delegated powers.

That is precisely how the ratifiers understood those words. We know this because the Constitution's supporters had to explain the scope of Congress's powers to the (often skeptical) state ratifying conventions. At the North Carolina ratifying convention, James Iredell, a future Supreme Court justice, described the enumerated powers of Article I as "a great power of attorney." As for the necessary and proper clause, delegate George Nichols told the Virginia convention that it "only enables [Congress] to carry into execution the powers given to them, but gives them no additional powers." Madison explained in Federalist No. 44 that the clause was simply a shorthand reference to powers that Congress needed "for carrying their other powers into effect." Elsewhere, Federalists insisted that the clause simply ensured that the enumerated powers "are to be executed by the proper laws" (William MacLaine, North Carolina) or "shall be effectually carried into execution" (James Wilson, Pennsylvania).

Even Marshall recognized that the necessary and proper clause involved a distinction between "ends" and "means." As he stated in *McCulloch v. Maryland*, the enumerated powers of Article I constitute a complete list of the ends for which Congress can legislate, but the necessary and proper clause gives Congress the choice of means to achieve those ends. To take an example, the Constitution allows Congress to "provide for the Punishment of counterfeiting" (Article I, Section 8), and to "declare the punishment for Treason" (Article III, Section 3). Even though the Constitution does not say so, it is reasonable to assume that Congress can also hire prosecutors to secure convictions of those crimes, and to build prisons (or gallows) to deal with those found guilty. Those are "necessary and proper" means to achieve one of Congress's express powers.

Notwithstanding his accurate statement of first principles,

Marshall went on in *McCulloch* to hold that it was "necessary and proper" for Congress to incorporate the Second Bank of the United States—thus parroting Hamilton's ludicrous but politically successful argument of 1791 with respect to the First Bank of the United States. As Madison had said of the First Bank, if that's what "necessary" means, then Congress's power could be expanded to "reach . . . every object within the whole compass of political economy." A fair description, one might say, of the federal government's role since the Depression.

THE SANTA CLAUSE

Even with a submissive Court at his command, FDR still faced an obstacle: not every New Deal program could be shoehorned into the commerce clause. The Social Security Act of 1935, for example, had no connection whatsoever with regulating commerce. Nor does any other provision in the Constitution suggest that Congress can create a system of old-age pensions. The Supreme Court overcame this obstacle in the 1937 case of *Helvering v. Davis* by finding that the Social Security Act was a proper exercise of Congress's "spending power" under the general welfare clause.

There was just one problem: there is no "spending power" in the general welfare clause. That clause, which is at the very beginning of Article I, Section 8, provides that "the Congress shall have Power to lay and collect Taxes, Duties, Imposts and Excises, to pay the Debts and provide for the common Defence and General Welfare of the United States"; enumerated powers follow.

As you can see, the entire provision is about taxing, not spending. It gives Congress the power to tax—a controversial power, and one that Congress lacked under the Articles. But the clause restrains this fearful power by specifying that any taxes must be justified in the name of (i) paying down the debt; (ii) defense; or (iii) the "general welfare." Granted, money collected from taxpayers will eventually be spent, but the validity of government spending is governed by the necessary and proper clause—congressional spending is one of those powers incidental to the enumerated powers.

As for the "general welfare," it simply means that taxation must serve the nation as a whole—which is why it is teamed up with the concept of the "common Defence"—as distinct from any narrow or regional interest. It's true that the phrase "general welfare" lacks specificity, but that is because the specific components of the general welfare are laid out in the rest of Section 8; namely, the enumerated powers. In Federalist No. 41, Madison explained that the phrase "general welfare" was not meant to convey some new, unspecified power but was instead a collective reference to Congress's specific powers. "Nothing is more natural nor common," he wrote, "than first to use a general phrase and then to explain and qualify it by a recital of particulars."

Certainly, nobody in the founding era thought that the Constitution gave Congress a blank check to spend money on anything it deemed conducive to the general welfare. Well, nobody except Alexander Hamilton. In his 1791 "Report on Manufactures," Hamilton argued that the general welfare clause necessarily gave Congress the power to appropriate money for purposes beyond those expressed in Article I. In particular, he asserted that the federal government possessed the power to promote "the general interests of learning, of agriculture, [and] of manufacturing." Such powers would have to be implicit, of course, since the Philadelphia convention had rejected any explicit power "to establish public institutions, rewards, and immunities for the promotion of agriculture, commerce, trades, and manufactures."

The Hamiltonian view of federal spending created an "odd loophole," as Robert Levy and William Mellor put it in their classic study of judicial activism, *The Dirty Dozen*. Congress would be limited to its Article I powers—unless it wanted to spend money, in which case it could do whatever it wanted. Odd, yes, but that's what the Supreme Court decided in *Helvering* when it translated the general welfare clause to mean that "Congress may spend money in aid of the 'general welfare.'" The Court left no doubt about the inspiration for its conclusion: "The conception of the spending power advocated by Hamilton," declared the majority, "has prevailed over that of Madison." Historian Clinton Rossiter would later describe the New Deal as the ultimate vindication of "the principles of nationalism and broad construction expounded by Hamilton and his disciples"—disciples like Marshall.

The triumph of the Hamiltonian view of federal spending has led to depressingly predictable results. Since 1937, the federal government has been on a tear, with taxes and spending escalating to ever more dizzying heights. Five years before *Helvering*, constitutional scholar Charles Warren presciently warned that the "practice of making drafts on the National Treasury to carry out purposes not within the enumerated or implied powers of the National Government" would lead to disastrous results, nicely encapsulated by the title of his book: *Congress as Santa Claus*. Santa Clause, indeed. How else to describe an institution that in 2009 doled out $787 billion in pork-barrel spending under the guise of "stimulus"? Among other things, jolly Santa Congress gave $5 billion to those who wanted to weatherize their homes, $7.2 billion to promote broadband Internet service, $200 million to spruce up air traffic control towers, and $50 million for the

National Cemetery Association—presumably to give the Constitution a decent burial.

Perhaps somewhere up in the sky, Alexander Hamilton has been observing all this federal largesse with satisfaction. After all, as columnist George Will observed in his 1992 book *Restoration*, "We honor Jefferson, but we live in Hamilton's country."

THE SUPINE COURT WAKES UP

Amazingly, between 1937 and 1995, the Supreme Court did not strike down a single federal law as exceeding Congress's power. One could argue that Congress had been scrupulously faithful to the Constitution in those years, but if you believe that, I've got a bridge to nowhere I'd like to sell you. The more likely explanation is that the Court, under FDR's appointees and, later, Earl Warren, set a pattern of abdicating any responsibility to enforce the enumerated powers of Article I.

A long-overdue correction arrived in the 1995 case of *United States v. Lopez*. The case involved the Gun-Free School Zone Act, which relied on the commerce clause to prohibit possession of a gun within 1,000 feet of any school. The Supreme Court struck down the law as beyond Congress's power to regulate commerce. Congress responded immediately by limiting the scope of the law to any "firearm that has moved in or that otherwise affects interstate or foreign commerce"—a constitutional fig leaf that was later blessed by the courts (see chapter 8). In 2000 the Supreme Court struck again, correctly holding that the Violence Against Women Act—however laudable its purpose—could not be justified under the commerce clause.

When the case of Diane Monson and Angel Raich reached

the Supreme Court in 2004, many observers thought that the justices would give Congress another smack-down. But constitutional law makes strange bedfellows. Conservatives Clarence Thomas and Antonin Scalia went separate ways in Monson's case. Thomas vigorously sided with advocates of medical marijuana, declaring that, to the Founders, "it would have been unthinkable that Congress could prohibit the local cultivation, possession, and consumption of marijuana." Scalia, however, hearing the siren song of *stare decisis* (see chapter 5), reasoned that since the Court had allowed Congress to regulate homegrown wheat in *Wickard*, Congress must also be able to regulate homegrown pot. He joined several liberal justices in upholding the power of the federal government to trample on California's medical marijuana law, a decision applauded by the *New York Times* in a June 8, 2005, editorial. Why? Because upholding a broad reading of the clause is necessary to preserve the modern regulatory state, no matter the collateral damage.

THE CONTROL FREAK CONSTITUTION

The Supreme Court's June 2012 decision upholding the Obama health care law, known as the Affordable Care Act (ACA), represents yet another victory for the Hamiltonian/liberal view that Congress's power to tax and spend is essentially unlimited. The ACA precedent means that Congress needn't search for commerce to regulate; it can forcibly create commerce and then regulate it.

Spilling out over more than 2,700 pages, passed via procedural gimmicks, unread, in the middle of the night, ACA is a monstrosity that turns the entire health care industry into a federal utility. Naturally, Congress inserted language into the law describing ACA as a garden-variety exercise of Congress's power to regulate commerce. Thanks to precedents like *Wickard* and *Raich*, scores of law professors agreed. But ACA takes federal power even further than the Court has previously allowed. The law is built upon the "individual mandate," by which Congress prohibited a specific form of inactivity; namely, the *failure* to buy an insurance policy. Under ACA, each and every citizen must—as part of the privilege of being alive—purchase a government-approved health insurance policy or face penalties, up to and including criminal sanctions. Never before has Congress required ordinary citizens to purchase a commercial product.

One supposedly originalist defense of the individual mandate is that Article I of the Constitution does not actually set the limits of congressional power. Rather (so the argument goes) Congress's power is defined by "Resolution VI," a proposal adopted in the early days of the Philadelphia convention. It is true that Resolution VI was part of the original "Virginia Plan" submitted to the convention in May 1787. The resolution stated, in part, that "the National Legislature ought to be empowered . . . to legislate in all cases to which the separate States are incompetent, or in which the harmony of the United States may be interrupted by the exercise of individual legislation."

Resolution VI was never intended as anything more than a placeholder until the convention could hammer out the specific powers of Congress. Indeed, after the Committee of Detail produced its first draft of the enumerated powers, Resolution VI was never mentioned again by the delegates. Because of the broad language of the resolution, however, left-wing lawyers have argued that the specific provisions of Article I, Section 8, are merely examples of the sweeping powers that the Founders intended to give Congress via Resolution VI. Thus, even if the individual mandate doesn't count as a regulation of commerce, surely it is something that individual states are "incompetent" to do, since no single state could enact a national mandate. Or maybe forcing people to buy health insurance promotes the "harmony of the United States." Liberal groups like the Constitutional Accountability Center (CAC) have cited Resolution VI in amicus briefs to establish the validity of the individual mandate on "squarely originalist" grounds, as CAC's chief counsel, Elizabeth Wydra, put it.

There's more than a whiff of desperation about the Resolution VI argument, depending, as it does, on the idea that the Constitution is nice, but a rough draft of the Constitution is even better. If the framers were so pleased with Resolution VI, why did they spend so much time spelling out Congress's powers? It boggles the mind to think that the framers, with their gift for economical language, would have composed the enumerated powers as a roundabout way of saying Congress can do anything that *might* be done better on the national level. Moreover, none of the state conventions that ratified the Constitution knew about Resolution VI because the proceedings of the Philadelphia convention had been kept secret—the convention notes were not published until the 1820s. Resolution VI, therefore, has absolutely no bearing on the original public meaning of Article I.

Less fanciful lawyers have insisted that the individual mandate is, in fact, an example of Congress's commerce power. In one ruling, federal district judge George Steeh endorsed an argument that has become popular with ACA proponents. Dismissing a lawsuit filed by the Thomas More Law Center, Steeh asserted that the commerce clause empowers Congress, not merely to regulate "commerce," or even "economic activity," but to regulate all "economic decisions."

Who can deny that the decision not to purchase insurance is "economic"? Not me. By that logic, what isn't covered by the commerce clause? Every day, we make decisions not to purchase things. Why, just today I declined to purchase a GM car, a set of solar panels, and a third martini. Presumably, all of those decisions were "economic," meaning that the government could use its power to force me to make different decisions.

At the Supreme Court, a majority of the justices actually rejected Obama's expanded version of the commerce clause, but then upheld the mandate under Congress's power to raise taxes for the "general welfare." The tax in question is the "shared responsibility payment" that will be imposed on individuals who fail to purchase health insurance. Of course, two years earlier, when trying to sell ACA, President Obama had declared on national television that "nobody" considers this payment to be a tax.

THE DOUBLE STANDARD

As we stare down the precipice of judicially sanctioned tyranny, it's nice to know that the *New York Times* editorial board is cheering us on. On October 27, 2010, the paper ran a rousing defense of Judge Steeh's decision, gushing that the judge "persuasively argued that refusals to buy health insurance are economic decisions that, in the aggregate, will have a substantial impact on interstate commerce." Upon reading those words, every enlightened reader of the *Times* could fold up the paper, finish his latte, and feel appropriate contempt for the knuckle-dragging Tea Partiers who can't see the sheer logic of Obamacare. *Do they really think that the federal government should let the Constitution stand in the way while people are persistently refusing—refusing!—to buy health insurance? Don't they realize that the Constitution has some . . . thingummy in the penumbra that empowers government to force people to do what's right?*

Liberals discover the virtues of limited government only when conservatives are in power. Almost exactly four years before the *New York Times* defended the government's power to crack down on citizens who "refuse" to buy health insurance, the paper ran an editorial urging Congress to repeal much of the Patriot Act, the law enforcement measure passed after the September 11 attacks. Why? The act "gives government too much power," said the *Times*, because, among other things, it allows federal agents to demand individuals' medical records, when the government has a belief that such records are relevant to antiterrorist investigations. Compare that to President Obama's health care regime, which mandates that doctors record all medical treatments in a centralized database that is always accessible to the government. In effect, the Obama administration has subpoenaed every citizen's health care records in perpetuity. And yet the newspaper of record appears unfazed by "too much power" in the hands of the Obama administration.

The Founders did not decide to limit the powers of government on a whim. The majority of them—excluding the Hamilton faction—had a profound distrust of concentrated power. The Constitution that they drafted and ratified reflects that distrust by separating government powers "horizontally" into three separate branches, and "vertically" between states and the central government. The latter was vested with specific powers; the states got the rest.

Reasonable minds may differ about the powers that Congress should have in an ideal world. We're stuck with the powers Congress was actually given. Nothing could be more alien to the framers' design than a system in which Congress has virtually unfettered discretion to define its own powers. The Constitution's checks and balances—which were intended to prevent one branch from accumulating too much power—have been missing in action, as we will see in the next two chapters.

CHAPTER FOUR

THE PRESIDENT

The Mouse That Roared

The executive power shall be vested in a President of the United States of America.

—ARTICLE II, SECTION 2

HARRY TRUMAN KEPT A THIRTEEN-INCH painted glass sign on his desk in the Oval Office proclaiming, "The Buck Stops Here." Truman loved the sign; he considered it *the* symbol of his presidency. In his 1953 farewell address to the nation, he explained that the sign meant that "the President—whoever he is—has to decide. He can't pass the buck to anybody. No one else can do the deciding for him. That's his job."

Truman's little sign neatly summarizes an important constitutional principle: the president is ultimately responsible for implementing and enforcing all federal laws. As the only member of the executive branch elected by the people (with the VP coming along for the ride), the president has the duty to answer for all of those unelected bureaucrats charged with carrying out the nitty-gritty details.

Nowadays, a "Buck Stops Here" sign would be out of place in the Oval Office: it's as kitschy as a singing big-mouth bass—

and just about as relevant to today's presidency. In a series of decisions that began even before Truman took office, the courts have allowed Congress to remove huge swaths of the executive branch from the president's control. Technically, the president can still claim that he never passes the buck, but that's only because Congress rarely gives him the buck in the first place.

Many liberals rejoice at the demise of the so-called imperial presidency, but what we got instead was an imperial *bureaucracy.* The results have not been pretty. Consider, for example, the saga of Beckstead and Watts.

PEEKABOO—I'LL CRUSH YOU!

Beckstead and Watts, LLP, was a small CPA firm in Henderson, Nevada, specializing in small-business audits. The firm had only three members, but for managing partner Brad Beckstead, it was the culmination of his personal American Dream to serve the needs of entrepreneurs.

In the beginning of May 2004, Beckstead received notice that his firm was to be inspected by a new federal regulator, the Public Company Accounting Oversight Board (PCAOB). The 2002 Sarbanes-Oxley Act had created the PCAOB—endearingly known as "Peekaboo"—and the agency was just beginning to flex its muscles.

Two weeks after the initial notice, the Peekaboo inspectors showed up, seven of them, at Beckstead's door. They crammed into Beckstead and Watts's thousand-square-foot office, and there they stayed for two weeks. They carried out detailed reviews of sixteen of the firm's audit files, with all the document requests and follow-up questions that they deemed necessary. Responding to the PCAOB's various inquiries ultimately consumed about five hundred man-hours of the firm's time.

The PCAOB took a full year to produce a draft inspection report, which they sent to Beckstead—and gave him exactly thirty days to respond. Holding Beckstead and Watts to the gold-plated standards of Big Four accounting firms, the report charged the firm with eight accounting deficiencies. Brad Beckstead's formal response had some choice words for the PCAOB. He pointed out that if the regulators continued to ignore the economic realities of small accounting firms, they would drive "this segment of the market" out of existence.

With its pride wounded, the Peekaboo board retaliated by launching a full-scale investigation of Beckstead and Watts. The firm was ordered to produce another five audit files for inspection. Brad Beckstead and the firm's audit manager were hauled in for three days of questioning before representatives of the PCAOB. And then came a demand for four more audit files, as well as copies of electronic and paper correspondence. And all of this dragged on while the firm was working to address the eight findings in the original report. The firm's profitability dropped 60 percent.

Beckstead and Watts was eventually cleared of all charges, but that was beside the point. "It was clear to me," Beckstead would later write, "that they wanted to make me the poster child for small audit firms, and that they ultimately wanted me out of business." Fair enough. Why shouldn't the federal government be able to destroy businesses on a whim?

But wait—I hear you saying—why didn't Beckstead call his congressman for help? In days of yore, that might have worked: the congressman could put political pressure on the president to curb the abuses of his servants, lest *he* take the blame for harassing innocent professionals. Such pressure, however, would have been useless in this case, because the president had no power to hire or fire the members of Peekaboo's board. Instead, Congress gave that power to the commissioners of the Securities and Exchange Commission (SEC). And even that power was extremely limited, since the PCAOB board members could be fired only "for cause," meaning that they can do what they please provided they don't break the law or commit gross malfeasance. Still, couldn't the president lean on the SEC? Unfortunately not. The SEC commissioners themselves were protected from "at-will" dismissal, and thus were also beyond the president's effective control.

Thus insulated by two layers of "for cause" civil service protection, the five members of the PCAOB board could ride roughshod over the accounting industry without interference unless one of them broke the law or was found in bed with a goat. Beckstead's only recourse was to the courts. So to the courts he turned. With the help of a public interest group called the Free Enterprise Fund, Beckstead sued the PCAOB.

THE UNITARY EXECUTIVE

In court, Beckstead argued that the PCAOB violated the Constitution's requirement of a "unitary executive," which is simply legal lingo for "the buck stops here." The text and structure of the Constitution demand that those who implement federal law must be answerable to a democratically elected president. But if the president has to go to court to establish "cause" every time he wants to fire an official, then he has—in the words of former solicitor general Ted Olson—"lost all effective control of that official." Certainly that was the case with the PCAOB board members: the president couldn't lay a glove on them.

The "unitary" part of the unitary executive emphasizes the obvious fact that the Constitution provides for only one president at a time. The framers did not want the executive power to be dispersed among dozens of petty chieftains. Not only did the framers create a unitary executive, but the Philadelphia convention voted down at least four separate attempts to include a "council" that would have shared executive power with the president.

Americans had learned the hard way to distrust plural executives. The generation of 1776—in its zeal to overthrow royal despotism—had originally created governments based loosely on the theme of "What if the kids ran the school?" There was, for example, no national chief executive at all under the Articles of Confederation; executive powers were sprinkled like fairy dust among the delegates to Congress. The states made similar mistakes. Some of them created plural executives, and even where there was ostensibly a single governor, he was generally subservient to some combination of the legislature and a council.

These hydra-headed governments got little done. At the national level, the only way to fix this problem was to draft a brand-new constitution. One of the "great objects" of the Philadelphia convention, wrote James Madison, was to create "a proper energy in the Executive." That word—energy—was often repeated by the framers. At the convention, James Wilson made the motion to create a single executive, arguing that it would give "energy, dispatch and responsibility to the office."

Hamilton, writing in Federalist No. 70, continued the theme at greater length. "Energy in the Executive," he wrote, "is a leading character in the definition of good government." Like Wilson, he believed that unity was the way to achieve "energy," as well as other important executive traits such as "decision, activity, secrecy and despatch." But executive unity could be destroyed, Hamilton warned, by "vesting [the executive power] ostensibly in one man, subject, in whole or in part, to the control and cooperation of others."

Even though the framers clearly provided for a single chief executive, liberals have come to regard the "unitary executive" as a fringe theory cooked up by Dick Cheney in his spare time during those lazy days after the September 11 attacks. Joe Biden, for example, when campaigning for Cheney's job, labeled the unitary executive as a "dangerous" theory developed by the Bush White House out of thin air. That accusation, incidentally, was made while Biden was lecturing his opponent, Sarah Palin, about how *Article I* of the Constitution "defines . . . the Executive Branch"—oops. But then again—Article I, Article II—what does it matter? During the George W. Bush presidency, the Constitution was merely a prop with which to beat the president. Who had time to read the thing?

The Bush years witnessed such bizarre spectacles as the president of the United States being criticized for attempting to "influence" *his own* EPA administrator. California congressman Henry Waxman held hearings to investigate whether Bush had improperly prevented the EPA from allowing California to impose draconian air pollution standards in the state's quixotic attempt to unilaterally defeat "global warming." The Natural Resources Defense Council labeled Bush's assertion of control over the EPA as "unprecedented and unlawful." Under the Living Constitution version of Article II, it is "unlawful" for an *elected* president to ensure that his own appointees are carrying out the policies for which he was elected.

By the end of Bush's second term, anyone listening to the mainstream media's endless critiques of the administration would have to wonder whether the president can properly exercise *any* control over his cabinet, or whether he must, like Jimmy

Carter, content himself with overseeing the White House tennis courts. The Supreme Court's liberal bloc evidently favors the Carter-style presidency.

A RARE VICTORY

Brad Beckstead initially lost at trial and in the D.C. Circuit Court of Appeals. But one of the appellate judges, Brett Kavanaugh, issued a stinging dissent describing the PCAOB board as "unaccountable and divorced from Presidential control to a degree not previously countenanced in our constitutional structure." A majority of the Supreme Court agreed with Kavanaugh. Chief Justice John Roberts put his finger on the problem when he noted that "the Executive Branch . . . wields vast power and touches almost every aspect of daily life," making it a serious "concern" that it "may slip away from the Executive's control, and thus from that of the People."

In Beckstead's case, officially known as *Free Enterprise Fund v. PCAOB*, all four liberal justices—the ones allegedly full of "empathy" for the little guy—voted to throw Brad Beckstead under the big government bus, much the same treatment that the Court's liberals had dished out to Diane Monson and Angel Raich (see chapter 3). Indeed, when it comes to big government versus the little guy, attentive readers might begin to detect a pattern.

THREE BRANCHES WALK INTO A BAR

As every middle-schooler knows, the Constitution creates a system of three separate branches of government: legislative (Article

I), executive (Article II), and judicial (Article III). The framers did not create this tripartite system because they liked the way it looked on an org chart. They did it because they believed that good government required it.

"No political truth is certainly of greater intrinsic value," James Madison wrote, than the "maxim that the legislative, executive, and judiciary departments ought to be separate and distinct." Separation of powers was a bedrock principle of the political philosophers John Locke and Baron de Montesquieu, whose influence on the Founders is well documented. According to University of Virginia law professor Saikrishna Prakash, Montesquieu, whose 1748 *Spirit of the Laws* argued for strict separation of the three governmental powers, "had perhaps the most influence of any political theorist on our Constitution's division of powers."

The rationale for separation was straightforward: without it, there are no checks and balances. And without checks and balances, "there can be no liberty," as Madison wrote in Federalist No. 47 (quoting Montesquieu). If the legislative and executive powers were combined, then the same person or body could "*enact* tyrannical laws [and] *execute* them in a tyrannical manner." The Massachusetts Constitution of 1780 also echoes Montesquieu when it states—in words drafted by John Adams—that maintaining separate branches of government is necessary "to the end that it may be a government of laws and not of men."

Once we appreciate the dominant political philosophy of the founding era, the first sentence of Article II should not be terribly difficult to interpet:

> The executive power shall be vested in a President of the United States of America.

The executive power. Not *some* executive power. Not "the executive power, except the bits about accounting." But *the* executive power—all of it. Note the difference between that sentence and the corresponding sentence of Article I, by which "all legislative Powers *herein granted* shall be vested in a Congress of the United States" (emphasis added). See the words in italics? The framers strictly limited Congress's jurisdiction to those enumerated powers "herein granted" in Article I (see chapter 3), but vested the president broadly with "the power" inherent in the executive. One reason the framers granted only limited powers to Congress but broad power to the executive was their fear that Congress would encroach on the executive's domain. They had observed, as Madison wrote in Federalist No. 48, the inclination of every legislature toward "extending the sphere of its activity, and drawing all power into its impetuous vortex."

Notwithstanding the clear distinction between Article I and Article II, many academics dispute the idea of inherent executive powers. In an influential 1994 law review article, Professors Larry Lessig and Cass Sunstein maintain that the first sentence of Article II contains an implicit "herein granted" clause. Therefore, "the executive power in Article II does not extend beyond the enumerated powers there." In other words, the president's power is limited to those tasks explicitly delegated in Article II: he can receive ambassadors, make a State of the Union speech, and so forth. But he has no general power to execute the laws.

Lessig and Sunstein are no slackers: they stand at the summit of the legal academy. Sunstein went on to serve as President Obama's regulatory czar, while Lessig is a renowned expert on intellectual property and, as I discuss in chapter 12, a forceful advocate of the Article V convention process. But their argument here represents bad originalism. They find it significant, for example, that the "herein granted" language of Article I was inserted late in the Philadelphia convention by the Committee of Style and, therefore, was probably not seen by the framers as terribly important. Original meaning, however, is not an attempt to guess what the framers were thinking. Who knows how much weight they put on any particular phrase? What matters is what the words meant to the ratifying public. The most reasonable reading of Articles I and II is that the former restricted Congress to express powers, while the latter granted the executive implied powers.

THE ORIGINAL MEANING OF EXECUTIVE POWER

What was the original meaning of "the executive power"? It embraced the power to "execute" the laws, meaning the power to implement and enforce the laws. Noah Webster's 1828 dictionary, for example, defines "executive" as "the body or person who carries the laws into effect, or superintends the enforcement of them." That definition reflects the teachings of Montesquieu, who believed that the executive must have the full power to execute the laws, including such tasks as prosecution, tax collection, and disbursement of public funds.

If you've ever sued anyone and tried to collect on the judgment, you'll know the difference between a piece of paper (say, a court order or a statute) and the action taken to enforce that piece of paper (e.g., seizing property or garnishing wages). Legislatures and courts can churn out pieces of paper all day long; that's their job. The job of the executive, whether it's a mayor, a governor, or the president of the United States, is to turn those pieces of paper into reality.

One of the best-known treatments of executive power during the founding era was *The Essex Result*, a document produced by a group of prominent Massachusetts Federalists in 1778. They had gathered in convention in Essex County to protest against a proposed constitution for the State. The *Result* pamphlet—authored by future Massachusetts chief justice Theophilus Parsons—summarized the reasons for rejecting the constitution. One of the worst defects of the document, according to the pamphlet, was that it failed to provide for an independent executive power. Describing what a good constitution ought to say, Parsons wrote:

> The executive power is . . . to enforce the law, and to carry into execution all the others of the legislative powers . . . to arrest offenders and bring them to trial, inflict punishments after criminal trial, and to enforce judgments in civil cases.

The Essex Result became, essentially, a road map for John Adams's 1780 Massachusetts constitution, with its emphasis on separation of powers. Adams's constitution, in turn, heavily influenced the U.S. Constitution.

If there were any lingering doubt about the meaning of Article II's vesting clause, it should be cleared up by the additional command that the president "shall take care that the laws be faithfully executed" (Article II, Section 3).

The people who ratified the Constitution were comfortable imposing a duty on the president to faithfully execute the laws. Would it have been reasonable to impose this duty without giving the president the power he needed to discharge it? Of course not. Moreover, this type of language had always been used in connection with a powerful executive branch. The "take care" clause was lifted almost verbatim from the 1777 New York Constitution, which had bucked the post-1776 trend by creating a strong unitary executive. The language was also found in the Pennsylvania Constitution, where it had been adapted from language going all the way back to a 1681 colonial charter. In every iteration, the clause applied to an executive (or executive branch) with full power to implement and enforce the laws.

HUMAN RESOURCES

The most important practical aspect of the president's control of the executive is his ability to hire and fire the top executive branch bureaucrats—which is why the *Free Enterprise* case matters. When it comes to hiring, the Constitution's text is quite clear. Article II, Section 2 provides that the president "shall appoint Ambassadors, other public Ministers and Consuls, Judges of the supreme Court, and *all other Officers* of the United States" (emphasis added). This provision is subject to two important conditions: (1) for high-level officers, their appointment must be confirmed by the Senate; and (2) for "inferior Officers," Congress can decide whether they are to be appointed by the president without Senate confirmation, or by "Heads of Departments," or by "Courts of Law." For example, Congress can give courts the power to hire their own law clerks without having to get the president and Senate involved. The bottom line, however, is that all executive branch officials must be appointed either by the president himself or by someone (a department head or federal judge) appointed by the president.

The Constitution does not say whether the president has the power to remove executive officers at will, but any other reading of the text produces the bizarre result of a president bound to faithfully execute the laws, yet powerless to control his administration. The first Congress—which included many of the Constitution's framers and ratifiers—came to the same conclusion in what came to be known as the Decision of 1789. When Congress was drafting legislation to create the first executive departments, it initially included language granting the president power to remove the department heads. But a majority of both houses later agreed to delete that language on the grounds that the removal power was not Congress's to give—it was inherent in the office of president.

Presidential control of the executive held firm for more than a century, but it began to run up against the ideal of the "administrative state," that is, rule by unelected bureaucrats. Historian Herman Belz dates the birth of the administrative state to 1887, the year that Woodrow Wilson published an essay ("The Study of Administration") arguing for a government of expert administrators "removed from the hurry and strife of politics." Wilson's express purpose was to adapt the bureaucratic systems of continental Europe to the United States. Also in 1887, Congress created the Interstate Commerce Commission, the prototype of the regulatory agencies that would come to dominate Washington, according to Belz. In the early decades of the administrative state, however, the bureaucracy remained under presidential control. As late as 1926—in the case of *Myers v. United States*—Chief Justice (and former president) William Howard Taft affirmed the president's unfettered power to remove all executive officers.

Article II began to "evolve" in the early days of the New Deal. Upon taking office in 1933, Franklin Roosevelt desperately wanted to fire William Humphrey, a member of the Federal Trade Commission. Humphrey was a staunch Republican appointed by Herbert Hoover, and his views were not simpatico with the New Deal. At first, FDR politely suggested that Humphrey should go and regulate somebody else. When Humphrey didn't take the hint, FDR dismissed him. Humphrey, however, insisted that the president had no power to fire FTC commissioners. The stalemate lasted for four months, at which point Humphrey dropped dead. His executor then sued the federal government for the four months' of wages that Humphrey believed he had earned after he was "fired." The outcome of the lawsuit, *Humphrey's Executor v. United States*, therefore, hinged on the validity of FDR's dismissal of Humphrey.

The Supreme Court—at that point hostile to FDR—held that the federal government owed Humphrey's estate four months' wages because the president did not have power to dismiss an FTC commissioner at will. The president might have such control over traditional executive departments, but not agencies like the FTC, whose powers are "quasi judicial and quasi legislative" and which are "charged with the enforcement of no policy except the policy of the law." If that sounds utterly vacuous, it's because it is. Justice Antonin Scalia aptly summarized the *Humphrey's* decision as "devoid of textual or historical precedent." It also shows that conservative judicial activism is no better than the liberal variety. In *Humphrey's*, a conservative court ignored the text, structure, and history of the Constitution in an attempt to blunt FDR's power. For the sake of creating a minor bump in the road for FDR, the Court legitimized the "independent" executive agency, something that has become a key tool for Congress to expand the size and scope of government.

Moreover, since the Watergate scandal of the early 1970s, Congress has asserted the right to appoint "independent counsels" to investigate and prosecute crimes—a "quintessentially executive function," as Justice Scalia has observed—without any accountability to the president. Congress let the independent counsel statute lapse in 1999 at the request of the Clinton administration—which had been embarrassed by an independent counsel investigation into the president's misdeeds—but the law could be revived anytime. The Supreme Court's 1988 decision in *Morrison v. Olson*, which upheld the independent counsel law, has never been overturned.

Independent agencies have become a shadow government, carving up the nation's resources with no accountability to the people or their representatives. And no accountability to the courts, either. It is nearly impossible to get a federal regulation overturned by a court because the Supreme Court has decreed that lower courts must defer to an agency's interpretation of the law unless it is completely irrational. This lax standard of review is known as "Chevron deference" — named after the 1984 Supreme Court ruling in *Chevron USA v. National Resources Defense Council.* In the upside-down world of constitutional law, federal judges have a free hand to overturn laws enacted directly by state voters (see chapter 5), but they must show deference to unelected bureaucrats. Some agencies are shielded from review altogether, such as the Independent Payment Advisory Board (IPAB), a fifteen-member junta created by the Affordable Care Act—the Obama health law—with the modest task of dictating medical costs for the nation. IPAB was designed so that its edicts "aren't subject to administrative or even judicial review," according to a March 9, 2012, editorial in the *Wall Street Journal.*

In the *Free Enterprise* case, Justice Stephen Breyer unwittingly illustrated the extent of the problem when he observed (in dissent) that the federal government relies on no fewer than forty-eight agencies, offices, bureaus, and boards whose members are, like the PCAOB, insulated from presidential control by at least two layers of "for cause" dismissal protection. Dozens more have one layer of "for cause" protection. Breyer's point was that independent agencies must work awfully well, since there are so many of them. If you measure success by regulatory output, he's certainly right. Independent agencies represent a large chunk of the three hundred–plus federal entities that, as of 2010, had issued 35,367 pages (225 volumes) of fine-print regulations, all with the force of law. But if the Constitution is your yardstick, we're in deep trouble. With no checks and balances, the permanent bureaucracy—with its built-in incentive to accumulate power—remains on "liberal autopilot," as the *National Review*'s Jonah Goldberg aptly described it.

ALL HAIL THE ADMINISTRATIVE STATE!

Harvard law professor Noah Feldman observed in the *New York Times Magazine* in September 2008 that "the New Deal ushered in systemic regulation and administrative agencies that had no real place in the three-branch system." Feldman then went on to assure the *Times* readership that "we now accept [such regulation and administrative agencies] as constitutional today." Do we?

Common sense tells that the Founding Fathers would be horrified to see our liberties held hostage by unelected and unaccountable bureaucrats. Early progressives like Woodrow Wilson proudly asserted that the administrative state was an improvement upon the Founders' design. According to Professors Lessig and Sunstein, however, the Founding Fathers had provided for the administrative state all along. In their 1994 article (which I discuss above), they contend that the Constitution does not vest the president with run-of-the-mill executive functions, which they call "administrative power." Rather, the Constitution vests the president only with the enumerated executive powers, like defense and foreign affairs, and leaves virtually all administrative powers in the hands of Congress. On this reading, the framers gave Congress the power to establish an administrative branch of government beyond the president's control.

The case for the administrative branch is built upon the necessary and proper clause of Article I—that all-purpose tool for big government advocates everywhere. As you'll recall, that clause comes at the end of Article I, Section 8's laundry list of congressional powers, and it grants Congress the power "to make all laws which shall be necessary and proper for carrying into Execution the foregoing Powers."

Eureka!—comes the cry from the faculty lounge—it says "execution"! That must mean that the framers vested Congress with its own "executive power," namely, the power to create any administrative body that it finds necessary and proper. Right?

Not exactly. As we saw in the last chapter, the necessary and proper clause was a legalistic redundancy that was originally understood to restrict, not expand, Congress's power. It is true that *execution* is related to *executive*, and that both words have to do with effectuating some plan. But consider the context. Article I, Section 8, contains a list of specified *legislative* powers. And then, to carry *those powers* into "execution," Congress has the power "to make laws." This is nothing more than a restatement of the fact that Congress has to produce pieces of paper ("make Laws") to exercise its jurisdiction over interstate commerce, and so on. It does not suggest that Congress has a stand-alone power to implement or enforce the laws that it makes.

There is not a shred of real evidence that the Constitution gives Congress vast administrative powers. To the contrary, the text of the Constitution itself provides for three distinct branches, each one set forth in a separate article. It beggars belief to think that the framers relegated the administration of the law to a mere inference to be drawn from the necessary and proper clause. Nor is there any record of the framers or ratifiers referring to an administrative power distinct from the executive. To the contrary, the framers were expressly devoted to Montesquieu (the "oracle," according to Madison), who clearly laid out the three branches as an exhaustive catalog of government powers. And it is interesting, as Professor Prakash has pointed out, that "not one of the Constitution's rather able advocates" even tried to rebut the Anti-Federalists' fears of executive tyranny by pointing out that it was the administrative branch rather than the executive branch that would actually execute the laws.

Ultimately, the argument that there are administrative powers outside the framers' tripartite scheme misses the branches for the trees. As an intellectual parlor game, one can think of government functions that are difficult to categorize. But that does not relieve us of the obligation to designate all functions as belonging to one branch or another. The Constitution was understood, above all, to protect individual liberty and state sovereignty. Nobody in 1789 would have understood the document as permitting individuals to exercise significant powers over individuals or states outside of the three branches. Only officers of the three branches are required to swear an oath to uphold the Constitution, and only officers of the three branches are subject to the framers' checks and balances.

Living Constitution advocates like Justice Breyer argue that the complexities of the modern world require us to abandon the text. According to Breyer, Congress must be empowered to set up agencies where "experts" can be protected from "political influence." But the dreaded "political influence" is nothing more than democratic control over executive officers. That control was a key concern in a young nation that had broken away from King George in part because he had "erected a multitude of new offices, and sent hither swarms of officers to harass our people and eat out their substance." Historian Gordon Wood observed that "the power of appointment to offices" was considered by the founding generation to be "the most insidious and powerful weapon of eighteenth century despotism."

THE ROAD TO FIEFDOM

Is despotism too strong a word? I think not. The very logic—such as it is—of *Humphrey's Executor* is that Congress is free to ignore separation of powers by creating bodies that are partly executive, but also "quasi legislative and quasi judicial." The use of "quasi" is the one artful piece of the decision. It makes the independent agencies sound like harmless dabblers—never exercising any real power, but just chugging along in their little-bit-country-little-bit-rock-and-roll bureaus. The reality is that the awesome power of the federal government has been concentrated in a series of independent fiefdoms like the National Labor Relations Board (NLRB), with jurisdiction over labor-management relations. The NLRB uses its "quasi" powers to issue regulations, investigate violations, prosecute offenders, and sit in judgment on their cases. Lawmaker, advocate, judge, and jury.

In April 2011, for example, the NLRB filed a complaint to block Boeing from opening a new $2 billion facility to produce its Dreamliner series of planes. The reason was that Boeing had decided to locate the facility in the right-to-work state of South

Carolina rather than using its existing (unionized) facility in Washington State. Thank heavens this decision was made by "experts" insulated from "political pressure." Those craven pols who have to face the voters might have thought twice before protecting "workers' rights" by shuttering a plant that would have employed a thousand people. The NLRB ultimately dropped the complaint against Boeing, but only after the machinists' union had extracted promises from Boeing to produce a new jet in the Seattle area.

Or take our friends over at PCAOB. A harmless little agency of helpful experts? The five PCAOB board members have nearly absolute power to regulate the accounting profession, particularly the manner in which publicly traded companies are audited. In its first year of operations, those regulations imposed more than $35 billion in compliance costs on the nation's businesses. The board members have the power to enforce compliance by investigating wrongdoers and levying fines of up to $15 million. They never have to ask Congress for money because they fund themselves via a tax on public companies. They even set their own salaries. In 2003, for example, they decided that each Peekaboo board member merited over $400,000, with the chairman raking in $556,000. And, as we've seen, they are virtually unremovable. Nice work, if you can get it.

Against the grim realities of the administrative state, the *Free Enterprise* decision represents only a modest victory. The Supreme Court did invalidate the original structure of the PCAOB, but only because its members were protected by *two* layers of "for cause" protection: the SEC had limited power to fire the Peekaboo board, and the president had limited power to fire the SEC commissioners. The court did not overturn *Humphrey's* (or *Morrison v. Olson*), meaning that we are still left with the alphabet soup of federal agencies shielded by "only" one layer of insulation from the president, including the FTC, SEC, FEC, NLRB, TVA, FCC, and—well, you get the idea. The constitutional mandate that the president "take care" that the laws be faithfully executed "no longer extends to vast areas of federally-regulated conduct and behavior," according to Ted Olson. In those areas, says Olson, "it is virtually impossible for the President to have an impact."

FROM THE HALLS OF MONTEZUMA . . .

Compared to the hard slog of domestic affairs, presidents enjoy tremendous freedom of action when it comes to making war. When I say "enjoy," I don't mean to suggest that presidents actually enjoy sending troops into combat. But they certainly have a tendency to do so. The constitutional question is: Can the president independently make war against another country, or must he get authorization from Congress?

It depends who you ask—and when you ask him. Barack Obama, for example, told the *Boston Globe* in 2007 that the president "does not have the power under the Constitution to unilaterally authorize a military attack in a situation that does not involve stopping an actual or imminent threat to the nation." The comment was intended as a rebuke to the Bush administration, which, according to the Left's narrative, was always plotting to invade yet another country. Specifically, then-senator Obama feared that Bush was going to attack Iran, which posed no "imminent threat" to the United States—except being led by a U.S.-hating, Holocaust-denying megalomaniac bent on acquiring nuclear weapons.

When Obama said that the president could not act unilaterally, he meant "without the consent of Congress." In short, then-senator Obama was simply asserting one of Congress's enumerated powers: the power "to declare War" (Article I, Section 8). The subtext, of course, was that war was a lot less likely to happen with Congress in charge rather than that "cowboy" George Bush.

. . . TO THE SHORES OF TRIPOLI

But then Obama became president and got himself a Nobel Peace Prize. Suddenly, starting a war became something of a challenge—sort of like getting a drink in Utah. The opportunity came during the "Arab Spring" of 2011, when a popular uprising in Libya was being crushed by dictator Moammar Qaddafi. Obama decided to dispatch the U.S. military to support the Libyan rebels after consultations with the leaders of France and Britain, NATO, the UN Security Council, and the Arab League; in fact, after consulting pretty much everyone except the U.S. Congress. His very first communication to Congress on the matter occurred on March 21—just hours before the bombing began. When pressed on their failure to consult with Congress, Obama and Secretary of State Hillary Clinton articulated a whole new doctrine: the president doesn't need Congress's permission when he acts as part of an international coalition.

Constitutionally speaking, the Obama of 2007 was a lot closer to the truth than the Peace Prize winner of 2011. But the Libyan War is a useful illustration of the signature feature of all war-powers debates: hypocrisy. The party that holds the White House invariably embraces presidential war power until the moment it finds itself in opposition. Not only did Obama reverse his earlier stand (a "full flop," according to the nonpartisan PolitiFact Web site), but the Democratic Party did as well. On April 5, 2011, Republican senator Rand Paul introduced a "sense of the Senate" resolution that simply repeated, verbatim, Obama's 2007 statement to the *Boston Globe.* Every single Democratic senator voted against it, including those who had spent years railing against the Bush administration's supposedly go-it-alone defense policy.

The Libyan adventure also helps to expose the paranoid fantasy that "presidential war power" is a doctrine invented by the Bush administration—no doubt in the same secret Skull and Bones ceremony that produced the "unitary executive" theory. In fact, presidential war power is a long-standing bipartisan tradition, wrongheaded though it may be. Consider this: Congress has not declared war on anyone since Pearl Harbor, but thousands of Americans have been sent into combat since the end of World War II. Every one of those military campaigns has been justified as an exercise of inherent presidential power.

George W. Bush did have a particularly articulate advocate of presidential power in John Yoo, who was a member of the Office of Legal Counsel (OLC) in the Bush Justice Department. Yoo, a scholarly lawyer who has since moved on to an academic career, was criticized by both the Left and the Right for taking an expansive view of presidential war powers. But on the basic question of who decides whether the United States goes to war, Yoo did little but restate—with footnotes—the assertions that the OLC had been making for decades. Clinton's OLC, for example, gave the green light to deploy troops to Somalia, Haiti, and Bosnia without congressional approval. Indeed, in the latter two conflicts, Clinton intervened despite pointed congressional disapproval.

Even Jimmy Carter—that cowboy—embraced unilateral presidential war powers. The Carter OLC declared, in the midst of the Iranian hostage crisis of 1979–81, that Carter could attack Iran without congressional approval if even one of the fifty-two U.S. hostages was harmed. In sum, there was nothing novel about Bush's assertion of presidential initiative in making war.

MAKE DECLARATIONS, NOT WAR

Despite the long tradition of presidential war powers, nothing in the Constitution empowers the president to start an offensive war. To the contrary, the framers assigned to Congress the power "to declare War; grant Letters of Marque and Reprisal, and [to] make Rules concerning Captures on Land and Water" (Article I, Section 8).

The clauses after the word *war* refer to lower-level hostilities that would fall short of full-fledged war. Letters of marque and reprisal would authorize private parties (usually shipowners) to take action against hostile powers, while captures would authorize private parties to seize the vessels and other property of hostile powers. The bottom line is that the people, acting through Congress, must authorize any military adventure. The president cannot evade this requirement by outsourcing the job to the private sector.

Advocates of presidential war powers argue that Congress's power under Article I is nothing compared to the president's power as "Commander-in-Chief of the Army and Navy of the United States, and of the Militia of the several States, when called into the actual service of the United States" (Article II, Section 2). The consistent view of the OLC, as summarized by John Yoo after the September 11 attacks, is that "the Commander-in-Chief Clause is a substantive grant of authority to the president and . . . the scope of the president's authority to commit the armed forces to combat is very broad." The historical evidence for reading this clause so broadly, according to Yoo, is that the Founders were familiar with "the British approach" to war-making powers, which involved "executive initiative and legislative appropriations." In other words, one should assume that the president possesses all the traditional powers of the British king unless the Constitution expressly says otherwise.

But the Constitution *does* say otherwise. That was the whole point of giving Congress, not the president, the power to declare war. According to Alexander Hamilton, this was a major reason why the president's role as commander in chief would be "much inferior" to that of the British king. Yes, the president would have "supreme command and direction" of the military, wrote Hamilton, but the king's power "extends to the declaring of war and to the raising and regulating of fleets and armies," which the Constitution delegates to Congress. As Hamilton would clarify later on, the president has "the direction of war when authorized or begun."

Notice Hamilton's choice of words: war can be "authorized *or* begun." The commander-in-chief power applies in two situations: when war is "authorized" (because declared by Congress) or "begun" (because somebody else has attacked us). That is why Article I speaks of "declaring" war. The original draft would have given Congress the power "to make war," but on a motion by Madison and Elbridge Gerry, the delegates replaced "make" with "declare." The point of the change, according to Madison's notes, was to leave the president free "to repel sudden attacks." This was a sensible change: if the nation is under attack, the president must be able to act decisively in "making war" on the aggressor. A declaration of war—which was a public announcement of hostilities—was hardly necessary once we had actually been attacked.

The presidentialist camp, however, goes further, insisting that declarations of war were considered a mere technicality in the eighteenth century and that nations fought undeclared wars all the time. Thus, according to Professors Yoo and Robert Delahunty, the "declare war" clause would have been understood as merely empowering Congress "to serve notice on American citizens, neutral nations, and intended or actual foreign enemies of the existence of a state of war." On this view, a declaration of war was simply an after-the-fact tweet to the world: *OMG, prez started another war. LOL.*

Yoo and Delahunty concede that when it came to an offensive action, declarations of war were considered "necessary (or at least advisable) for securing the legitimacy or lawfulness of an offensive war." The notion that Congress would get around to declaring war only after the president had decided to wage war is belied by the framers' words. Even Hamilton, who favored an "energetic" executive, wrote that "the Legislature alone . . . can transfer the nation from a state of peace to a state of hostility." Again, this formulation leaves the president room to defend the nation, because if we've already been attacked, he's not "transfer[ring] the nation" from peace to war.

Moreover, it's unlikely that the Constitution would have been ratified if it had been understood merely to give Congress the power to rubber-stamp every presidential military adventure. There was a strong Anti-Federalist movement that feared the potential power of the commander in chief. As Thomas Woods and Kevin Gutzman note in *Who Killed the Constitution?*, "no

Anti-Federalist would have been appeased" by the argument that Congress can issue empty declarations while the president calls the shots.

George Washington and other early presidents understood the Constitution to give Congress the initiative in waging offensive war. During the Washington administration, the United States fought against various Indian tribes on the northwestern frontier. In his 1793 State of the Union, Washington noted that he had taken offensive measures against the Wabash Indians—as Congress had authorized—but had not done so against the Creeks. As he explained to South Carolina governor William Moultrie in that same year, "The Constitution vests the power of declaring war with Congress; therefore, no offensive expedition of importance can be undertaken" without congressional authorization. Granted, Washington hedged a bit—he reserved the right to conduct offensive operations that were not "important"—but that may simply reflect the fuzzy nature of a border war, where "defense" might require an incursion across the frontier. In any event, it's a far cry from the grand assertion that the president can invade any country, at any time, without Congress's say-so. For that doctrine, we have to thank not George Bush and John Yoo, but Harry Truman.

THE IMPERIAL PRESIDENCY

On June 24, 1950, the army of Communist North Korea invaded South Korea. The next day, the UN Security Council passed a resolution denouncing the invasion and called on UN members to render "assistance" in executing the resolution. By the following evening, Truman and his top aides had decided to commit forces to the defense of South Korea. A few days later, Truman made a fateful decision. Relying on the advice of Secretary of State Dean Acheson, Truman decided not to seek a declaration of war but instead to mobilize the army based on his inherent power as commander in chief. The unfortunate result was three years of bloody conflict and eleven seasons of *M*A*S*H*.

To justify his faulty advice to Truman, Acheson had some State Department mandarin produce a memo listing eighty-seven instances in which a U.S. president had supposedly deployed troops without congressional authorization. In *The Imperial Presidency*, the late Arthur Schlesinger observed that the memo contained "precedents for limited action to suppress pirates or to protect American citizens. . . . They were not precedents for sustained and major war against a sovereign state." Like Obama in 2011, Truman would try to rely on the existence of a UN resolution, but such resolutions—while nifty instruments of international law—cannot replace Congress's prerogative to declare war. As Schlesinger concluded, Truman "dramatically and dangerously enlarged the power of future presidents to take the nation into a major war."

Ironically, Schlesinger, a stalwart Democrat, had defended Truman at the time of the Korean War. When Republican senator Robert Taft argued in 1951 that Truman's Korean troop deployment was unconstitutional, Schlesinger branded him as "demonstrably irresponsible." Schlesinger came to write *The Imperial Presidency* in reaction to a different war, Vietnam, and a different president, the Republican Richard Nixon. Unlike many other Democratic commentators, however, Schlesinger had the decency to apologize for his earlier statement. When, one wonders, will Barack Obama apologize for his 2007 criticism of George W. Bush?

CONGRESS GETS IT BACKWARD

In 1973—the very year that *The Imperial Presidency* came out—Congress attempted to restore the constitutional balance of war-making powers by enacting the War Powers Resolution. Like most latter-day attempts to improve upon the framers' design, the resolution succeeds mainly as evidence that Darwin was wrong.

The resolution capitulates to the president on the question of offensive war, allowing the executive to send troops into hostilities anywhere in the world with nothing but a forty-eight-hour heads-up to Congress. Once the fighting begins, Congress has up to ninety days to authorize the war, or not. But this is no power at all, because once a war has begun, there will be overwhelming pressure on Congress to rally around the troops by showing resolve. Besides, Congress already had the ability—via its power of the purse—to stop any military campaign by cutting off the funds.

As if to make up for its surrender of constitutional power, Congress also took away some of the president's power. The War Powers Resolution imposes the same forty-eight-hour/ninety-day shot clock on any deployment abroad of troops "equipped for combat," with certain exceptions. But not all troop deployments amount to "war." In a Constitution that authorizes a standing army (Article I, Section 8), the commander in chief should be able to move his troops around without getting Congress's say-so. As long ago as 1916, Chief Justice William Howard Taft made the seemingly uncontroversial assertion that the commander-in-chief power authorizes the president to "order the army and navy anywhere he will, if the appropriations furnish the means of transportation"; that is, if Congress has provided the money for ships, trains, horses, etc.

Is it possible that the president can provoke a war by amassing troops on a sensitive border or other hot spot? Sure—just as he could provoke a war (at least in an earlier era) by expelling another country's diplomats. In any system of divided powers, one branch might be able to force the hand of another branch; but the idea that the president must check in with Congress whenever moving troops abroad is just as unconstitutional as giving the president a three-month free trial period for any new war. The only good thing about the War Powers Resolution is that it is basically a dead letter, having been consistently flouted by presidents of both parties.

Notwithstanding the Left's anti-Bush hysteria, the Bush administration's conduct of war came much closer to the constitutional design than Clinton's had been, or Obama's would prove to be. The wars in Afghanistan and Iraq, as well as the broader offensive against al-Qaeda, were all authorized ahead of time by Congress. Shortly after the September 11 attacks, Congress empowered the president to use military force against "those nations, organizations, or persons he determines planned, authorized, committed, or aided the terrorist attacks." This language easily fits the original understanding of a declaration of war as a "simple and overt declaration" of the nation's hostile intentions, as Connecticut delegate Oliver Ellsworth had described it to the Philadelphia convention. Likewise, in October 2002 Congress passed a joint resolution authorizing the president to use force against Iraq to enforce UN Security Council resolutions or to protect the national security of the United States. That was five months before the invasion began.

MILITARY INTELLIGENCE

Once a war is "authorized or begun," as Hamilton noted, the president assumes "supreme command and direction" of the armed forces. That's what *commander in chief* means. The Philadelphia constitution followed the model of the 1780 Massachusetts constitution, which also granted the executive commander-in-chief powers that, it explained in lurid detail, included the power to "kill, slay, destroy, if necessary, and conquer by all fitting ways, enterprize and means."

One of the "ways, enterprize and means" by which commanders defeat the enemy is by spying on them. Intelligence gathering was a well-established part of war by 1787: Nathan Hale had been an American spy; Benedict Arnold was a double agent. Not surprisingly, at the outset of the War on Terror, President Bush directed the National Security Agency to conduct electronic surveillance to gather intelligence on terrorist plots against the United States.

When this warrantless wiretapping program came to light, it became a cause célèbre for liberals and some conservatives because the administration had not followed the requirements of FISA—the Foreign Intelligence Surveillance Act of 1978. Under FISA, the administration must get approval from a special FISA court in order to gather "foreign intelligence," which includes, for example, information bearing on an "actual or potential attack" against the United States. Bush's response was that, in time of war, he had the inherent authority to conduct intelligence without micromanagement. Jonathan Alter of *Newsweek* moaned that Bush was trying to "scrap the Constitution," while Bruce Fein, a former Reagan administration lawyer, argued that Bush's real motivation was "to chill dissent by creating an aura of intimidation." Yes, of course: you'll remember how dissent withered away during the Bush presidency.

Bush was right. Being commander in chief includes the power to gather intelligence on the enemy. Abraham Lincoln was of the same view. During the Civil War, his administration hired spies to go down South and pick up every possible scrap of information about the Confederacy's war effort. When the legitimacy of this spying program came into question in a case called *Totten v. United States*, a unanimous Supreme Court held that Honest Abe "was undoubtedly authorized during the war, as commander-in-chief . . . to employ secret agents to enter the rebel lines and obtain information respecting . . . the enemy." Lincoln did not obtain warrants to spy on the enemy, nor did future presidents. As a federal appellate court summarized in 2002, "all . . . courts to have decided the issue [before the enactment of FISA] held that the president did have inherent authority to conduct warrantless searches to obtain foreign intelligence information."

FISA, however, makes virtually no concession to presidential war powers. Even after an official declaration of war, the statute gives the president just fifteen days to gather intelligence on his own initiative; after that, everything has to be blessed by a FISA court. In other words, FISA says that even in time of war, the commander in chief must seek judicial approval to gather intelligence about imminent attacks on the United States. Whatever its merits in time of peace, FISA is surely an unconstitutional fetter on the president's power in time of war. Indeed, nothing in the Constitution gives Congress the authority to limit the inherent powers of the other two branches. Subjecting the president to FISA is a little like requiring the Supreme Court to seek congressional approval before accepting a case.

ROUND UP THE USUAL SUSPECTS

Similarly, most of the arguments against Bush's program of detaining enemy combatants ignored the reality of presidential war powers. In a time of war, the commander in chief must be able to detain captured enemy fighters during the hostilities without putting each POW on trial. This was what the Supreme Court had affirmed in *Johnson v. Eisentrager* (see chapter 2). Granted, it was at one time controversial to apply the word *war* to the struggle against Islamic terrorism, but since Barack Obama declared in January 2010 that "we are at war against al Qaeda," that argument seems to have fallen away.

There are, of course, limits to presidential powers, even in wartime. Those limits derive from the Constitution itself. No branch of the federal government can exercise its vested powers in such a way as to violate another provision of the Constitution. It was wrong, for example, for FDR to round up Japanese Americans and put them in detention camps during World War II, thus depriving them of liberty without due process. Truman's attempt to seize the nation's steel mills during the Korean War was not a proper "executive" act because it did not implement any law—Congress had not authorized the seizure. But in that case, at least, the Supreme Court stepped in to stop the expropriation in the *Youngstown Sheet & Tube* case.

President Bush went too far, however, when he claimed that the War on Terror authorized him to detain *U.S. citizens* without charges. Under the Constitution, citizens who engage in war against the United States or who give "aid and comfort" to her enemies are guilty of treason. Article III lays out specific procedures for the government to prove this serious crime: the traitor must confess in open court, or the government must produce testimony from at least two witnesses. Moreover, due process requires that a citizen deprived of liberty must be able to challenge his detention through a habeas corpus proceeding.

In the 2004 case of *Hamdi v. Rumsfeld*, unfortunately, the

Supreme Court upheld the executive's power to detain even U.S. citizens indefinitely as enemy combatants. The decision drew a sharp dissent from Justice Antonin Scalia, joined by the liberal justice John Paul Stevens. Scalia rightly argued that where a U.S. citizen is concerned, the government is obliged either to charge him with treason or release him — unless Congress suspends habeas corpus, which it had not. (For more on *Hamdi*, see chapter 2.)

Barack Obama was one of many politicians assailing Bush for detaining U.S. citizens without trial. Little did we know that as president, Obama would devise an interesting alternative: kill U.S. citizens without trial. In February 2010, media outlets revealed that the Obama administration was keeping a list of terror suspects targeted for assassination. The list included U.S. citizens who were to be summarily executed by drone strike or otherwise. Due process? That's for sissies.

One of the targeted citizens was Anwar al-Awlaki, whose father Nassar sued the U.S. government with the assistance of the ACLU. The district court judge tossed Nassar's case out on procedural grounds, but if that hadn't worked, the Obama administration's next move was to invoke the state secrets doctrine, ably summarized by the liberal magazine *Mother Jones*: "You can't challenge your presence on the secret government assassination list because the list is a secret." On September 30, 2011, U.S. drones killed al-Awlaki as well as Samir Khan, a U.S. citizen of Pakistani origin.

No administration—not even those Bush cowboys—has ever asserted the president's authority to kill any American, anywhere in the world, whenever he deems that person to be a threat. Had George W. Bush attempted to claim such powers, then-senator Obama would have dashed to the nearest teleprompter to deliver a stinging rebuke. But that's the temptation of presidential war powers: they turn our commander into a Hypocrite in Chief.

WHAT ARE YOU, A MAN OR A MOUSE?

The argument of this chapter might seem schizophrenic—building up presidential power in the first half, only to tear it down (partly) in the second. Originalism, however, is neither pro-president nor pro-Congress, it's pro-text. The Constitution envisions a unitary executive with the power to control the implementation and enforcement of the laws that Congress enacts. But it also creates a very clear division of war powers in which only Congress can declare war, and only the president can conduct a war.

Perversely, we've ended up with a system in which the executive branch has seen its core functions eaten away by independent agencies, while successive presidents appoint czars and start wars based on nonexistent war powers. The late constitutional scholar Charles Hardin, in his classic 1974 study *Presidential Power and Accountability*, observed that "in recent decades the presidency has escaped the political controls essential to constitutional, i.e., *limited* government" (emphasis his). Despite the president's apparent authority, however, Hardin recognized that "the president's power often disappears in bureaucratic independence."

Although he correctly diagnosed the problems, Hardin's prescription was strong medicine; perhaps too strong. He proposed sweeping constitutional changes intended to ensure that the president would always represent the majority party in both houses of Congress—similar to a parliamentary system. With executive and legislature thus aligned, the constant attempts of one branch to undercut the other would come to an end. But then again, we would also lose all the other benefits of divided government. Washington gridlock—often derided by commentators—has saved the Republic from more than one piece of foolish legislation. Rather than establishing a quasi-parliamentary system, I propose more targeted changes to restore the proper scope of executive power, such as a line-item veto, in chapter 12.

CHAPTER FIVE

THE COURTS

Supreme Power Grab

The judicial Power shall extend to all Cases, in Law and Equity, arising under this Constitution, the Laws of the United States, and Treaties.

—ARTICLE III, SECTION 2

IN THE 2008 GENERAL ELECTION, California voters overwhelmingly backed Barack Obama—and Proposition 8, a ballot initiative that added the following sentence to the state constitution: "Only marriage between a man and a woman is valid or recognized in California."

Proposition 8 enjoyed widespread support, including roughly 70 percent of the black vote and a majority of the Hispanic vote, according to exit polls. This was, in fact, the second time Californians had voted to define marriage in this manner, having approved exactly the same language in a 2000 referendum. In the intervening years, voters in twenty-three other states had approved laws banning same-sex marriage. In the 2008 presidential campaign, both major candidates spoke out against gay marriage.

The will of the people, however, is no match for a single determined federal judge. When a lawsuit challenging Proposition 8 ended up in the courtroom of Judge Vaughn Walker, the law was doomed. Barely able to conceal his contempt for the ballot measure, Walker tried to intimidate Proposition 8 supporters out of testifying by ordering that the trial be televised. He also ordered Proposition 8 supporters to hand over their internal campaign communications, so that opponents could look for signs of antigay bias. These procedural orders were reversed by appellate courts, but Walker got the result he wanted. After all, he was the judge.

After the trial, Walker issued a 136-page opinion declaring that Proposition 8 violates the "fundamental right" of gay marriage under the U.S. Constitution. Not that the Constitution actually says anything about marriage, or gender, or sexuality. If it did, Walker could have written a one-page opinion. But it takes a lot more ink to convince people that the Constitution says things that it manifestly does not.

According to Judge Walker, the 7 million California citizens who voted for Proposition 8 (and presumably the voters in those twenty-three other states) acted "irrationally" in denying this previously unheard-of right. The judge knew—somehow, he just knew—that those 7 million voters had been motivated by nothing more than a bigoted belief "that opposite-sex couples are morally superior to same-sex couples." That would be the same bigoted electorate that supported California's domestic partnership law, which, as Judge Walker conceded, provides gay couples with "essentially the same rights and obligations" as traditional marriage. Such partnerships, however, are not good enough: apparently the Constitution not only mandates state recognition of gay unions, but it also requires that states use the word *marriage* to describe them. Walker was not merely rewriting the Constitution that day; he was adding fine print.

All of this innovation was justified by a scholarly-sounding discussion of the history of marriage in which Walker scolded California voters for failing to recognize "the movement of marriage from a gendered institution" and the "evolution in the understanding of gender." Unbeknownst to the majority of California voters, the notion of marriage as a union of man and woman is "an artifact" of a time when society dictated gender roles. "That time," Walker ominously intoned, "has passed." Those naughty voters. Who do they think they are?

My point is not that the Constitution *forbids* gay marriage. To the contrary, every state in the Union could endorse gay marriage without offending the Constitution in the least. Several have. That is for the simple reason that the Constitution does not address marriage one way or another. Governmental recognition of marriage is one of those innumerable policy issues that the Constitution leaves to the voters and legislatures of the states (see chapter 11).

But there's no need to take my word for it. The ultimate indictment of Judge Walker's decision is the fact that it was upheld by the Ninth Circuit Court of Appeals, the most consistently wrong court in the nation. In a February 2012 ruling penned by Judge Stephen Reinhardt, a left-wing jurist known for his passionate opposition to the Pledge of Allegiance (see chapter 7), the court held that Proposition 8 is unconstitutional because it "stripped away" a right that had previously been enjoyed by Californians. But Reinhardt barely mentioned the fact that the only reason gay marriage was ever deemed a right in California was an earlier activist decision by the state supreme court in 2004—precisely the decision that the voters overturned by approving Proposition 8. By Reinhardt's logic—which even the reliably liberal *Washington Post* described as a "wobbly piece of jurisprudence"—the Constitution is a one-way liberal ratchet. Once a court invents a new right, the voters have no power to change course.

THE LEAST DANGEROUS BRANCH?

The ease with which federal courts have disenfranchised millions of California voters on a quintessential matter of state law is, alas, but a symptom of a judiciary run amok. The judicial branch was established by Article III of the Constitution to decide "cases" and "controversies," that is, concrete disputes in which a judge must *apply* the law to the facts. Instead, federal judges have established themselves as a superlegislature: making up novel "rights," raising state taxes, redrawing election districts, dictating the exact level of religiosity of Nativity scenes in public parks—and that's just for starters.

The courts have also become a superexecutive. Since the 1970s, the federal bench has snatched more and more power away from the nation's governors and mayors. Today, federal judges run schools, hospitals, public housing authorities, and prisons. Lots of prisons. According to one estimate, by 1993, courts had taken over 80 percent of all state prison systems and a third of the five hundred largest local jails.

Alexander Hamilton predicted that the judiciary "will always be the least dangerous branch to the political rights of the Constitution." How could it be otherwise? With no political base, no taxing power, and no army at its command, a bunch of judges seem ill equipped to usurp political power from the other branches. But that is what has happened. Contrary to Hamilton's prediction, the federal judiciary has systematically taken over legislative and executive powers while everyone else stood by and watched.

The courts have used a variety of methods to grab power, like manipulating "standing" rules to allow favored interest groups—think Sierra Club—to challenge laws. But the two most important tools of judicial supremacy are (1) judicial legislation, i.e., constitutionalizing policy issues that should be decided by legislatures; and (2) expansive use of "equity" powers to usurp power from executive bodies.

JUDICIAL LEGISLATION

Pity the poor federal judge. There he is: ambitious, intelligent, and protected by lifetime tenure. Is he really supposed to sit around deciding the narrow "cases" and "controversies" set before him while those yokels in Congress and—even worse—the state legislatures get to say what the law is? Of course not, especially when all it takes is a little creative interpretation to make new laws. As Justice Scalia remarked, the Supreme Court's "temptation is . . . towards systematically eliminating checks upon its own power; and it succumbs."

Constitutional lawmaking is an especially indelible kind. A garden-variety statute can always be repealed by a later statute. But a constitutional decision—if accepted by the Supreme Court—will stay in place unless a later majority of the Court decides to overturn it (rare) or the people rise up to amend the Constitution (*very* rare). Former judge and senator James Buckley expressed it beautifully when he suggested that the federal judiciary has developed "an approach to constitutional interpretation that has permitted American judges to carve their policy preferences in constitutional granite."

How do we know that judges are supposed to *apply* the law but not *create* the law? First of all, the framers established a whole branch of government for the very purpose of creating laws: Congress. Indeed, the Constitution plainly vests Congress with *all* of the legislative powers granted therein. Wouldn't it be odd if the ratifiers had understood the judiciary to have those same powers?

Second, the Philadelphia convention rejected numerous attempts to give federal judges a policy-making role. The Virginia delegation had proposed to give a veto power to a "Council of Revision," which would include the executive and "a convenient number of the National Judiciary." But such a council was repeatedly rejected. Apparently, a majority of delegates concluded that the most "convenient" number was zero. Variations of the Virginia proposal were floated four times and defeated each time. Elbridge Gerry of Massachusetts objected that it was "quite foreign" to the nature of a judge's office "to make them judges of policy and public measures." His fellow Bay Stater Rufus King added that judges should "expound the law as it should come before them, free from the bias of having participated in its formation."

Third, the framers weren't stupid. They were well aware that aggressive judicial interpretation of laws represented a threat to separation of powers. Influential political philosophers such as Montesquieu warned against this very danger. The *Essex Result*, an important precursor to the Constitution (chapter 4) also rejected a proposed constitution for Massachusetts because it lacked strong checks and balances, including safeguards against "artful construction" of the laws by judges.

The framers' concerns about "interpretation" were magnified when it came to judges interpreting the Constitution itself, a prospect that struck fear in the hearts of many of the Philadelphia delegates. Gerry warned in 1789 that "all construction of the meaning of the Constitution is dangerous or unnatural . . . I am decidedly against putting any construction whatever on the Constitution." Even James Madison expressed grave reservations about granting federal courts jurisdiction to hear cases "arising under the Constitution." The judiciary should not, he said, have the power "of expounding the Constitution" beyond the traditional right of judges to apply the written law.

And finally, let's not forget that the Constitution has its own procedure for making amendments: Article V. The framers deliberately made this procedure difficult, requiring action by Congress or a national convention, plus three-fourths of the states. It's hardly likely that the same framers implicitly gave the judicial branch the power to change the Constitution without formal amendment.

THE DEATH OF RESTRAINT

Justice Harlan Stone once observed, "The only check upon our own exercise of power is our own sense of self-restraint." Stone knew this better than most. No model of restraint himself, he spent the 1930s as an associate justice of the Supreme Court, enthusiastically twisting the Constitution to accommodate the New Deal—for which Franklin Roosevelt elevated him to chief justice.

If any residual sense of restraint remained after the New Deal, it evaporated as soon as Earl Warren took the helm as chief justice in 1954. A popular ex-governor of California, Warren had no interest in the dreary task of interpreting the law; he preferred to make law. Although nominally a Republican, Warren found himself commanding a court full of New Dealers, so he drove them in the only direction they would go: leftward. From 1954 to 1969, the "Warren Court" graciously supplied all sorts of new laws to the state governments, thus relieving legislators of the bother and inconvenience of writing bills. This was the high-water mark of judicial legislation, better known as "judicial activism."

Judicial activism violates the principle of separation of powers because it involves judicial encroachment on the powers of the other branches. Activism is a temptation to all judges—and signs of activism can be seen in the earliest decisions of the Supreme Court, such as *Marbury v. Madison*. But it was with the New Deal that the Court began systematically legislating from the bench (in fact, the term *judicial activism* had been coined in 1947 to describe some of the New Deal justices). The Warren Court, nonetheless, elevated this particular type of power grab to an art form—leading Eisenhower to lament Warren's appointment as "the biggest damned-fool mistake I ever made."

While conservatives are nearly unanimous in their condemnation of activist judges, liberals can't seem to make up their minds. One school of thought urges us to embrace activism as good for the country; perhaps even for our souls. An example of this school is David Dow's 2009 *America's Prophets*, a book that opens with the modest claim, "Jesus was a judicial activist."

But wait: not just Jesus! "The great Jewish rabbi Hillel" was also a judicial activist. And "so were the great Muslim scholar Al Nawari, the Buddhist Samyatta Nikaya, and even Confucius himself." I love the "even Confucius" bit—he's obviously the most distinguished guy on the list.

Dow's argument is that judicial activists help to nudge humanity toward progressive goals. Without activist judges, we would have been stuck with race and gender discrimination for a much longer time. Putting aside the preposterous notion that unelected judges are supposed to lead society into the future, Dow's assumption that judicial activism is invariably progressive is pure hogwash. Judicial activism is an equal-opportunity offender. For example, in the *Dred Scott* case, an activist Court invented a racial test for citizenship that had no basis in the text (see chapter 2). Among other enlightened activist decisions are those that blessed state-sponsored segregation (*Plessy v. Ferguson*) and sanctioned FDR's wartime detention of Japanese Americans (*Korematsu v. United States*).

Activism is the logical result of the Living Constitution philosophy—a philosophy that empowers judges to rewrite the Constitution and praises them when they do so. In the 1980s, when people like Reagan attorney general Ed Meese were starting to talk about the need to get back to the original meaning of the Constitution, then-justice William Brennan declared that it was far better for judges to treat the Constitution as a blank slate. "The genius of the Constitution," said Brennan, "rests not in any static meaning it might have had in a world that is dead and gone, but in the adaptability of its great principles to cope with current problems."

If the Constitution isn't actually a document with fixed meaning, but rather some eternally youthful "genius" always casting about for ways to "cope" with today's problems, then activism makes perfect sense. Judges aren't rewriting the text of the Constitution, so long as they are fulfilling its "great principles." Why enforce the original meaning of the First Amendment, for example, if it interferes with our coping strategies?

THE LEFT DISCOVERS "TRADITION"

The other school of liberal thought holds that judicial activism is bad, but it is conservatives who are the activists. Why? Because they want to overrule earlier liberal precedents, and every departure from "settled" law is "activist." This argument ignores the nature of judicial activism, which is a separation-of-powers problem. It happens when judges usurp power from the legislative or executive branch by writing or implementing laws. The decision of one court to follow—or not—the previous decision of another court has nothing to do with judicial activism.

Yes, American courts do operate on a principle of *stare decisis* (let the decision stand), a Latin maxim that expresses a preference for not disturbing earlier holdings. But until relatively recently, the Left couldn't have cared less about the law being settled—an attitude exemplified by Brennan's sneering reference to "a world that is dead and gone." No liberal bemoaned the Warren Court's energetic overturning of precedent. Nor did any of the Supreme Court's liberals think twice about striking down laws forbidding homosexual sodomy in 2003 (*Lawrence v. Texas*), even though that decision overturned the Court's own precedent from only fifteen years earlier (*Bowers v. Hardwick*). To the contrary, the Court's majority brushed aside such concerns, saying that *stare decisis* "is not . . . an inexorable command."

But now that liberal precedents are in danger, *stare decisis* is all the rage. In a 2004 *Washington Post* essay, Doug Kendall, a lawyer with Community Rights Counsel, criticized Justice Clarence Thomas for his lack of respect for *stare decisis*. He lectured that "the excitement of approaching every constitutional question anew comes at the cost of constitutional tradition."

Ah, tradition! Not exactly what one expects to hear from

a "community rights" lawyer, is it? That is, until one realizes that "constitutional tradition" is code for a series of cases decided from the 1940s to the 1970s that turned the Constitution on its head. That's why liberal activists are careful to cite "constitutional tradition" rather than the actual Constitution.

Ronald Reagan once joked that *status quo* is Latin for "the mess we're in." The same can be said of *stare decisis*—it's the mess that the law is in—which is why liberals are suddenly so keen on it. Unfortunately, conservatives all too often accept the conventional wisdom that they must slavishly follow precedent. In commercial law, that makes some sense—businessmen need certainty. But not in constitutional law. Under *stare decisis*, the Supreme Court's mission statement is not, "Life, liberty, and property," but instead the dreary refrain, "Don't rock the boat."

The "constitutional tradition" that we are now told to worship stands for a federal regime of unlimited jurisdiction. It stands for a government by unelected, unaccountable, and unremovable bureaucrats. This tradition—not the Constitution—dictates that policemen give a highly specific set of warnings to suspects, lest the confession be for naught (*Miranda v. Arizona*). And the tradition allows a federal judge to strike down any state law that, in his opinion, does not serve a "legitimate" local interest. To paraphrase Yogi Berra, tradition ain't what it used to be.

CAN YOU SPOT THE ACTIVIST DECISION?

There have been thousands of federal court rulings since the New Deal, and to be fair, not every one is an activist decision. To the untrained eye, it might be difficult to know whether a judge has overstepped his or her bounds. In case you find yourself wondering about a particular court opinion, here are five red flags that let you know you're reading an activist decision:

1. Emphatic denial that the court is imposing its own beliefs.
2. Solemn invocation of "fundamental rights."
3. Pretentious pseudo-learned prose.
4. Ample use of metaphor, e.g., "living" and "evolving."
5. Multifactor balancing tests.

These techniques have been most energetically used in the due process and equal protection cases that overturned democratically enacted laws in the name of "rights" the Founders never dreamed of.

Judge Walker's decision in *Perry v. Schwarzenegger* (the Proposition 8 case) fits the pattern, including an insistence that "plaintiffs do not seek recognition of a new right," an assertion that gay marriage is a "fundamental right," and a pseudo-learned survey of the characteristics of marriage "throughout the history of the United States." Oddly enough, Walker's catalog of the historical characteristics of marriage left out the fact that states have traditionally defined it as a union of man and woman. Even today, in over half of the states, gay marriage is explicitly barred by the state constitutions. But the issue is not whether gay marriage should be legally permitted. The question is, Who gets to decide such issues: judges or the people? What makes this decision particularly sad is that Judge Walker, a Reagan appointee, had rendered many fine decisions earlier in his career, including the Half Moon Bay wetlands case (see chapter 9). But *Perry* wasn't one of them.

IS THAT A PENUMBRAL EMANATION, OR
ARE YOU JUST HAPPY TO SEE ME?

The Warren Court's 1965 decision in *Griswold v. Connecticut* set a new standard for judicial activism. In that case, Planned Parenthood challenged a Connecticut law forbidding use of contraceptives, even by married couples. It was admittedly an outdated law even by the standards of 1965, but it was not unconstitutional. The framers did not see fit to mention contraceptives in the Constitution; nor is the topic implicated by any fair reading of the text. But the Warren Court voted seven to two to overturn the law, with Justice William O. Douglas given the task to make up a reason.

If you needed someone to invent constitutional law out of thin air, Justice Douglas was a good choice. A politically ambitious man appointed by FDR, Douglas, like Warren, found the business of applying the law rather dull—he wanted to make a splash. In *Griswold*, Douglas swept aside the lack of any constitutional provision dealing with contraception because "specific guarantees in the Bill of Rights have penumbras, formed by emanations from those guarantees that help give them life and substance."

So there's your first clue: ample use of metaphors. Penumbras (shadows), emanations, life, and substance—a whole string of meaningless puff meant to prettify the Court's desire to strike down a perfectly valid, albeit old-fashioned, state law. Douglas goes on to say that the right to use contraceptives is found within a "zone of privacy" based on "emanations" from the First, Third, Fourth, and Fifth Amendments.

A virtuoso performance. He even worked in the sadly neglected Third Amendment, which prohibits soldiers from being "quartered in any house" in peacetime. Thus, your right to keep soldiers out of the house leads inexorably to your right to keep Trojans in it. Douglas emphatically denied that he was imposing a policy choice on the states. There's clue number two. "We do not sit as a super-legislature to determine the wisdom, need, and propriety of laws that touch . . . social conditions." Heaven forbid. The Court was not legislating, it had merely discovered some long-lost privacy rights wedged between a couple of other amendments like so many coins beneath the sofa cushions.

Douglas also proclaimed the "fundamental" nature of this new right. To allow the state to search the "sacred precincts of the marital bedroom" for contraceptives "is repulsive to the notions of privacy surrounding the marriage relationship." Douglas knew a thing or two about marriage. At the time of *Griswold*, he was on his way to his fourth marriage, this time to a waitress he'd picked up on the lecture circuit.

In dissent, Justice Hugo Black made the rather obvious point that the framers took the trouble of specifying precisely which rights would be protected by the federal government. Had they meant to create a "zone," they could have done so. In a particularly prophetic passage, Black observed, "One of the most effective ways of diluting or expanding a constitutionally guaranteed right is to substitute for the crucial word or words of a constitutional guarantee another word or words more or less flexible and more or less restricted in meaning."

GRISWOLD = MC²

David Dow in his *America's Prophets* calls *Griswold* "a brilliant breakthrough," on par with "Einstein's special theory of relativity." Presumably this puts Justice Douglas right up there with Confucius, or at least that Jesus guy. Dow rhapsodizes that Douglas's opinion is not just about penumbras and emanations but also "constitutional architecture" because it "evokes the idea of space, physical . . . as well as metaphysical." Enough already with the metaphors!

You might be wondering how emanations from the Bill of Rights—enacted as a series of limitations on the *federal* government—could be used to invalidate a state law like the one in *Griswold*. The answer is the Fourteenth Amendment, which was adopted immediately after the Civil War (together with the Thirteenth and Fifteenth) to ensure that the states did not infringe the rights of the newly freed black citizens. To that end, the Fourteenth Amendment forbids any state from depriving "any person of life, liberty, or property without due process of law."

The due process clause of the Fourteenth Amendment, like the due process clause of the Fifth Amendment, from which it was copied, was originally understood as a guarantee of judicial fairness. Indeed, *due process of law* was an ancient and well-known term in Anglo-American law, standing for all the procedural safeguards of the common-law courts. The due process clause was understood to mean that courts could not forfeit your property, or sentence you to prison or death without observing such well-established procedures as habeas corpus, grand juries, and rights to appeal. "The words 'due process,'" Alexander Hamilton assured the people of New York in 1787, " . . . can never be referred to an act of legislature."

That was the original idea. But the temptation to use due process as a club to beat up on legislatures proved impossible to resist. It all started with *Dred Scott*—remember that nicely antiquated relic from chapter 2? In the midst of his Civil War–provoking opinion, Chief Justice Roger Taney grumbled that any federal law that purported to deprive a man of his slave "could hardly be dignified with the name due process of law." And with those words, Taney kick-started a doctrine that came to be known as substantive due process; that is, the concept that certain policy choices of state and federal legislatures can be so bad as to violate the due process clause.

The beauty of substantive due process—for an activist judge—is that it is an empty vessel. It is impossible to say when a legislature violates due process, because the very question is nonsensical: When does a *legislature* fail to observe *judicial* procedures? Always? Never? The upshot is that courts can go ahead and imbue due process with any policy preference they like. One version of substantive due process holds that the Fourteenth Amendment "incorporates" the Bill of Rights (or most of them) and makes them applicable to the states. From an originalist perspective, this is bad enough. Even the notably left-wing justice Felix Frankfurter conceded that all the relevant evidence demonstrates conclusively that the congressmen and legislators who ratified the Fourteenth Amendment did not understand the due process clause as "incorporating" the Bill of Rights. For one thing, the due process clause itself was a copy of one clause of the Fifth Amendment. It would be odd, to say the least, to use the language of one amendment as a shorthand way of saying that the states are bound by the whole Bill of Rights.

But at least the incorporation doctrine has some boundaries. It could be stretched only so far as the language of the Bill of Rights would allow—admittedly pretty far, but still not far enough for activist judges. Thus, the Supreme Court has nurtured an even more flexible rule: that the Fourteenth Amendment prohibits state legislatures from infringing, or even "burdening," any right that is "so rooted in the traditions and conscience of our people as to be ranked as fundamental" (*Snyder v. Massachusetts* [1934]). There's that word again—*fundamental*.

The People do, of course, possess rights beyond the Bill of Rights. The Ninth Amendment says just that: "The enumeration, in the Constitution, of certain rights, shall not be construed to deny or disparage others retained by the people." No doubt there are traditional rights beyond the black letter of the Bill of Rights, such as the right to earn an honest living (see chapter 9). But the question is, who should interpret the "traditions and conscience" of the American people? The elected representatives of the people, or nine life-tenured justices whose contact with ordinary Americans is limited to such phrases as "Table for two, please?" We've ended up with a system where the people and their representatives must wait until the Court reveals to us what our fundamental rights are.

Justice Douglas, the main perpetrator of the *Griswold* decision, once referred to the due process clause as "the wildcard to be put to such use as the judges choose." When judges like Douglas create new rights in the name of substantive due process, they are not applying the law, they're creating it. They're legislating.

THE MYSTERY OF LIFE

Now you know why the incantation of "fundamental rights" is one of our red flags for judicial activism. In the Orwellian world of left-wing courts, the rights that are "fundamental" are the ones that nobody ever bothered to put in the Constitution. And by the magic of the Fourteenth Amendment, each new fundamental right removes yet another issue from the democratic control of the states. After *Griswold*, it took only eight years for the Supreme Court to invent its most infamous fundamental right. This was a right so deeply "rooted" in our "traditions and conscience" that it has split the nation in two, leading to mass protests, bombings, an avalanche of litigation, and a completely poisoned process of judicial confirmation. I refer to abortion.

Roe v. Wade (1973) involved a challenge to a Texas law that prohibited abortion, except when necessary to save the mother's life. The Constitution itself—that black-and-white parchment thingy—has as much to say about abortion as it does about contraception or gay marriage: nothing. And because the Constitution gives the federal government no power over abortion, it is one of those issues "reserved to the States . . . or the people" under the Tenth Amendment (see chapter 11). At the time of the nation's founding, nobody would have dreamed that the document conferred a federal right to abortion, particularly since the common law (which all the states embraced) treated abortion as a serious felony. Likewise, at the time of ratifying the Fourteenth Amendment, abortion was a crime in every state. Up until January 1973, abortion remained a matter of state law, with most states opting to prohibit or restrict the procedure.

All of that changed with a stroke of Justice Harry Blackmun's pen. Writing for the majority in *Roe*, Blackmun pulled out all the stops in his quest to create a brand-new federal right to abortion on demand. There was much pseudo-learning in his opinion, including a survey of ancient Greece, Rome, and Persia, in which Blackmun finds that abortion was uniformly popular among the ancients, except for a few Pythagoreans. There was the ritual invocation of "fundamental rights." There was a multifactor balancing test, as Blackmun instructed all lower courts to evaluate the validity of state abortion laws by balancing such factors as the stage of pregnancy, the viability of the fetus, the life and health of the mother, and the existence of a "compelling state interest."

And there was, naturally, the usual denial that the Court was doing anything new; rather, it was simply applying the existing right to privacy—that venerable doctrine dating all the way back to 1965! But how was abortion a matter of privacy? Evidently, the right to engage in private acts of intercourse includes the right to destroy any offspring that results. I say "evidently" because Blackmun never actually explains his rationale; he simply recites various cases finding that "privacy" bears a relation to things like family and procreation. He couldn't even bring himself to say for certain which part of the Constitution supported this newly expanded right. It was probably the Fourteenth Amendment, he said, but it might be the Ninth Amendment. Same difference.

The decision was an "exercise of raw judicial power," as Justice Byron White said in dissent, that "constitutionally disentitled" the people and the legislatures of the fifty states from weighing the pros and cons of abortion for themselves. Worse yet, because the Court held that any state restriction on abortion would have to pass muster under its multifactor balancing test, the Court once again set itself up as a superlegislature.

PROFILES IN JUDICIAL COURAGE

Over the next two decades, as more Republican appointees joined the Supreme Court, expectations mounted that the justices would overturn *Roe*. Speculation grew intense in 1992, when the Court heard a case involving Pennsylvania's decision to place certain conditions on abortion, such as the requirement that a married woman notify her spouse before terminating a pregnancy (*Planned Parenthood v. Casey*).

Here was the perfect opportunity to jettison *Roe* and return the issue where it belonged: the state legislatures. Instead, three Republican appointees—Sandra Day O'Connor, Anthony Kennedy, and David Souter—jumped on the *stare decisis* bandwagon and upheld *Roe*'s abortion "right." They did not pretend that *Roe* had any constitutional validity, but rather, they asserted that the only way to protect "liberty" was to remove any "doubt" about the legal status of abortion.

The Super Friends of Liberty went on to proclaim a new balancing test, under which federal courts could strike down any state law that placed an "undue burden" on abortion. The utter ambiguity of "undue burden" was an open invitation to courts to continue to make up the law. In *Casey*, the Super Friends held that spousal notification *did* impose an "undue burden," but that other provisions of the Pennsylvania law, such as parental notification for minors, did not. How's that for removing doubt? The fact that Justice O'Connor signed on to this travesty is particularly sad. As we'll see in later chapters, O'Connor has written strongly originalist opinions in fields such as property rights and federalism.

What the pro-abortion justices lack in the way of logic, they make up for with euphemism. For these cases are never actually about abortion. Rather, for Blackmun, *Roe* was about privacy, while for Justice Douglas, it was about the right "to care for one's health and person." In *Casey*, the Super Friends insisted that *Roe* protects all "intimate and personal choices . . . central to personal dignity." In fact, they continued, *Roe* is about "the right to define one's own concept of existence, of meaning, of the universe, and of the mystery of human life." Put it that way, and it doesn't even sound like killing a fetus.

As for "undue burden," that phrase has turned out to be just as slippery as the *Casey* decision itself. One thing, however, is clear. For liberals, any—and I mean any—regulation of abortion amounts to an undue burden. In the Supreme Court's most recent abortion decision, *Gonzales v. Carhart* (2007), a narrow five-to-four majority just barely managed to uphold the federal partial-birth abortion ban enacted by Congress in 2003. The Court's four liberal justices at that time (Ginsburg, Souter, Stevens, and Breyer) insisted that the ban represented an undue burden.

Now, forgive me, but in order to understand where the Court's liberals stand, I must describe exactly what "right" was being burdened. The law in question deals with a particular type of abortion known as "dilation and extraction," or "D&X." In this procedure—described by the stalwart liberal Justice John Paul Stevens as "gruesome"—a doctor partially delivers a still-living fetus and then kills it by collapsing its skull using one of several possible methods: crushing, suction, or even decapitation. No other procedure is banned by this law, and even D&X is permitted if a physician finds it necessary to protect the life of the mother. The statute was carefully drafted, in part, to get around an earlier Supreme Court decision that struck down a Nebraska partial-birth abortion ban that was not quite so narrowly tailored.

Reading the dissent in *Gonzales*, you would think the majority had summarily ordered all women to remain barefoot, pregnant, and disenfranchised. Justice Ruth Bader Ginsburg declared it "alarming" that the Court would sit back and let Congress prohibit the crushing of fetal skulls. According to her, "a woman's autonomy to determine her life's course" depends upon her ability to have a D&X abortion on demand. The reaction from the legal commentariat was equally sensational. In April 2011, *Slate*'s Dahlia Lithwick cited the *Gonzales* decision as evidence of "the death of *Roe v. Wade*." According to Lithwick, any judicial tampering with the unfettered right of *Roe*—even by the Supreme Court itself—violates "the rule of law," presumably because *stare decisis* creates an invisible shield around liberal precedents. Perhaps the most telling comment came from law professor Geoffrey Stone. Writing in the University of Chicago Faculty Blog on April 20, 2007, Stone attributed the decision to the "painfully awkward" fact that "all five justices in the majority in *Gonzales* are Catholic." There speaks the voice of enlightened scholarship.

At what point, one wonders, does a baby have rights that might outweigh the mother's autonomy? In 2001 and 2002, the Illinois legislature defeated the Born Alive Infant Protection Act, a law that would require physicians to preserve the life of babies born as a result of unsuccessful abortions. Then–state senator Barack Obama opposed the legislation because it would represent—you guessed it—a "burden" on a woman's right to choose an abortion. And why stop there? A February 2012 article in the *Journal of Medical Ethics* makes the case in favor of infanticide as merely "after-birth abortion." Similarly, Princeton University bioethics professor Peter Singer thinks infanticide should be legal because "killing a newborn is never equivalent to killing a person." Killing an infant could be appropriate, for example, if "the baby has a serious disability." But just because he supports killing babies doesn't mean that Singer is hard-hearted. In fact, he is a strict vegetarian and animal rights advocate.

Gonzales was a triumph of judicial restraint, for it simply allowed the clearly expressed will of the people to stand. The statute upheld by the Court had been passed by Congress three times, but the first two times it was vetoed by President Clinton. In the decade before the Court's decision, some thirty state legislatures had enacted partial-birth abortion bans. If *Gonzales* signals the death of *Roe*, it's because the people killed *Roe*, not the Court.

SMALL RIGHTS YOU MAY HAVE MISSED

In the meantime, the federal judiciary's rights factory will continue to churn out new liberties that might otherwise elude the people. One new frontier is suggested by the 2006 book *Transgender Rights*, which describes the legal rights of "transsexuals, transvestites, cross-dressers, drag queens and drag kings, butch and femme lesbians, feminine gay men, intersex people, bigendered people, and others." The Supreme Court has yet to address the topic, but the ACLU opined, in a November 2009 "Know Your Rights" bulletin, that the "determination" and "expression" of one's gender "are interests that we believe the Due Process Clause recognizes and protects." Add cross-dressing to the ever-growing list of fundamental rights.

Another cutting-edge field is "environmental rights." In his 2003 book *Environmental Justice in America*, Indiana University professor Edward Lao Rhodes predicted that the United States is "on the verge" of recognizing the enjoyment of "equitable levels of environmental costs and benefits" as a "fundamental right." The United States should create such a right, the argument goes, because lots of other countries have; at least a hundred countries have constitutional provisions on the environment. In 2005 a group of Inuits brought a petition before the Inter-American Commission on Human Rights, charging the United States with violating their human rights by failing to stop global warming—that's right, Eskimos were complaining that it's getting too hot. Although the commission declined to hear the case, the petition's prime mover, Sheila Watt-Cloutier, has gone on to international stardom, including a 2007 nomination for the Nobel Peace Prize. Given the inclination of some Supreme Court justices to import international and foreign law into the U.S. Constitution (see chapter 10), we may well find ourselves with a fundamental right to enjoy pristine glaciers. We might have to give up cars, but, hey, it's what our Founding Fathers would have wanted.

Don't get me wrong. I have nothing against Eskimos, cross-dressers, or even cross-dressing Eskimos. But to pretend that the Constitution affords them special protections that have no basis in the text of the Constitution threatens the rule of law. In a democracy, the most important right of all citizens—even cross-dressing Eskimos—is the right to be heard through one's elected representatives, without the interference of overreaching judges.

THE EQUAL PROTECTION RACKET

The due process clause is the most popular source of judicial leg-islation, but the equal protection clause runs a close second. Also found in the Fourteenth Amendment, that worthy clause holds that no state may "deny to any person within its jurisdiction the equal protection of the laws." The point of those words—ratified in the midst of Reconstruction—was to require that states treat blacks and whites equally. Once upon a time, the clause was un-derstood to be so specific to race relations that it was rarely cited in federal court. Oliver Wendell Holmes once referred to it as the "last resort of constitutional arguments."

Equal protection got an extreme makeover in a 1942 decision (*Skinner v. Oklahoma*) in which the Court held that the equal protection clause forbids any sort of "unequal" classification, at least where "basic rights" are concerned. The majority opinion, written by—surprise!—Justice Douglas, created a "substantive equal protection" doctrine that opened up whole new vistas of judicial lawmaking. That's because all laws create classifications; indeed, that is the essence of legislation. A state's motor vehicle law, for example, dishes out "unequal" treatment to those under the age of sixteen, the legally blind, drunk drivers, and so forth. When judges reserve the right to strike down state laws because they treat different classes of people unequally, they have effectively given themselves a veto over all state legislation. It's a power that has been exercised in scores of cases.

The most curious equal protection decision is also the most famous: *Brown v. Board of Education.* I say "curious" because the Court took a needlessly activist approach to a case that called for a straightforward application of the Fourteenth Amendment's text. In *Brown*, the Court considered laws in four states that either mandated racial segregation of public schools or allowed local authorities to mandate such segregation. It is true, as Justices Felix Frankfurter and Robert Jackson privately conceded, that the men who drafted the Fourteenth Amendment did not intend to desegregate the schools. Even in the North, there were segregated schools in 1868. But remember: originalists are not concerned with the secret intentions of the drafters. What matters is the original public meaning of the words. If nothing else, the equal protection clause stood for the proposition that state laws must treat blacks and whites equally. In *Brown*, the litigation in the lower courts produced plenty of evidence that segregation laws were a pretext to justify inferior schools for blacks. Because "separate but equal" was never really achieved and was, in any event, impossible for courts to police, it was no great stretch to strike down school segregation laws. And that's what the Court did—unanimously.

Brown, however, was the first opinion to be written by the newly installed chief justice, Earl Warren, and he used it to announce a new approach to constitutional law. Warren started out by declaring that the original meaning of the equal protection clause is irrelevant because "we cannot turn the clock back to 1868 when the amendment was adopted." Seizing upon a single sociological study cited in the courts below, Warren found that black children in segregated schools experience "feelings of inferiority as to their status in the community." It was the evolution of "psychological knowledge," according to Warren, that dictated a new reading of the equal protection clause. The Court reached the right result, but bequeathed a lesson—heartily embraced by generations of law school professors since—that it was necessary to abandon original meaning in order to end segregation. Or, as Professor David Strauss puts it in *The Living Constitution*, "if originalism were to prevail . . . [r]acial segregation of public schools would be constitutional."

Here's a better way to look at it. If Earl Warren had actually applied the Fourteenth Amendment's original meaning, we could have avoided decades of disastrous judicial micromanagement of public schools. The year after the initial *Brown* decision, the Supreme Court ruled that states must implement the decision "with all deliberate speed." But what did it mean to implement *Brown*? Heeding Warren's revelation that the equal protection clause is really about preventing feelings of inferiority, judges soon concluded that even de facto segregation violates equal protection because it produces the same feelings. Thus, the legal imperative of desegregation soon became a mandate of integration. It was not enough for state and local governments to remove legal barriers; they had to guarantee outcomes.

By 1971, the Supreme Court had upheld a lower court order against a Virginia school district that included a forced busing plan and racial targets for individual school populations (*Swann v. Charlotte-Mecklenburg Board of Education*). Shortly thereafter, the Court approved the decision of a federal judge in Denver who found that the city's policy of building schools close to where children live—what were they thinking?—was unconstitutional because kids in predominately black neighborhoods would go to predominately black schools. As a result, the judge had placed the entire Denver school system under his personal supervision (*Keyes v. School District No. One, Denver, Colorado*). That was just the beginning of a national wave of receiverships and decrees by which federal courts assumed control of schools.

Before the 1960s, federal courts had often legislated, but they had never assumed such awesome power to run the day-to-day affairs of cities and school districts. One may ask: Where does this power come from? In *Swann* (the Virginia case), Chief Justice Warren Burger asserted what has become the standard answer: busing and other forced integration measures are within a federal court's power to craft "equitable remedies." An "equitable remedy" is an order by a court requiring that a person do—or refrain from doing—a certain act. That restraining order you got against your ex? That's an equitable remedy. The Constitution gives federal courts jurisdiction over "all Cases, in Law and *Equity*, arising under this Constitution" (Article III, Section 2; emphasis added). Ergo, federal judges can order anybody to do anything in the name of upholding the Constitution.

The original understanding of "Cases, in . . . Equity" was far more limited. At the time of the founding, equity was a well-established branch of Anglo-American law, but it was not a free-floating grant of judicial power. Rather, it was a "system of relief" that allowed courts to grant remedies other than money damages, which had been the only form of relief at common law. But equitable remedies were available only in certain types of cases. Hamilton—a highly successful lawyer—noted that equity jurisdiction could be invoked by allegations of "fraud, accident, trust or hardship."

More important, equitable remedies are supposed to be as narrow as possible, normally requiring no more than "a single simple act," according to the classic treatise *Principles of Equity*. And equitable remedies are supposed to be imposed on the wrongdoer. A court can issue a restraining order on your ex, but it can't force your ex's best friend to keep an eye on him. In the case of busing, however, it was not any wrongdoer but innocent schoolchildren who were being made to bear the burden of remedying past discrimination. This fundamentally unfair use of judicial power was greeted by three cheers from legal academia. In 1976 Abram Chayes, a Harvard law professor, celebrated the judiciary's new power "to adjust future behavior" of government entities, rather than the traditional, but boring, role of trying to "compensate for past wrong." Chayes briefly acknowledged that when judges run the government, there is a slight separation-of-powers concern, but he cheerfully concluded that the judiciary is "unlikely" to displace the other two branches.

Technically, Chayes was right. The judiciary has not completely displaced the other branches. People still show up to work at Congress and the White House, and you and I continue to pay them. But those people don't work for us anymore; they serve the judiciary.

THAT CARPET HAS GOT TO GO!

The two trends I've been discussing—the expansion of the equal protection clause and of the Court's invention of a new brand of equity power—converged in a case called *Missouri v. Jenkins*. A real-life version of Charles Dickens's *Jarndyce v. Jarndyce* (the case that dragged on so long that nobody could remember what it was about), *Jenkins* lasted two decades, with two trips to the Supreme Court. The issue was the alleged segregation of the Kansas City, Missouri, school system. By the time the lawsuit was filed in 1977, segregation laws had been repealed for twenty years, but the plaintiffs alleged that the city's failure to erase the "vestiges" of segregation constituted a violation of equal protection. The trial judge, the late Russell Clark, agreed, finding that de facto segregation of the city schools—there were twenty-five schools with 90 percent or more black enrollment—meant that the students were doomed to an inferior education. That itself was a startling conclusion, based, as Justice Clarence Thomas observed, "upon the idea that any school that is black is inferior, and that blacks cannot succeed without the benefit of the company of whites."

By 1985, Judge Clark was busy issuing equitable decrees to eliminate all "vestiges" of segregation. To do so, he embarked on a utopian scheme to create a "magnet" school district within Kansas City that would be sufficiently irresistible to attract affluent white students from the surrounding suburbs. In 1987, he imposed a long-term capital improvement plan on the school district, dictating a level of "visual attractiveness" that eschewed such blemishes as "floor coverings with unsightly sections of mismatched carpeting and tile, and individual walls possessing different shades of paint." He also declared that the equal protection clause required the city to adorn the school system with a 2,000-square-foot planetarium, a twenty-five-acre farm with an air-conditioned meeting room for a hundred people, a model United Nations wired for simultaneous translation, film production facilities, and a 3,500-square-foot diesel mechanics room, among other things. All this cost money, so Judge Clark used his equitable power to order the school district to raise taxes. This truly outrageous abuse of power went up to the Supreme Court, which in 1990 upheld the judge's tax hike.

Unfortunately, even the erection of Xanadu-like schools could not reverse the white flight from Kansas City to the suburbs. And so the judge, now in his seventh year of running the school system, mandated an across-the-board pay raise in the name of attracting the best teachers (although in a fit of generosity, the judge also gave a pay raise to nonteaching staff as well). That decree also made it up to the Supreme Court, and here the justices finally drew the line. Finding that there was no connection between teacher salary levels in 1995 and a system of de jure segregation that had ended in 1957, the Court came to the sensible—and long overdue—conclusion that the judge had exceeded his authority.

The Court's liberals were furious. According to Justice Ginsburg, the only problem with the district court's micromanagement was that it hadn't gone on long enough. What was a mere seven years, she wondered, considering that discrimination in Missouri goes back to 1724, when "Louis XV of France issued the Code Noir, the first slave code for the colony of Louisiana, an area that included Missouri?" Note the pseudo-learned reference—not just an old law, but an old French law! By Ginsburg's logic, the court's jurisdiction could extend for two hundred years—and perhaps include a tax on all Frenchmen to remove the vestiges of the Code Noir.

Justice David Souter, writing separately, found there to be "nothing exceptionable" in Judge Clark's salary decree. Unfortunately, Souter had a point. By 1995, federal judges had displayed such flair in managing other people's business and spending other people's money that they certainly seemed to have unfettered power. One judicial decree covering the Bryce Mental Hospital in Alabama, for example, specifies the exact temperature of the water for bathing (110° F) and for laundry (180° F). A federal judge in North Carolina ordered state officials to buy recreational equipment for the prison system, including three sets of horseshoes, three guitars, five Frisbees, fifty decks of playing cards, and a piano. As Justice Thomas pointed out in his concurring opinion in *Jenkins*, "judges have directed or managed the reconstruction of entire institutions and bureaucracies, with little regard for the inherent limitation of their authority."

The madness has got to end somewhere, and the 1995 decision in *Jenkins* was at least a step in the right direction. Under the current law, one can only hope that judges will rediscover the virtue of restraint. Unfortunately, few judges today would accept this undue burden on their imperial authority.

CHAPTER SIX

FREEDOM OF SPEECH

Some Speech Is More Equal Than Others

Congress shall make no law . . . abridging the freedom of speech, or of the press.

—First Amendment

IN LATE 2007 THE CONSERVATIVE nonprofit group Citizens United produced *Hillary: The Movie*, a distinctly unflattering documentary about then-senator Hillary Clinton. The plan was to release the movie during the 2008 presidential primaries on the theory—which seems almost quaint in retrospect—that Clinton was the most dangerous Democrat seeking the presidency that year. Citizens United also planned to run TV ads promoting the film.

All things being equal, none of this should have been any business of the federal government. After all, the First Amendment imposes an absolute prohibition: "Congress shall make no law"—none whatsoever—"abridging the freedom of speech." The amendment does not purport to create any right; rather, it protects an already existing right. The framers understood free speech to be a natural, God-given right: part of the unalienable liberty that the Declaration of Independence talks about. Freedom of speech and press, particularly the right to criticize the government, was at the heart of the Revolution.

It would be odd—would it not?—to think that the First Amendment allows Congress to prohibit certain classes of Americans from criticizing a sitting member of Congress. And yet that is effectively what Congress did. In 2002 it passed the McCain-Feingold Act, which, building on earlier federal law, made it a crime for corporations and unions to use their general treasury funds to "expressly advocate" the election or defeat of a federal candidate. Every member of Congress who seeks reelection is, of course, a federal candidate and thus would be shielded from corporate speech, while enjoying the taxpayer-funded advantages of incumbency. Under federal law, any corporation or union seeking the privilege of speaking about an election had to form a political action committee (PAC), a separate entity, subject to onerous regulation.

On the basis of McCain-Feingold, the Federal Election Commission prohibited Citizens United from running TV ads to promote the documentary. As David Bossie, president of Citizens United, told the *Washington Post*, the FEC's decision "completely and totally shut down" the marketplace for *Hillary: The Movie*. So Bossie sued the FEC, launching a lawsuit (*Citizens United v. Federal Election Commission*) that would eventually reach the Supreme Court.

What gave David Bossie the crazy idea that he could get around McCain-Feingold by producing a documentary? He was inspired by none other than radical left-wing filmmaker Michael Moore. In 2004, the multimillionaire college dropout decided to make a documentary ridiculing George W. Bush for being rich and stupid. The film, *Fahrenheit 911*, was released in the summer of 2004 for a single purpose, as reported in *Businessweek*: "to deny Bush reelection." In fact, Moore used the film as an "organizing tool" to sign up anti-Bush campaigners. Among other things, *Fahrenheit 911* claimed that Bush had committed voter fraud in 2000, that his family had a business relationship with the bin Laden family, and that he had created an "atmosphere of fear" throughout the United States.

Moore's film was corporate speech: financed, produced, and distributed entirely by corporate entities. Surely *Fahrenheit 911* was nothing less than a massive campaign ad for Bush's 2004 opponent, John Kerry—in direct violation of McCain-Feingold. But the FEC rejected conservative challenges to the film, declaring that *Fahrenheit 911* represented "commercial" activity and that—laughably—it did not "expressly advocate" the defeat of President Bush. It was in the wake of that decision that Citizens United decided to get into the documentary film business.

At the Supreme Court, the government's lawyer, Deputy Solicitor General Malcolm Stewart, vigorously defended McCain-Feingold, pointing out that it did not merely apply to films but also to political books! Actually, Stewart didn't go out of his way to make that point, but he conceded it when asked by Chief Justice John Roberts. Would McCain-Feingold apply to a book, asked Roberts, if it mentioned the name of a federal candidate just once?

"That's correct," said Stewart.

The chief justice clarified his hypothetical. "It's a five-hundred-page book, and at the end it says, 'and so vote for X,' the government could ban that?"

After some hemming and hawing, Stewart agreed. If the corporation failed to pay for the book using a separate PAC, then, yes, "We could prohibit the publication of the book."

This answer was so alarming that the Court scheduled

an unusual second round of argument five months later. This time, Solicitor General (and now Justice) Elena Kagan came to court herself. Kagan immediately said that the government had changed its position on books, but when pressed for specifics, she did not deny that McCain-Feingold gave the federal government the power to ban political books if they are funded by corporations. The best she could do was point out that the FEC had never actually done so in the past, and therefore it would be awfully unusual for them to start banning books. Mere "political pamphlets," on the other hand, were fair game. The good people at the FEC could be trusted to distinguish books from pamphlets.

Unwilling to "put our First Amendment rights in the hands of FEC bureaucrats," as Chief Justice Roberts put it, a majority of the Court issued an opinion overturning those sections of McCain-Feingold that prohibited corporations and unions from subsidizing speech. Although it was a straightforward application of the First Amendment, the decision was supported only by the Court's conservatives and Justice Anthony Kennedy. The Court's liberal bloc voted to uphold the book-banning law, for reasons set out in Justice John Paul Stevens's ninety-page dissent. For the most part, Stevens's opinion is a ramshackle tirade against corporations (but not unions); however, the dissent does nicely illustrate some of the key First Amendment issues that separate the Naked Constitution from the Living Constitution.

WHAT IS SPEECH?

In his dissent, Justice Stevens asserted that the "original understanding" of the First Amendment was that it applied only to "oral communications of human beings." Since corporations are not human beings, it follows that the First Amendment does them no good. What's more, according to Stevens, the Founding Fathers positively hated corporations: a little-known fact supposedly demonstrated by such gems as a letter written by Thomas Jefferson twenty-five years after the First Amendment was ratified, expressing concern about the power of "monied corporations."

Stevens's dissent represents the worst sort of pseudo-originalism. Who knows what the framers had in mind? What matters is the text that they proposed, and that the states ratified. That text protects all speech, not particular classes of speakers. It's true, as Justice Antonin Scalia pointed out in his concurring opinion, that all the provisions of the Bill of Rights set forth the rights of individual human beings, "not, for example, trees or polar bears." But the individual's right to speak "includes the right to speak in association with other individual persons." For that is all a corporation, or a union, is—an association of individuals.

If the Court's liberals truly believe that only individuals acting alone can avail themselves of the Bill of Rights, we're in deeper trouble than most people realize. If, for example, the Fifth Amendment's "takings" clause applies only to individuals, what's to stop the government from seizing a corporation's property without "just compensation"? Is there any reason why federal agents would need a warrant to search a corporation's office if the Fourth Amendment applies only to individual human beings?

McCain-Feingold does exempt one category of corporation from its restrictions: media companies. They can spend unlimited sums from their general treasuries to advocate for or against candidates. Thus, a corporation that has the decency to buy a newspaper or radio station can endorse candidates before the election. The media carve-out looks like a nod to freedom of the press, but in reality, it's just the opposite. It assumes that media outlets owned by corporations (basically, all of them) have the right to speak about elections only to the extent permitted by Congress. No matter, the overwhelmingly liberal media loved McCain-Feingold and hated *Citizens United*. One of the main beneficiaries of McCain-Feingold's media exemption, the *New York Times*, denounced the *Citizens United* majority for its "insistence that corporations are . . . entitled to the same First Amendment rights [as people]."

If the First Amendment protects anything, it protects political speech. That would have been obvious to the ratifying public of 1791. Look at the context: the framers put the rights of speech and press together with the rights "peaceably to assemble, and to petition the Government for a redress of grievances." A citizen's right to criticize the government, or individual officials, is "the heart of what the First Amendment was meant to protect," according to Justice Scalia. Unfortunately, the Court has been a more consistent advocate for unfettered child pornography than for free political speech.

As for Stevens's claim that the First Amendment covers only oral communications, it's a strange assertion from a man who has repeatedly voted to grant First Amendment protection to all manner of "expressive conduct." In one case, Stevens urged that erotic dancing—which (I'm told) doesn't involve a lot of talking—is constitutionally protected speech. So protected, in fact, that Stevens held that the First Amendment forbids state legislation that would require pasties and G-strings in "adult entertainment" establishments. Presumably, none of those dancers had incorporated, or they would have lost Stevens's sympathy. The majority in that case (*Barnes v. Glen Theater*) agreed with

Stevens that nude dancing is covered by the First Amendment, but upheld that pasties-and-G-string requirement as a reasonable regulation.

MONEY TALKS

Yet another argument from the censorship crowd is that "money is not speech," and therefore it's okay to pass laws like McCain-Feingold that limit political expenditures. Imagine a law that says, "Registered Republicans are free to express themselves, but they can't spend money on Web sites or Internet service." Would that pass muster? Okay, substitute "Democrat" for "Republican" and try again. The point is that if you want to communicate with more than a few people at a time, you're going to have to spend money, whether it's to publish a magazine, build a Web site, or rent a microphone.

The Founders understood that a tyrannical government can restrict speech by making it too expensive. Remember the Stamp Act? That 1765 law imposed a heavy tax on the sales and advertising revenue of colonial newspapers. The point of the law was to drive out of business the low-rent newspapers that tended toward sensational, rabble-rousing stories. Technically, the Stamp Act did not ban any newspaper; it was just about "money." But Americans understood it to be a gross violation of press freedom, and it became one of those British outrages that precipitated the independence movement. In 1983, excise taxes on ink and paper were struck down by the Supreme Court on First Amendment grounds. Similarly, a 1936 decision struck down a latter-day Stamp Act that imposed duties on newspaper ad revenues.

Those decisions, however, protected the mainstream

media—they're the good guys, according to the liberal narrative. When it comes to political speech, liberals claim that the fight against "corruption" trumps the First Amendment. In *Citizens United*, Stevens tells us that the Founders "would have been appalled" by the corruption arising from political campaigns and would have favored any government restriction on speech necessary to halt "moral decay." No doubt the Founding Fathers would be appalled by many things in today's society—secular culture, abortion on demand, and tofurkey, to name just a few. But we cannot rewrite the Constitution based on what we think the framers would say today. We have to go by what they wrote; and if we don't like it, we can amend it.

Only in the fantasy world of the Living Constitution could the language of the First Amendment be construed to allow rampant government censorship. That amendment, it bears repeating, contains an absolute prohibition against "abridging" the freedom of speech. To abridge means to limit or truncate something— like the abridged version of a book. The framers could easily have told Congress not to "eliminate" or "destroy" free speech; but instead they barred any diminution of free speech. In so doing, they greatly improved upon Britain's common-law tradition, in which free expression was more narrowly protected against "prior restraint" by the king's censors. As James Madison observed in 1800, the First Amendment ensured that the press—and by extension, all speech—would be free from both "prior restraint" and "subsequent penalty of laws."

Nothing could be more alien to Madison's vision than the vast web of federal election laws at issue in *Citizens United*. As of 2010, those laws required 568 pages of regulations and thousands of pages of advisory opinions explaining exactly who is allowed to say what about federal elections, and when. The law recognizes seventy-one distinct entities capable of engaging in thirty-three different categories of speech. It takes a platoon of lawyers to sort through the different permutations of entity plus speech.

Prior restraint? With the threat of criminal charges lurking in the background, corporations and unions looking to express political views are more or less forced to seek advance permission from the FEC. Good news if you're Michael Moore. Not so good for conservatives.

KEEPING UP APPEARANCES

The original sin that led to today's labyrinth of campaign finance laws is the Supreme Court's 1976 decision in *Buckley v. Valeo*. In that case, New York senator James Buckley challenged the Federal Election Campaign Act, which limited the amounts that individuals and groups could contribute to a federal candidate and put limits on campaign expenditures—even restricting the amount that independent groups could spend "relative to a clearly-identified candidate." The Court struck down the expenditure limits on First Amendment grounds but in a bout of schizophrenia upheld the contribution limits because of the government's "compelling interest" in avoiding even the "appearance of corruption."

The effect of *Buckley* was to give would-be censors in Congress and the state legislatures an easy way to evade the First Amendment. So long as they could plausibly argue that their "reform" laws were needed to combat the "appearance of corruption," they were home free. McCain-Feingold itself was dressed up with pages of congressional "findings" about the inherent corruption of campaign spending by corporations.

Over decades of litigation, no court has ever really explained why it is corrupt for a corporation to express its views (that is, the views of its shareholders) about an election. The closest the Supreme Court came to articulating a rationale was that corporate money "distorts" the political marketplace—a view expressed in *Austin v. Michigan Chamber of Commerce. Austin* was an important precursor to McCain-Feingold, since it upheld a law forbidding corporations from using general treasury funds to support or oppose any candidate.

The antidistortion principle mangles the First Amendment to the point of—dare I say it?—distortion. The First Amendment guarantees *freedom* of speech, but not *equality* of speech, in which no speaker can have a bigger megaphone than anyone else. The Living Constitution fantasy assumes that the framers sought to achieve something that had never existed on earth: a world in which everyone's voice is equally heard. Moreover, the supposed equality is an illusion. Incumbent politicians have an enormous advantage given their name recognition and their ability to deliver pork-barrel projects. Any law that attempts to level the playing field will tend to favor incumbents. Why else would they be so keen to vote for such laws?

LIBERALS GONE WILD

In *Citizens United*, the Supreme Court rejected *Austin* and its antidistortion principle, and overturned the part of *McConnell* that had blessed the independent expenditure limits on corporations and unions. The Court finally recognized that the government might just be "abridging" free speech by requiring certain groups of citizens to set up political action committees for the privilege of expressing their opinions.

Liberals went berserk. No, literally. President Obama immediately denounced the decision as a "major victory for big oil, Wall Street banks, [and] health insurance companies." Evidently those groups don't deserve First Amendment rights. The president then showed his deep commitment to separation of powers by publicly scolding the members of the Court who were attending his State of the Union address. Democratic senator Chuck Schumer called for hearings—about what, it wasn't clear. With breathtaking hypocrisy, Michael Moore, the corporate-backed millionaire auteur, bellowed on the Democracy Now! Web site that Citizens United would unleash a conservative "propaganda machine" that would "manipulate an uneducated American public." Poor Michael Moore: he thought he had exclusive rights to manipulate the uneducated.

Democrats in Congress tried to undo *Citizens United* with the DISCLOSE (Democracy Is Strengthened by Casting Light on Spending in Elections) Act. This legislation "strengthened" democracy through such enlightened reforms as limiting the speech of government contractors as well as corporations with as little as five percent foreign ownership. It imposed such heavy burdens on speech that even the normally liberal ACLU came out against it. DISCLOSE failed twice in Congress, after which President Obama—eager to start strengthening democracy—tried to ram it through as a clandestine executive order. Once a draft of the order became public, the administration decided to drop the whole thing.

Liberals claim that *Citizens United* was unfaithful to the Constitution because it "gives" rights to corporations that belong only to individual human beings. Vermont's socialist senator, Bernie Sanders, along with other members of Congress, has proposed a constitutional amendment to strip for-profit corporations of all constitutional rights. As we saw in chapter 2, the demonizing of "constitutional personhood" completely misses the point. *Citizens United* does not stand for the proposition that corporations are persons; rather, it stands for the proposition that the people don't lose the right to free speech when they act collectively, through corporations or other groupings. "If the First Amendment has any force," wrote Justice Anthony Kennedy for the majority, "it prohibits Congress from fining or jailing citizens, *or associations of citizens*, for simply engaging in political speech" (emphasis added). A corporation is simply one variety of association. Indeed, even under the amendment proposed by Sanders et al., the members of nonprofit corporations—say, the Sierra Club—would retain their constitutional rights. Only those people who associate for the purpose of making a buck would lose their rights. This effort to discriminate against for-profit corporations fits perfectly with the broader liberal assault on property rights and those who dare to exercise them (see chapter 9).

THE MYTH OF GOVERNMENT NEUTRALITY

The lesson of *Citizens United* is that the First Amendment protects speech, not particular categories of speakers. The government has no business abridging the political speech of certain people—including those who organize themselves as corporations or unions.

There is a long and honorable tradition of Supreme Court decisions striking down various attempts to silence unpopular participants in the "marketplace of ideas," to borrow Oliver Wendell Holmes's metaphor. In 1969, for example, the Court recognized the free speech rights of the Ku Klux Klan, refusing to uphold the conviction of a KKK leader who had advocated violence. Since then, the Court has come to the aid of white supremacists, Nazis, flag burners, and other members of fringe groups.

There is, unfortunately, another tradition. Over the years, certain groups have been forced to suffer severe restrictions of their First Amendment rights. During the Cold War, for example, the Supreme Court allowed the government to suppress the rights of Communists to speak and associate. The Court did so by developing a balancing test that gives judges the power to decide who merits First Amendment protection. In cases like *Konigsberg v. State Bar of California* (1961)—in which California was allowed to withhold a law license from a man who refused to answer questions about his association with the Communist Party—the Court assumed the power to balance the text's guarantee of free speech against "the governmental interest" in suppressing speech. In his *Konigsberg* dissent, Justice Hugo Black pointed out the hazards of any doctrine "that permits constitutionally protected rights to be 'balanced' away whenever a majority of this Court thinks that a State might have interest sufficient to justify abridgement of those freedoms." That is precisely why the "multifactor balancing test" is one of the red flags of judicial activism (see chapter 5).

The First Amendment balancing test is typically described as being protective of liberty because the Court employs so-called strict scrutiny when the state attempts to abridge a particular point of view. What this means is that the government cannot tip the scales in favor of censorship unless it can establish a compelling interest in doing so. Even this superficially tough standard, however, is too lax for anyone who believes in original meaning. Why should *any* abridgment of free speech be allowed, even if the government can put forward a "compelling" reason?

The First Amendment is unconditional: "Congress shall make no law . . ." The framers could have added a clause saying, "unless Congress has a really good reason," but they did not.

In the old days, Communists lost out under judicial "balancing." Today, it's pro-lifers. In Massachusetts, for example, a 2007 law prohibits any person from having any contact—verbal, nonverbal, telepathic, whatever—with any other person within thirty-five feet of an abortion clinic. Even silently offering a pamphlet near an abortion clinic is a criminal offense. Chanting and singing are out of the question. In 2009 a federal appeals court upheld the law, even though the Commonwealth had no "compelling interest" in silencing abortion protests. Nonetheless, the Court held that the law could survive because it is "content-neutral"; that is, it restricts all speech equally regardless of the content.

That's a relief. For a minute, I thought the Massachusetts law was aimed at anti-abortion protests! But in fact it applies "neutrally" to all those *other* groups that gather around abortion clinics. The Marines, for example, will just have to stop recruiting at abortion clinics; likewise, the Girl Scouts will have to abandon their traditional practice of selling cookies at abortion clinics. And try as they might, the Elks Club simply cannot hold its next convention on the grounds of a Massachusetts abortion clinic

The alleged neutrality of the Massachusetts law—farcical though it is—makes all the difference for First Amendment purposes. Laws that are deemed to be "content-neutral" don't qualify for strict scrutiny; rather, they are reviewed under a balancing test known as "intermediate scrutiny." Under that test, the government need only establish a "significant," rather than "compelling," reason to suppress speech. And that semantic downshift makes it far easier for judges to uphold laws that happen to advance their personal agendas.

In the language of constitutional law, laws are content-neutral if they regulate the "time, place, and manner" of speech without favoring or disfavoring any particular content. Let's stipulate that some laws really are content-neutral. Noise pollution laws, for example, that set a maximum decibel level in residential neighborhoods do not target any particular content. Beyond that, however, one has to tread carefully. In theory a ban on flag burning is content-neutral if it applies to all flags—American, French, Chinese, etc. But such laws are obviously aimed at protecting the American flag.

Since 1994, the Supreme Court has upheld a variety of measures that supposedly regulate the "time, place, and manner" of abortion protests. In *Madsen v. Women's Health Center*, the Court approved a Florida court's order creating a thirty-six-foot "buffer zone" around the entrance of an abortion clinic in which anti-abortion protesters were forbidden from "congregating, picketing, patrolling, demonstrating or [even] entering." Imagine, if you will, a law establishing a no-speech zone around a nuclear power plant or a military installation. Would the Left agree that such a law is content-neutral? Of course not. But in *Madsen*, the Court declared the injunction to be content-neutral, while openly conceding that it prohibited only one flavor of political speech, since there were no equivalent demonstrations by pro-abortion advocates.

The Supreme Court has even endorsed the concept of "floating" buffer zones; that is, no-speech bubbles around every person in the vicinity of an abortion clinic. In 2000, the Court upheld a Colorado law making it a criminal offense to approach within eight feet of any person near an abortion clinic for the purposes of "protest, education, or counseling" (*Hill v. Colorado*). It is a bizarre turn of events when the American Left—the movement that prides itself on demonstrations, teach-ins, vigils, and the like—enthusiastically supports government suppression of the most basic form of protest. Even the liberal Harvard professor Laurence Tribe blasted *Hill* as "slam-dunk wrong."

Not that most liberals apply the *Hill* standard to themselves. In 2011, lawyers representing Occupy Wall Street and similar protest groups around the country argued that the First Amendment guaranteed not only their right to speak but also their right to take up permanent residence in public parks. In a variety of decisions, however, courts held that the act of seizing a public park is not "speech." Even if "occupation is the message," as some of the Occupy lawyers argued, the government clearly has a significant interest in regulating the "time, place, and manner" of such protests so as to keep public parks from becoming squalid encampments for a handful of protesters. But in a case like *Hill*, what is the government's significant interest in prohibiting such mild forms of expression as "education" and "counseling"? Apparently, education and counseling *could* lead to other things, like "nuisance [and] following," according to the majority in *Hill*. Oddly, two members of the *Hill* majority, Justices Stephen Breyer and Ruth Bader Ginsburg, would later go on to argue that the First Amendment guarantees the right to engage in "teaching and advocacy" in support of terrorist organizations. In *Holder v. Humanitarian Law Project*, Breyer and Ginsburg urged the Court, unsuccessfully, to strike down a federal law that barred U.S. nonprofits from providing "training," "expert advice," and other favors to Kurdish and Tamil terrorist groups that had carried out numerous attacks. In his dissent, Breyer argued that the Constitution does not permit the government to prosecute Americans for engaging in "coordinated teaching and advocacy"—not even to serve the "compelling interest in combating terrorism."

For at least some of the Court's liberals, therefore, it is acceptable to prosecute Americans for anti-abortion "education and counseling," but not for pro-terrorist "teaching and advocacy." Under the Living Constitution, there may be some complicated way to reconcile these positions. But the reality is far simpler: the Court's majority will do anything possible to uphold laws that stifle the continuing protest unleashed by its own misbegotten decision in *Roe v. Wade* (see chapter 5).

FREEDOM FOR POLITICALLY CORRECT IDEAS

Anti-abortion picketing is not the only form of speech that loses out under the Living First Amendment. The censors of the nanny state have identified other forms of expression that are too dangerous to be tolerated.

Jokes, for example. In 1995, the Montana Human Rights Commission ordered the City of Great Falls to pay damages based solely on off-color jokes and cartoons distributed by city employees. The city was also ordered to do whatever it took to prevent any further "harassing" jokes. *Harassment*—that's the magic word that renders the First Amendment powerless. The Montana Commission determined that the dirty jokes were a form of sexual harassment, even when not directed at any particular employee. Other states and cities, as well as the federal Equal Employment Opportunity Commission (EEOC), have taken a similar stand against dirty jokes. A U.S. Department of Labor pamphlet, for example, instructs employees that they have suffered harassment if "someone made sexual jokes or said sexual things you didn't like." St. Petersburg, Florida, announced a "zero-tolerance" policy on sexual humor, while the New Jersey Department of Law and Public Safety has proclaimed that "sexual or smutty jokes" are forms of illegal sexual harassment.

As a general rule, dirty jokes are not terribly funny. But they are *speech*. As we saw earlier, the original understanding of the First Amendment, as articulated by James Madison not long after its ratification, was that speech must be exempt from both prior restraint and "the subsequent penalty of laws." This principle applies no matter how hateful the speech. Even protesters who disrupt the funeral of a fallen marine are immune from liability, according to the Supreme Court's 2011 decision in *Snyder v. Phelps*. In that case, members of the Westboro Baptist Church picketed the funeral of Lance Corporal Matthew Snyder—who was killed in the line of duty in Iraq—to protest against the toleration of gays in the military. Snyder himself was not gay, but that did not matter. On the day of the funeral, Snyder's loved ones were greeted with signs saying things like "Thank God for Dead Soldiers." Snyder's father, Albert, sued Westboro founder Fred Phelps, and a jury awarded him $2.9 million for intentional infliction of emotional distress. But, unfortunately, that judgment amounted to a government-imposed penalty for particular speech. The Supreme Court, in an eight-to-one decision, reversed the lower court, holding that the First Amendment means that "we must tolerate insulting, and even outrageous, speech."

The Westboro protesters were harassing Albert Snyder and his family, but it was not harassment with a capital *H*, like those naughty jokes in Montana. Under a patchwork of federal and state precedents, speech can be punished if it creates a "hostile environment" in the workplace or any other place of "public accommodation." I am not referring here to things like intimidation ("Sleep with me, or you're fired"), which is a mixture of illegal *conduct* and speech. Rather, these cases involve pure speech—provided the speech displays hostility based on certain characteristics: race, religion, sex, or, depending on where you live, things like age, obesity, occupation, tobacco usage, and Appalachian origin. When it comes to the marines, however, you can be as hostile as you like.

Although the Supreme Court has endorsed the concept of "hostile environment" as a form of unlawful discrimination, it has yet to address the First Amendment implications of such a wide-open doctrine. Lower courts, however, have generally upheld the government's right to punish politically incorrect speech. In 1991 a federal court in Florida sustained a sexual harassment claim against the Jacksonville Shipyards. The claim was brought by a female worker who was shocked and dismayed to discover that dockworkers—dockworkers!—have a tendency to display their favorite centerfolds, tell dirty jokes, and make lewd comments. There was no First Amendment problem, the court explained, because hostile environment law "constitutes nothing more than a time, place, and manner regulation of speech." In other words, it is "content-neutral"—it treats all dirty jokes the same. The same justification has been trotted out to impose liability on a mining company for miners' lewd remarks, and on Avis Rent-a-Car for "racial epithets" uttered by one of its supervisors.

Content neutrality is a mere pretext for government censors to silence speech that they find offensive. Professor Eugene Volokh of UCLA has pointed out that hostile environment law is not only content-based, it zeroes in on one particular viewpoint. An employee in the lunchroom can go on and on about the equality of women, but if one of his coworkers responds with a barefoot-and-pregnant comment, he or his supervisors could be guilty of a crime. Even the judge in the Jacksonville Shipyard case, Carter appointee Howell Melton, hardly trusted his own "content-neutral" conclusion, for he went on to argue that even if it were content-based, hostile environment law can withstand strict scrutiny. Why? Because it serves a "compelling governmental interest in cleansing the workplace of impediments to the equality of women."

Maybe it's just me, but isn't the word *cleansing* just terrifying? Not as bad as "ethnic cleansing," perhaps, but based on the same assumption that certain "undesirable" traits must be purged by an omnipotent government. Nor is Judge Melton alone in viewing the judiciary's role as social engineering rather than defending the Constitution. In 1988 a panel of the Sixth Circuit Court of Appeals stated that employers are obliged to prevent "bigots" from "expressing their opinions" in the workplace so that "people may eventually learn that such views are undesirable *in private*, as well" (emphasis added).

There's no need to imagine the slippery slope that might emerge from such statements. The slope is already there, and our First Amendment rights are hurtling downward. Employers have been forced to change job titles such as "foreman" and "draftsman" to gender-neutral equivalents. The Kentucky Commission on Human Rights has even found that the use of Men Working signs "can be viewed as perpetuating a discriminatory work environment."

Even beyond the workplace, states and cities have applied hostile environment law to any "public accommodation"; that is, any place that offers services to the general public. Depending on your state, public accommodations can include restaurants, stores, hospitals, gyms, barbershops, hotels, libraries, bookstores, concert halls, mortuaries, and trailer parks. Nowadays, the proprietors of all such places have to worry about saying the wrong thing. Even the wrong *tone* can get you in trouble. In 2010 the

Delaware Human Relations Commission fined a movie complex $80,000 for reminding patrons to turn off their cell phones. Although such reminders are commonplace, members of the predominately black audience alleged that it had been delivered in a "condescending tone." The commission's decision was later reversed by the courts—but not on free speech grounds.

Liberal academics, grasping at straws to defend government censorship, have declared that the word *speech* in the First Amendment does not include racist or sexist remarks. Professor Rodney Smolla, for example, argues that racial epithets have "no cognitive message at all," but rather convey "raw unvarnished feeling." According to Smolla, feelings are beyond the First Amendment, which is concerned only with "ideas"—bad news for those erotic dancers. In a similar vein, feminist legal scholar Catharine MacKinnon has argued that harassing speech is not actually speech, but rather an act; namely, sex. As an unwanted sex act, sexist speech can be punished with the same severity as rape.

The one remaining bastion of free speech appears to be universities, such as those that employ Smolla and MacKinnon. Courts have consistently struck down university speech codes that attempt to chill offensive speech. In 2010 an appellate court tossed out a hostile environment claim against a community college for failing to stop a professor who sent three "racially charged" mass e-mails to the college staff. Although the logic in that case—*Rodriguez v. Maricopa County Community College*—could be applied to other workplaces, the Court's decision focused on the particular importance of free speech on campus.

Predictably, for some academics, even robust protection of speech isn't enough, unless the government subsidizes their speech. Holly Hughes, for example, an associate professor at the

University of Michigan, was one of four performance artists who sued the National Endowment for the Arts for violating their First Amendment rights by denying their grant applications. All four of them specialized in sexually explicit performance pieces intended to shock the very middle classes whose tax dollars they demanded. The "NEA Four" lost their case in the Supreme Court, but only after the Court conceded that the failure to fund speech *might* constitute an "abridgement" of speech in some circumstances—a conclusion that Justice Scalia labeled as "preposterous."

For most of us, then, freedom of speech remains a precarious right, subject to the whims of judicial balancing tests. But university professors, at least, are free to discuss—perhaps with the help of a government grant—strategies for shocking, offending, and silencing everyone else.

CHAPTER SEVEN

RELIGION

One Nation, Under . . . Never Mind

Congress shall make no law respecting an establishment of religion, or prohibiting the free exercise thereof; . . .

—First Amendment

On March 11, 2010, Judge Stephen Reinhardt revealed that the federal government was conspiring with the states to "indoctrinate" and "coerce" our nation's children with a state-held religious belief. To Reinhardt's horror, this campaign of brainwashing was taking place every morning, when students were forced to perform a religious "ritual" in school. You might know it as the Pledge of Allegiance.

In 2002 the Ninth Circuit Court of Appeals, of which Judge Reinhardt is a member, had declared the pledge to be unconstitutional. The problem was the bit that refers to America as "one nation, under God." In 2010, however, the Court reversed course, deciding that the pledge was constitutional after all. Judge Reinhardt was not happy. Considered one of America's most liberal judges, Reinhardt has been on the bench since 1980, when he was appointed by Leonid Brezhnev. Oops, I meant Jimmy Carter. Reinhardt thought that he and his colleagues had finally driven

God out of the pledge in 2002, but when the Court flip-flopped in 2010, he wrote a furious 130-page dissent, accusing his fellow judges of bending to Tea Party pressure and decrying the "under God" version of the pledge as a blatant attempt to "impose on [children] a religious belief."

The antipledge lawsuits—both in 2002 and 2010—were orchestrated by Michael Newdow, a California-based atheist who has also sued the government (unsuccessfully, so far) to remove "In God We Trust" from all U.S. coins and banknotes. There was no evidence of children actually complaining about the words "under God" in the pledge, but Newdow and the other plaintiffs argued that their children's rights were getting trampled every morning that they had to mumble their way through the pledge. Well, actually, they didn't *have* to recite the pledge, because students are always free to decline to do so.

The Ninth Circuit's original 2002 decision agreed with Newdow, holding that the Pledge of Allegiance, even if technically voluntary, exerts a "subtle coercive pressure" on students to acknowledge the existence of God. And that "pressure" is enough to violate the First Amendment's ban on laws "respecting an establishment of religion." That decision was greeted by a unanimous resolution of Congress reaffirming the inclusion of "under God" in the Pledge. Even then-senator Barack Obama jumped on the bandwagon, declaring in 2006 that he, for one, had never felt "oppressed" by having to recite the pledge as a kid. But no politician could change the legal precedent. As far as the courts were concerned, the last word on the subject—until 2010—belonged to Ninth Circuit judge Alfred Goodwin, who held that the declaration of "one nation, under God" is "identical" to saying that we are "a nation under Vishnu, [or] a nation under Zeus."

Funny he should mention Vishnu. According to some government officials, Vishnu is not "identical" to God, but far superior. In 2007, a San Diego school district decided that it was perfectly acceptable for teachers to display banners in their classrooms featuring Hindu and Buddhist teachings, but not with the dreaded words "one nation, under God." The taboo banners, put up by high school math teacher Bradley Johnson, also included a quotation from the Declaration of Independence: "All men are created equal, they are endowed by their Creator . . ."

The school district ordered Johnson to remove the banners because they "over-emphasized" God and conveyed "a Judeo-Christian viewpoint" that might offend a (purely hypothetical) Muslim student. But the other teachers were allowed to keep their banners promoting non-Western religions and atheism. In one classroom there hung a banner featuring the lyrics to John Lennon's "Imagine," including:

> *Imagine there's no heaven,*
> *It's easy if you try*
> *No hell below us,*
> *Above us only sky . . .*
> *Imagine there's no countries,*
> *It isn't hard to do*
> *Nothing to kill or die for,*
> *And no religion, too . . .*

Who needs to imagine while the ACLU is in business? The American Civil Liberties Union assisted the school district in its legal battle with Johnson. Although Johnson won in the district court—where the judge held that the school could not selectively censor one religious viewpoint—he lost in Stephen Reinhardt's home court, the Ninth Circuit Court of Appeals. The result is that a school can legally bar one teacher from quoting the Declaration of Independence, while allowing another teacher to encourage students to "imagine . . . no religion."

THE ESTABLISHMENT CLAUSE—NOT THE "SEPARATION CLAUSE"

The pledge controversy centers on the meaning of the establishment clause, which is one of two provisions on religion in the First Amendment (the other one is the free exercise clause, which I'll discuss later in this chapter). Contrary to popular belief, the establishment clause does not mandate separation of church and state. Rather, it forbids *Congress* from making laws "respecting an establishment of religion."

For the first 150 years of its existence, the establishment clause was a sleepy provision, generating almost no lawsuits. But in recent decades, it has become a full employment bill for liberal activists looking to fulfill Ebenezer Scrooge's wish that "every idiot who goes about with 'Merry Christmas' on his lips should be boiled with his own pudding and buried with a stake of holly through his heart." But of course they can't go around boiling people to death, so they settle for the next best thing: they sue. Every December, hordes of self-proclaimed civil libertarians scour the countryside, ready to file a lawsuit against every hapless town clerk foolish enough to allow a Nativity scene or menorah to sully public property.

In 1985, then–chief justice William Rehnquist lamented that the establishment clause had become a "crucible of litigation" that had produced only "consistent unpredictability" in court results. Establishment cases are unpredictable because the "living" version of the establishment clause bears no relation to the constitutional text, or to any other fixed principle. But there is a strategy: the liberal bloc of the judiciary seeks to drive religion from the public square whenever they can get away with it. The Pledge of Allegiance is a perfect example: the Ninth Circuit thought they got away with secularizing the pledge in 2002, but when it became clear that the American people were outraged, the court found a way to reverse itself.

IT'S ABOUT FEDERALISM

The vast majority of establishment-clause cases should never see the light of day for one simple reason: that clause does not create an individual right to be free from religion. In fact, it isn't about individual religious liberty at all—it's about state sovereignty.

The point of the establishment clause is to preserve state autonomy in supporting, or not, various religions. For the Founders, an "establishment of religion" referred either to an official state church (as in the "established" Church of England), or a denomination that is officially favored by the state. At the time the Constitution was ratified, the states had starkly different attitudes about religious establishments: Rhode Island, New Jersey, and Pennsylvania abolished them. But at least six states had established churches; that is, they had an official state church, or they provided aid to all (Protestant) churches on a nonpreferential basis.

The establishment clause, then, is "a federalism provision," as Justice Clarence Thomas describes it; "it protects state establishments from federal interference but does not protect any individual right." That explains why the framers prohibited *Congress* from making laws "*respecting* an establishment of religion"—they didn't want Congress to meddle one way or the other. The federal government could not foist an established church on Pennsylvania, but it also could not abolish the established church in Massachusetts. In 1833 Supreme Court justice Joseph Story aptly observed that the establishment clause was meant not to discredit state establishments, but to "exclude from the National Government all power to act on the subject."

ESTABLISHMENT CLAUSE, INCORPORATED

Everything changed with the Supreme Court's 1947 decision in *Everson v. Ewing.* In *Everson,* the Court struck down a New Jersey program that allowed public funds to subsidize school buses for kids in religious schools as a violation of the establishment clause.

To reach its result in *Everson,* the Court abandoned 150 years' worth of precedent, declaring that the establishment clause could be used as a weapon against the states. That was not a minor deviation from original meaning; it was a 180-degree turn. Before 1947, states had been free from federal interference when it came to the relationship between church and civil government. After 1947, the relationship between states and religion became a matter of federal law—or more bluntly, a matter of Supreme Court whim.

The *Everson* Court did not confess to making up the law— judges never do; rather, the majority declared that the Fourteenth Amendment required them to enforce the establishment clause against the states. That came as something of a surprise, particularly since the Fourteenth Amendment had already been around for seventy-nine years without ever requiring such a result. The Fourteenth Amendment itself says nothing about establishments. Those who ratified the amendment in 1868 certainly would not have understood it to destroy state autonomy over religion. Indeed, six years *after* the Fourteenth Amendment was ratified, there was a national movement to adopt a constitutional amendment to prohibit the states from "establishing" religion. It is unlikely, to put it mildly, that anybody would have bothered pushing for such an amendment if they thought the Fourteenth Amendment had already accomplished the same purpose.

Granted, by the time *Everson* came around, the Supreme Court had already held various provisions of the Bill of Rights to be "incorporated" against the states by the magic of the Fourteenth Amendment (see chapter 5). But even the made-up incorporation doctrine has its limits. Nobody suggests, for example, that the Fourteenth Amendment incorporates the Tenth Amendment, which reserves powers to the states (see chapter 11), because it would be silly to apply a states' rights amendment *against* the states. For the same reason, "it makes little sense" to read the establishment clause into the Fourteenth Amendment, as Justice Thomas observed.

In 1963, Justice Potter Stewart remarked on the "irony" of a situation in which "a constitutional provision designed to leave States free to go their own way [has now] become a restriction upon their own autonomy." But that was long ago—what was once ironic is now considered a pillar of constitutional law.

TEAR DOWN THIS WALL

But wait: the *Everson* Court wasn't finished rewriting the establishment clause. Even if we assume that the clause applies to states, what does a modest subsidy for school buses (the issue in *Everson*) have to do with an "establishment of religion"?

The answer, according to the Supreme Court, is that the establishment clause "means at least this: no tax in any amount, large or small, can be levied to support any religious activities or institutions." In other words, government effectively "establishes" a religion unless it is "neutral in its relations with groups of religious believers and nonbelievers." Well, that's obvious: one day you're helping children get to their parish school, the next day you're taking orders from the pope.

Everson's doctrine of "neutrality" is an accurate summary of the Constitution—of North Korea. Here in the United States, however, neutrality flies in the face of the text and history of the Constitution. The *Everson* Court made no serious attempt to analyze the original public meaning of the First Amendment, but it made a pretense of originalism by sprinkling its opinion with quotations from Madison and Jefferson that supposedly buttressed the Court's radical conclusion. Most famously, the Court invoked Jefferson: "In the words of Jefferson, the clause against establishment of religion by law was intended to erect 'a wall of separation between church and State.'" And—lest anyone accuse the Founders of dabbling in substandard walls, the Court added that Jefferson's wall was meant to be "high and impregnable."

Just one year after *Everson*, Justice Stanley Reed made the seemingly obvious observation that "a rule of law should not be drawn from a metaphor." But he was preaching, as it were, to the unconvertible. "No metaphor in American letters has had a more profound influence on law and policy," says Professor Daniel Dreisbach of the American University. The wall metaphor has proven irresistible to liberal secularists, who repeat it ad nauseam. It adds the appearance of intellectual heft to groups like Americans United for Separation of Church and State and the ACLU. Barack Obama extolled the "wall of separation" in a 2006 speech, while admonishing conservatives for failing to understand "the critical role" of the "separation of church and state."

There are just a few small problems. First, as always, the key to original meaning is the text itself. If the framers wanted to mandate a strict "separation of church and state," they could have inserted those very words into the Constitution. There's simply no evidence that those who ratified the First Amendment understood it as an absolute command of secularism. Second, Jefferson's interpretation deserves little weight, since he was neither a framer nor a ratifier of the First Amendment. He had been serving as minister to France, and did not get back to America until November 1789, after the entire Bill of Rights had been approved by Congress and sent on to the states. Third, the wall metaphor comes from a single letter that Jefferson wrote *eleven years after* the ratification of the Bill of Rights.

Finally, notwithstanding his deft use of metaphor, Jefferson never once suggested that states could not support religion. To the contrary, as a Virginia legislator and governor, he supported laws against blasphemy and in favor of government-sponsored days of fasting and thanksgiving. As Dreisbach explains, Jefferson's wall—like the establishment clause itself—was about federalism. The wall "was erected between the national and state governments on matters pertaining to religion and not, more generally, between the church and *all* civil government."

So much for the "wall of separation." As for Madison, although he participated in drafting the Bill of Rights, he "plainly implied on the floor of Congress that the Establishment Clause embodied views other than his own," according to former law professor (now Goldwater Institute fellow) Robert Natelson in a 2005 law review article. The premise that Jefferson and Madison provide the keys to unlocking the establishment clause is "wildly inaccurate," says Natelson.

Serious observers immediately saw through *Everson*'s fatuous "wall of separation." Just two years after the decision, constitutional scholar Edward Corwin argued that the Court had been "sold . . . a bill of goods." True, except the justices were willing buyers. The Court reached a result that reflected the virulent anti-Catholic sentiment of the era. With the large influx of Catholic immigrants in the early twentieth century, groups like the Ku Klux Klan turned their fearmongering attention to Catholics. Separation of church and state became a popular rallying cry for the KKK, with the goal of excluding Catholics from public life because they owe "allegiance" to the pope.

Legal historian Philip Hamburger has documented one particularly strong connection between *Everson* and KKK ideology: Justice Hugo Black, the author of the *Everson* opinion. Black had been an active Klansman in his native Alabama; in the goofy but sinister parlance of the Klan, he had served as Kladd of his Klavern. No doubt Black could have gone all the way to become King Kleagle of the Klan, but instead got himself elected to the Senate—thanks, in part, to the support of the Alabama Klaverns. Ironically, Black was known to criticize his fellow justices for their activist tendencies, as we saw in chapters 5 and 6. But in *Everson*, he rewrote the establishment clause in a way that just happened to advance the KKK's agenda. Not that Justice Black would have admitted any Klan influence while on the bench; why, he was just applying the Konstitution.

THE FOUNDERS WEREN'T NEUTRAL

Nobody in 1791 expected any American government—state or federal—to be neutral as between religion and irreligion. The

Founders did not have a take-it-or-leave-it attitude about religion; to the contrary, they generally agreed with John Adams's admonition, "Our Constitution was made only for a moral and religious people." The federal government was expected to promote and encourage religion in general because, as Madison had argued in Federalist No. 51, the security of "religious rights" depends upon a "multiplicity of sects." A robust diversity of religions would be the best safeguard against the sort of religious oppression that Europe had witnessed. In short, the Founders hoped to encourage sects, but not violence. To say this is not an attempt to guess at the secret intentions of the framers. Their support of religion is reflected in the text itself.

For one thing, the Constitution bars atheists from holding public office. Article VI requires that all legislators, and all executive and judicial officers—on both the federal and state level—take an oath to support the Constitution. But under the law at the time, only those who believed in God *and* in an afterlife could swear an oath. Atheists could not, for example, serve as witnesses in court—to whom would they swear to tell the truth? As late as 1820, New York's highest court observed, "It is fully and clearly settled, that infidels who do not believe in God, or if they do, do not think that he will either reward or punish them in the world to come, cannot be witnesses in any case . . . because an oath cannot possibly be any tie or obligation upon them."

At the North Carolina ratifying convention, lawyer and future Supreme Court justice James Iredell explained that the oath requirement would ensure a basic level of religious belief among officeholders because an oath is a "solemn appeal to the Supreme Being, for the truth of what is said, by a person who believes in the existence of a Supreme Being and in a future state of rewards and punishments." Madison acknowledged the religious nature of the oath in a letter of October 1787—just one month after the constitutional convention adjourned.

Although the Constitution requires a minimum level of religiosity for all officeholders, it does not favor any particular denomination—Article VI also prohibits any "religious Test" for holding federal office. As a whole, Article IV perfectly illustrates the framers' vision of the federal government's role in religion. The government could not, for example, require that all congressmen be Anglicans, or even Christians, but it does require that they be theists. Indeed, the framers were so scrupulous about the ecumenical nature of the oath that they specified that officeholders could "swear or affirm" to uphold the Constitution—affirmation being the method for Quakers and other individuals who objected to "swearing."

NEVER ON A SUNDAY

The early actions of the federal government also tend to debunk the neutrality canard. The very same Congress that approved the First Amendment also provided for paid chaplains in the House and Senate, and called upon President Washington to proclaim "a day of Public thanksgiving and prayer, to be observed by acknowledging, with grateful hearts, the many and signal favors of Almighty God." That same Congress also reenacted the Northwest Ordinance, which declares the government's policy that the teaching of "religion, morality and knowledge" shall "forever be encouraged."

The Court's liberals respond to all this with a phony brand of originalism that recasts the framers as secular humanists.

Happy to ignore the text of the establishment clause, the neutrality crowd prefers to focus on things that the framers didn't say. In *Marsh v. Chambers*, for example, Justice William Brennan found it highly significant that the framers "did not invoke the name of God" in the Constitution. Well, except that they did—in Article VII, which records the date of the document as "the Seventeenth Day of September in the Year of *our Lord* one thousand seven hundred and Eighty seven" (emphasis added). Who, one wonders, did Justice Brennan imagine "our Lord" to be?

Another provision that would be inexplicable to any proponent of strict neutrality can be found in Article I, Section 7. When Congress passes a bill, that clause gives the president ten days to decide whether to veto it; that is, ten days, "Sundays excepted." Why exclude Sundays? Wait—don't tell me—I know this one.

NEUTRALITY IN ACTION

The year after *Everson*, the Court struck down a program in Champaign, Illinois, that allowed children to be released from school for brief periods of religious instruction. The program was requested by parents, and to minimize the length of the children's absence, the instructors taught on school property. But that was the problem—to allow a religious instructor to set foot in a state school would constitute an "establishment of religion."

In 1962, the Court struck down a New York State law that allowed local schools to adopt a program of voluntary morning prayers. That case (*Engel v. Vitale*) involved the New Hyde Park School District, which had adopted a mild prayer to "Almighty God [to help] us, our parents, and our Country." Not exactly a tub-thumper, but according to the Court, it was enough to breach the "wall of separation."

In 1994, the obsession with neutrality reached the point where the Court struck down a New York law creating a special public school for handicapped children for the sole reason that all the students belonged to the same religion (*Board of Education of Kiryas Joel Village School District v. Grumet*). The school had been created by the New York legislature, with the governor's support, to accommodate a group of Hasidic Jews known as the Satmar Hasidim. It was not a religious school; it offered no religious curriculum. But the mere existence of the school—which simply allowed the Satmar to use their own tax dollars to support a public, secular school serving their own community—was enough to violate the neutrality principle, according to an opinion written by Justice David Souter. His fellow liberal, Justice John Paul Stevens, wrote a separate opinion to emphasize that the really offensive thing about the school was that it "increased the likelihood that [the children] would remain . . . faithful adherents of their parents' religious faith." And where would we be then?

The Founders would be "astonished," as Justice Scalia pointed out in dissent, to see the establishment clause used to prohibit this "characteristically and admirably American" accommodation of a religious group. As we've seen, the clause was originally understood to ensure that states would continue to have the power to make such accommodations without federal interference.

THE FEEL-GOOD CONSTITUTION?

The Court continued more or less along the Stevens-Souter trajectory until 2000, when it slightly modified the neutrality principle in *Mitchell v. Helms*. In that case, the Court upheld a law that authorized the state to lend computers to all students—those enrolled in religious as well as public schools—on a neutral basis. Neutrality was still key, but the Court allowed religious students to benefit from a government program on a nonpreferential basis. For the Court's liberals, however, this was the death of real neutrality. In dissent, Justice Souter wailed that the majority was just a small step away from "formally replacing the Establishment Clause."

Two years later, the Court upheld a Cleveland, Ohio, program of scholarship vouchers that could be used at any school, public or private. Parents were free to select religious schools, but it was entirely their own choice. The law was "neutral" as to religion. But again, the Court's liberals balked. Justice Stevens extended the *Everson* trope, warning that the Court had "remove[d] a brick from the wall that was designed to separate religion and government." Together with Justices Souter and Breyer, he argued that no law can be considered "neutral" if it allowed any religious school to benefit from any government program.

It was all very heartfelt and compelling, except that the liberal trio could not have believed what they were saying. Not even Justice Stevens—I think—would object to the local fire department putting out a blaze at a religious school, even though the school would thereby "benefit" from a taxpayer-funded goodie. In the real world, churches and religious schools benefit from local government services every day without any threat of creeping theocracy. Moreover, all religious institutions enjoy at least one *non-neutral* benefit from the government—they're tax-exempt. The Supreme Court upheld the religious tax exemption in 1970, and shows no sign of revisiting the issue.

Neutrality does not work in practice. It's impossible to make everyone equally happy. Take the case of Bradley Johnson, the teacher with the banners. The school district's policy evinced a clear hostility to Johnson's Judeo-Christian messages, but that was upheld as suitably neutral. In 2005 federal judge David Hamilton held that the Indiana legislature could not open its sessions with a Christian minister invoking the name of Christ, but later said that the legislature could invite a Muslim imam to pray to Allah. Decisions like that do have consequences, of course. In 2009, President Obama elevated Hamilton to the Court of Appeals.

As Judge Ferdinand Fernandez said in the 2002 pledge case, "I recognize that some people may not feel good about hearing [the phrase "under God"] recited in their presence, but, then, others might not feel good if they are omitted." Perhaps the fundamental mistake, as Fernandez put it, is the assumption that the Constitution is "a feel-good prescription." It is not. Even the ultraliberal Justice William Douglas—the inventor of penumbral emanations—once acknowledged that "we are a religious people whose institutions presuppose a supreme being."

PASSIVE/AGGRESSIVE RELIGIOUS DISPLAYS

Nowhere is the Court's obsession with neutrality more outlandish than in cases dealing with passive displays on public property— things like nativity scenes and depictions of the Ten Commandments.

In 1980 the Supreme Court made short work of a Kentucky statute that required the posting of a copy of the Ten Commandments, purchased with private funds, in each classroom in the State (*Stone v. Graham*). It was conceded that the only potential effect of such a law would be "to induce the schoolchildren to read, meditate upon, perhaps to venerate and obey, the Commandments." *Not on my watch*, said the Court. The justices struck down the law in a rare "summary reversal," without even requesting briefs or oral argument.

The *Stone* majority devoted not a word—not one—to the original understanding of the establishment clause. Instead they reached back to a venerable ten-year-old precedent, *Lemon v. Kurtzman*, for inspiration. In *Lemon*, which involved state subsidies for teacher salaries in religious schools, the Supreme Court held that any law touching on religion will violate the establishment clause unless:

1. It has a "secular purpose."
2. Its "principal or primary" effect is neither to advance nor inhibit religion.
3. It does not foster "excessive entanglement" with religion.

Like all such multifactor balancing tests, the *Lemon* test exists for the convenience of judges—it gives them ample flexibility to superimpose their own policy choices on the Constitution. How much entanglement is "excessive"? And who is to say what the real "purpose" of a law is? Certainly not the legislature that enacted it. In *Stone*, the Court disregarded the Kentucky Assembly's position that the Ten Commandments are an important part of Western civilization, whether you subscribe to them or not. The Court concluded that there could be no valid "secular" purpose for displaying the Ten Commandments.

Given precedents like *Stone*, one has to concede that Judge Reinhardt's 130-page rant in the 2010 pledge case actually had a valid point—if one can momentarily overlook the rhetorical spittle flying from the pages. What, after all, was Congress's "secular purpose" in inserting "under God" into the pledge, as it had done in 1954? There was no secular purpose—Congress wanted to celebrate America's God-fearing culture as compared to the godless states behind the Iron Curtain. But *Lemon* says that there must be a secular purpose, and so the Ninth Circuit argued that the words "under God" were added to reinforce "a concept of a limited government." Of course, the absurdity of the Court's reasoning proves that it's time to junk the *Lemon* test, not the pledge.

Unfortunately, the *Lemon* test is only one of *three* different balancing tests used in establishment clause cases. Judges who can't get the *Lemon* test to produce the desired result can choose to apply the endorsement test and/or the coercion test. All three tests are considered equally valid. Why not? When you replace the Constitution with a metaphor, there's no point in being exclusive about your balancing tests.

The endorsement test emerged in a 1984 case involving a city-sponsored nativity scene in Pawtucket, Rhode Island (*Lynch v. Donnelly*). In that case, Justice Sandra Day O'Connor announced that the establishment clause basically means that the government cannot "endorse" religion. That's because "endorsement sends a message to nonadherents that they are outsiders." O'Connor's apparent purpose was to simplify the three-pronged *Lemon* test, and she succeeded. Under her test, the establishment clause boils down to this: Is the government doing something that would make an atheist uncomfortable? In *Lynch*, O'Connor and a majority of the Court decided that the crèche did not endorse religion, since Pawtucket had thrown in so many secular symbols—a tree, a dancing elephant, a robot, and clowns—that your average atheist would feel right at home. Indeed, the only people likely to be offended were religious Christians. And they don't count.

Five years later, a somewhat more religious (and, presumably, less tacky) crèche in Pittsburgh was found to violate the establishment clause. In that case, the Court determined that a hypothetical nonbeliever would conclude that the display was religious, partly because of a banner proclaiming *Gloria in Excelsis Deo* ("Glory to God in the Highest"). It is unclear just how many Latin-speaking atheists in Pittsburgh were actually offended by the nativity scene. But no matter, the Court's hypothetical observer is just like every other fictional character: he bears no resemblance to any real person, living or dead.

By 2005, the hypothetical "reasonable observer" had acquired almost superhuman powers to root out religion from public life. In *McCreary County v. ACLU*, Justice Souter used the "reasonable observer" to assess displays in two Kentucky courthouses titled "Foundations of American Law and Government." The displays consisted of nine documents of equal size, including the Declaration of Independence and the Magna Carta—but also the Ten Commandments. Although the displays would appear to have a secular, educational purpose, the Reasonable Observer concluded that it was a "sham." Why? Because the Reasonable Observer knew that the counties would have preferred a less secular display—but they had been enjoined in an earlier lawsuit. Evidently the Reasonable Observer had been keeping an eye on the counties for years.

The establishment clause has now been turned upside down. Far from banning "establishments," it now positively mandates an orthodox secularism. It may well be that the Kentucky counties did not show any *outward* preference for religion, but they had lusted in their hearts, as it were, for religion. But what would the Reasonable Observer say about the Supreme Court itself? The

Court's building has a frieze on the outside depicting Moses carrying the Ten Commandments (in convenient tablet form!). Inside the building, there are symbols of the Ten Commandments on the doors leading into the courtroom, as well as on the gates lining the courtroom. Even worse, the Court opens each of its sessions with a prayer: "God save the United States and this honorable court." Justice Scalia recited all of these facts in his *McCreary* dissent, but Justice Souter responded that there was "no risk" that the Reasonable Observer would conclude that the Supreme Court had violated government neutrality. That's a relief!

McCreary was an awful decision. But just to show their zany, unpredictable side, the justices reached the opposite result in a different case on the very same day. In *Van Orden v. Perry*, a different majority of the Court held that a display of the Ten Commandments on the Texas state capitol grounds did not violate the establishment clause. Credit for honesty goes to Justice Breyer, who conceded that the Court wasn't really applying a "test" but rather exercising its own "legal judgment." The only problem is that the Supreme Court is supposed to lay down principles that lower courts can follow, and "legal judgment" isn't a principle.

With Justice Breyer advocating a jurisprudence of unfettered "judgment," it's no surprise that lower courts sometimes do their own thing. In 2010, the Court of Appeals for the Tenth Circuit held that the state of Utah had violated the establishment clause by allowing the Utah Highway Patrol Association—a private organization—to erect memorial crosses on the side of public highways. The appellate court disregarded the fact that only a few months earlier, a plurality of the Supreme Court had stated, "A cross by the side of a public highway marking . . . the place where a state trooper perished need not be taken as a statement of government support for sectarian beliefs."

Sure, the justices may have said that, but the Reasonable Observer trumps the Supreme Court. According to the Tenth Circuit, the sight of an occasional memorial cross near the highway would lead the Reasonable Observer to fear that Christians would receive preferential treatment from the Utah Highway Patrol, in general and—bizarrely—with respect to "hiring practices." Evidently, the Reasonable Observer aspires to be a state trooper himself, but won't submit his résumé until those crosses come down. Here's some advice for the Reasonable Observer: Don't even think about applying for that groundskeeper position at Arlington Cemetery.

As for the third test—the "coercion test"—it asks whether the government has done something to coerce citizens to exercise or support a particular religion. "Coercion" accurately captures what the framers were trying to avoid: the establishment clause forbids Congress from harnessing the power of the federal government to impose a particular religious orthodoxy by force of law. In practice, however, even the coercion test has proven to be an empty vessel. In *Lee v. Weisman*, a majority of the Supreme Court led by Justice Anthony Kennedy held that having a rabbi give a benediction at a high school graduation ceremony amounted to "coercion," even though students were not required to attend the ceremony at all. *Weisman*, in turn, was the intellectual underpinning of the Ninth Circuit's 2002 decision against the Pledge of Allegiance.

FREE EXERCISE

The effort to turn the establishment clause into an individual-rights guarantee has left the law in a state of hopeless confusion. And for no good reason. The Constitution already contains a guarantee of individual religious liberty; in fact, it is found in the six words immediately after the establishment clause: "or prohibiting the free exercise thereof." The free exercise clause is the flip side of the establishment clause; the latter prevents the federal government from dictating religious policy to the states, while the former prohibits the government from suppressing individual worship. It was inserted to address Anti-Federalist fears of government-sponsored suppression of religion.

Like freedom of speech, which comes next in the First Amendment, free exercise was expressed as an absolute right: "Congress shall make *no law* . . . prohibiting the free exercise [of religion]" (emphasis added). Over the years, however, the clause has come to mean that Congress and the state legislatures shall make no law prohibiting free exercise—unless they have a really good reason. Using the same balancing tests developed in the free speech context (see chapter 6), the Supreme Court has held that religious freedom must yield to sufficiently important government interests.

There's no textual basis for such balancing tests, but if the Court is going to use them, it should at least set the bar high when dealing with religion. That is what the Court did in *Sherbert v. Verner* (1963), holding that a state could not burden an American's free exercise unless it has a compelling interest for doing so— "compelling interest" is the magic formula for "strict scrutiny," the toughest standard of review that the Court employs. For decades, this high standard made it relatively difficult for states to get away with interfering with private religious practices.

RELIGIOUS FREEDOM—FOR THE MAJORITY

Today, however, attacks on religious freedom are far more likely to succeed, thanks to a 1990 decision in which the Supreme

Court held that federal, state, and local governments could infringe religious liberty all day long without having to come up
with a "compelling interest" for doing so.

Employment Division v. Smith involved two Native Americans, Alfred Smith and Galen Black, who worked as counselors
at a private drug clinic in Oregon. Smith and Black were fired because they had ingested peyote—a psychotropic drug made from
cacti—as part of a religious ceremony of the Native American
Church. The state of Oregon denied them unemployment benefits
on the grounds that they had been fired for "work-related misconduct."

Tripping out on peyote, it's true, would normally be
considered conduct unbecoming of a drug counselor, but in
this case, both Smith and Black were bona fide members of a
church that used peyote as a sacrament. The Oregon Supreme
Court held that the state could not constitutionally treat the
exercise of religion as "misconduct" so as to force the believers
to forfeit state benefits. Reasonable minds could differ about
that conclusion, but nobody disputed that the relevant standard was the compelling interest test. Oregon conceded the
point; it simply argued that the fight against drugs was sufficiently "compelling" to justify its zero-tolerance policy on
peyote.

Enter the U.S. Supreme Court. Without being asked to do
so by either party, the Court decided that it was time to ditch the
compelling interest test. The majority opinion—written, surprisingly, by Justice Antonin Scalia—virtually ignores the original
meaning of the First Amendment, except to say that various interpretations of the text are "permissible." And then the Court
simply declares that the compelling interest test "contradicts . . .
constitutional tradition." Constitutional tradition—that's what

judges rely on when they cannot find what they want in the constitutional text.

The "tradition" was in any event nonexistent. According to the majority in *Smith*, the Supreme Court had "*never* held that an individual's religious beliefs excuse him from compliance with an otherwise valid law prohibiting conduct that the State is free to regulate" (emphasis added). "Never" proved to be something of an overstatement. In 1972, for example, the Court had held that a compulsory school attendance law, although "neutral on its face," was unconstitutional because it "unduly burdens the free exercise of religion" among Amish families (*Wisconsin v. Yoder*). The Court had reiterated the compelling interest test in many cases since then, including at least three times in the year before the *Smith* decision.

Building upon its imaginary tradition, the *Smith* Court held that states are never required to exempt religious adherents from complying with "neutral laws of general applicability," even if those laws interfere with "free exercise of religion." In other words, the Oregon drug laws were acceptable, not because they served a compelling interest but because they were "neutral"— they didn't single out Native Americans for enforcement. The ramifications of this decision are mind-boggling. After all, the drinking age is also a "neutral law of general applicability." Can the police raid a Catholic Church and bust the padre for serving communion wine to minors? Or arrest Jews for serving wine to kids at Passover?

It all depends on the whim of the majority, according to *Smith*. Whether or not the state should accommodate a religious practice should be left to the "political process." Admittedly, that will put minority faiths at a "relative disadvantage," says that Court, but that's the price of "democratic government."

WHAT DID "FREE EXERCISE" MEAN?

Smith turns the First Amendment upside down. The whole point of that amendment—indeed, of the Bill of Rights—is to protect against majority oppression. If all the framers meant to say was, "Speech and religion will be tolerated to the extent permitted by Congress," there would have been no need for the First Amendment at all. Law professor (and former judge) Michael McConnell rightly branded *Smith* a "revisionist" version of the First Amendment.

Under the new, living First Amendment, the only religious freedom that is guaranteed is the freedom to believe. But the real First Amendment goes much further: it protects the freedom to "exercise" one's religion. The framers and ratifiers of the First Amendment understood, as we do today, that the word *exercise* conveys action, not merely thought. Samuel Johnson's *Dictionary*—the most influential of the founding era—defines *exercise* to include things like "Labour of the body" and "Use" and "*Act* of divine worship" (emphasis added). In *Smith*, Justice Scalia conceded that the exercise of religion may require "physical acts [such as] assembling with others for worship service, . . . sacramental use of bread and wine, proselytizing, abstaining from certain foods or certain modes of transportation." But the linchpin of his opinion is an 1879 precedent (*Reynolds v. United States*) in which the Supreme Court upheld laws against Mormon polygamy on the grounds that the free exercise clause protects only beliefs and not conduct. Not that the Court had any real evidence to that effect—the best it could do was dredge up Jefferson's "wall of separation" letter. The real motivation for *Reynolds* was the Court's horror of polygamy: a practice that "has always been odious among the northern and western nations of

Europe, and . . . was almost exclusively a feature of the life of Asiatic people."

Although later Supreme Court decisions did away with *Reynolds*'s belief/conduct dichotomy, the practical effect of *Smith* is to revive it. Beliefs may be protected, but there is no variety of religious conduct that cannot be prohibited by a law that is ostensibly neutral. And we've seen how well "neutrality" works as a protector of liberty in both the free speech and establishment clause contexts.

Had the *Smith* Court consulted original meaning—as Justice Scalia normally does—it could never have invented a neutrality exemption for infringements of free exercise. Granted, there must be some limits to religious ritual—human sacrifice, for example, is probably out of bounds—but the Founders had a strong bias against government-imposed limits. As Professor McConnell has demonstrated in several exhaustive law review articles, the Founders understood free exercise to require government to accommodate religious practices except when doing so would threaten the "peace and safety of the State." That understanding was reflected in colonial laws going back to the Maryland Charter of 1649, which declared that "noe person . . . shall bee any waies troubled or discountenanced for or in respect of his or her religion nor in the free exercise thereof," so long as—and here's the crucial bit—that person is not "unfaithfull to the Lord Proprietary [i.e., the Governor], or molest or conspire against the civill Government." In short, the colony could not "trouble" any person's free exercise of religion, except in cases amounting to treason.

After independence, the early state constitutions protected the individual's right to exercise religion "provided he doth not disturb the public peace" (New Hampshire) or "the peace or safety of this State" (New York). Similarly, the Northwest Ordinance of 1787 prohibits the government from disturbing the "mode of worshiping" of all persons who behave in "a peaceable and orderly manner."

Free exercise was not a matter of legislative whim in the early states or in the Northwest Territory. Rather, the government had to accommodate religious practices to the extent consistent with public safety. If that was the meaning of "free exercise" in the states and territories in 1791, why would anyone have read the First Amendment as providing less protection?

It is true that none of those early charters used the words "compelling interest"; however, "compelling interest" is a decent summary of the reasons that were thought to justify abridgment of religious freedom—peace, safety, and the prevention of "licentiousness." Certainly, "compelling interest" is a lot closer to original meaning than anything in the *Smith* decision, for which there is no historical antecedent. You will search in vain, I'm afraid, for any ancient charters providing for "newtrall lawes of generall applickabilitee" that would trump religious liberty.

Besides, religious accommodation was not just a matter of words on paper, it was a well-established American tradition by 1791. Since the mid-seventeenth century, colonial and, later, state governments allowed Quakers to "affirm" rather than swear an oath—even though the laws requiring oaths were "neutral" and of "general applicability." As we've already seen, the framers built this accommodation into the text of the Constitution. Religious exemptions from military service also date back to colonial times. In 1775, the Continental Congress granted an exemption for all those who "from religious principles, cannot bear arms in any case."

In 1787 Oliver Ellsworth, who would soon have a hand in

drafting the First Amendment, and would later go on to become chief justice of the Supreme Court, argued that the government had "no business" meddling with religion except to "prohibit and punish gross immoralities and impieties." This was the philosophy that animated the free exercise clause.

THERE'S RELIGION, AND THEN THERE'S RELIGION

Why did Justice Scalia abandon original meaning in *Smith*? One reason is suggested by Scalia's expressed concern that the compelling interest test had created "a system in which each conscience is a law unto itself"—quoting *Reynolds*. Perhaps peyote is the new polygamy: a sacrament so outlandish that it cannot be what the framers had in mind when they wrote about free exercise.

To be sure, the Founders probably were not thinking about polygamy or peyote when they wrote and ratified the free exercise clause. They almost certainly could not have predicted the rise of "churches" such as the Hawaii Cannabis Ministry and the Church of Marijuana—the latter of which was the subject of a split Tenth Circuit decision, with the dissenting judge insisting that the church "must be presumed" to be a legitimate religion.

What happened was a separate line of cases in which courts had moved the goalposts for determining what counts as a religion. At the time of the founding, religion took many forms, but it had to involve a belief in a Supreme Being. Remember Daniel Ellsworth? He wrote that the only exception to free exercise was "to prohibit and punish gross immoralities and improprieties." But he went on to write, in the same essay, that he "heartily approve[s] of our laws against . . . professed atheism." According to Natelson, Ellsworth's views were "entirely typical." There was no "free exercise" for nontheists.

The Supreme Court has long equated the word *religion* with any belief system that "occupies a place in the life of its possessor parallel to that filled by the orthodox belief in God" in theistic religions (*United States v. Seeger*). For free exercise purposes, religion has expanded to include ethical culture, secular humanism, Krishna consciousness, and other nontheistic belief systems. In 1986 the Fourth Circuit Court of Appeals held that the Virginia Department of Corrections was constitutionally required to accommodate the beliefs of a prisoner who claimed to practice Wicca (i.e., witchcraft), which he had studied via a correspondence course (*Dettmer v. Landon*). Worse yet, the court completely missed the obvious question—if the guy was really a witch, why was he still in prison?

Cases like *Dettmer* might seem to justify Scalia's fear that free exercise absolutism would make every conscience "a law unto itself." But *Dettmer* is not a result of the compelling interest test so much as of the watered-down definition of religion. Surely the answer to such cases is not to gut the free exercise clause, but to return to its original boundaries. There's no reason why the Court could not lay down a rule that, as far as the free exercise clause is concerned, religion is limited to theistic faiths. People who want to worship the sun or the moon or trees or marijuana or "secular humanism" would still be free to do so as a matter of free expression. And the state and federal governments may decide to accommodate the practices of such nontheistic faiths—but they wouldn't be *required* to do so under the free exercise clause. A return to the original meaning of religion would undoubtedly be greeted by howls of protest from every politically correct organization in the United States, but that would merely be an incidental benefit.

FURTHER ADVENTURES IN NEUTRALITY

It's not as though the facts of *Smith* were so extreme as to force the Court to give up the compelling interest test. Justice O'Connor, for example, reached the same result as Scalia by applying the compelling interest test; that is, she simply concluded that Oregon had a compelling interest in enforcing its drug laws. But O'Connor's reasoning did not attract a majority of the Court. Scalia's decision allows states to pass laws hostile to religion so long as they are careful to dress them up as "neutral laws of general applicability." In the wake of *Smith*, Congress passed the Religious Freedom Restoration Act (RFRA), which declared that the compelling interest test was the true measure of free exercise. A nice idea, but it didn't last long: in 1997 the Supreme Court held that the act was inapplicable to the states because the Court, not Congress, must have the last word on interpreting the Constitution.

Today, religious believers remain largely at the mercy of the "neutral" laws. In Massachusetts, for example, gay marriage is a civil right; therefore, it is "neutral" to require adoption agencies to place children with same-sex couples. Because that requirement contradicts Catholic teaching, Catholic Charities has been forced to exit the adoption business in the Bay State. Now, there's a victory for free exercise.

It is also neutral to require schoolchildren to learn the virtues of gay marriage in Massachusetts. Since at least 2005, the Lexington, Massachusetts, school district has had a compulsory reading program concerning same-sex relationships, which begins in kindergarten with such classics as *King and King*, a story about—well, you get the idea. When Christian parents tried to pull their kids out of the program, the school refused, even though Massachusetts law allowed parents to opt out of any program teaching "human sexuality." Then the parents sued—asserting a free exercise claim similar to that made by the Amish families who objected to compulsory school attendance in *Wisconsin v. Yoder*. But *Yoder* was decided in 1972, and this was 2007. With ample citation to *Smith*, the federal judge had no trouble concluding that the reading program was a neutral law with the modest goal of "chang[ing] attitudes and stereotypes [before] they have developed." Never mind that those "attitudes and stereotypes" reflect religious teachings. If parents want a curriculum that does not "conflict with their religious beliefs," said the judge, they "may send their children to a private school."

If courts were being consistent, then the type of conduct involved in "establishing" a religion ought to be similar to the conduct involved in "exercising" religion. But that's not the way things worked out. In the contradictory world of the First Amendment, it is ridiculously easy to "establish" a religion, but it's almost impossible to burden "free exercise." On the establishment side, the merest invocation of religion—a banner, a crèche, a Boy Scout oath—will suffice to breach the "wall of separation." In 2005, a federal court in Pennsylvania invalidated a school district's policy of requiring biology teachers to recite a four-paragraph statement encouraging students to "keep an open mind" about both Darwinian evolution and intelligent design. That was it. The school didn't actually teach intelligent design, but that four-paragraph statement was enough to violate the establishment clause.

Got that? A suggestion to "keep an open mind" is sufficiently religious to be an "establishment of religion," while a policy of forcing kindergartners to participate in a program celebrating gay marriage presents no burden on their parents' "free exercise."

After *Smith*, state and federal governments have used their power to coerce people to distribute contraceptives and even facilitate abortion, regardless of religious objections. States have threatened to revoke the licenses of pharmacists who refuse to distribute morning-after pills such as "Plan B," an abortifacient drug that prevents implantation of a fertilized egg. In Washington State, pharmacies could decline to dispense Plan B for secular reasons (e.g., lack of expertise, or concern over fraudulent prescriptions) but not because of religious scruples. In 2009, the Ninth Circuit held that the Washington State regulations were "neutral" within the meaning of *Smith*. A lower-court judge, however, struck down the regulations in February 2012, arguing that regulations fail the *Smith* test because they were not neutral in operation. If that decision (*Stormans v. Selecky*) is upheld—a big *if*, especially in the Ninth Circuit—it will represent a major correction to *Smith*.

At the federal level, the Obama administration has treated religion with the same sort of contempt that the *Reynolds* Court reserved for polygamists. In 2009, President Obama and his top cabinet officers stopped talking about "freedom of religion" and instead started extolling the virtues of "freedom of worship"—a rhetorical shift noted with alarm in *First Things* magazine. By equating religious liberty with "worship," the administration exploited the *Reynolds/Smith* view of the First Amendment: a dose of worship on the weekend is fine, but don't expect to practice your religion during the rest of the week. There's no telling where that might lead.

In January 2012, the Obama Health and Human Services Department proposed a rule requiring all employers—including religious hospitals, charities, and universities—to provide their employees with insurance coverage for contraceptives and abortifacients. The rule was part of the Affordable Care Act's "preventive services" mandate—pregnancy being the disease to be prevented. The only religious organizations excluded would be those that exist purely for their own members; namely, churches. But not church-affiliated groups. Following a public outcry, President Obama announced a "compromise": religious organizations would not have to cover abortion and contraception, but their insurance companies would have to do so—for free! By the time the Bible-thumpers realize that they've been subsidizing contraceptives via higher premiums—the reasoning seemed to go— Obama would be well into his second term.

The federal birth control mandate was modeled on a California law that was largely drafted by the ACLU, an organization tireless in its defense of liberty for those who manage to make it out of the womb alive. Indeed, the organization has urged the federal government to compel religious hospitals to perform abortions in "emergency" situations, which can include things like the mother's "emotional" well-being. In theory, health care workers and institutions have the right to refuse to participate in surgical abortions under the federal Church Amendment, but there is no effective way to enforce the right. In 2009, a court tossed out the lawsuit of a nurse at New York's Mount Sinai Hospital who had been forced to assist in the abortion of a twenty-two-week-old fetus. According to the court, individuals cannot bring lawsuits to enforce their rights under the Church Amendment. A right without a remedy is meaningless.

During the Bush administration, the Department of Health and Human Services had adopted regulations to strengthen the conscience rights of health care workers. Within two months of Barack Obama's inauguration, his administration announced that it would dismantle those regulations. Since his days as a senator, Obama has been an outspoken advocate for the Freedom of Choice Act, a proposed piece of legislation that would in a single stroke wipe out all pro-life conscience laws and force religious hospitals to perform abortions, emergency or otherwise. In fact, on the campaign trail in 2007, Obama declared, "The first thing I'd do as president is sign the Freedom of Choice Act. That's the first thing I'd do." But of course. One would expect nothing less from a former constitutional law professor.

CHAPTER EIGHT

TO KEEP AND BEAR ARMS

The Right the Left Left Behind

A well regulated Militia, being necessary to the security of a free State, the right of the people to keep and bear arms, shall not be infringed.

—SECOND AMENDMENT

RHONDA EZELL IS A MILD-MANNERED African American woman from the South Side of Chicago. She likes a quiet evening at home as much as anyone, but unfortunately, the criminals in her neighborhood had other ideas. In 2007, local thugs tried, unsuccessfully, to break into Ezell's home. And then they tried again. And again. After the third attempted burglary, Ezell concluded that she could not rely on the Windy City's finest for protection. She bought a gun.

Ezell also wanted to learn how to use her gun so that she would be prepared for emergencies. As any gun owner will tell you, the only way to learn how to properly handle a firearm is to practice at a firing range. The city of Chicago heartily agreed about the importance of firing ranges. In fact, Chicago made range training a mandatory condition of owning a gun. The city would not issue a firearms permit to Ezell—or any other citizen—without proof that she had completed a one-hour course at a firing range.

There was just one catch: *Chicago also banned firing ranges within city limits.* You've got to give them credit: the city fathers had produced one of those nonsensical decrees that one expects from Franz Kafka, George Orwell, or the EPA. You cannot have a gun permit without range training, and you cannot have range training.

And so Rhonda Ezell, in her mid-forties and seriously ill—in fact, awaiting a kidney transplant—traveled to a suburban firing range for the mandatory instruction and got her permit. But she would have to continue traveling to far-flung suburbs any time she wanted to practice her skills. Along with fellow Chicagoan Joseph Brown, a decorated World War II veteran, and others, Ezell sued Chicago for infringing her Second Amendment rights. She also asked the court to temporarily suspend (or "enjoin") the firing range ban until the lawsuit was resolved. Ezell's complaint went to the heart of the Second Amendment. As Chief Justice Thomas Cooley of the Michigan Supreme Court explained in 1868, "to bear arms implies something more than the mere keeping; it implies the learning to handle and use them." Chicago had blocked citizens from the only safe means of learning "to handle and use" guns. The district court, however, refused to enjoin the law, holding that Ezell and her fellow citizens were unlikely to prove that Chicago had interfered with their rights.

The most astonishing part of Ezell's saga is that the district court's decision effectively upholding the firing range ban came *after* the Supreme Court had declared, not once but twice, that the Second Amendment guarantees an individual right to keep and bear arms. In 2008 the Court held that the federal government could not ban an entire class of weapons—handguns—that citizens traditionally use for self-defense (*Heller v. District of Columbia*). And then in 2010 the Court stated that the Second Amendment also applies to the states. The latter case—*McDonald v. Chicago*—struck down an earlier Chicago law that contained an outright ban on handgun possession. Four days after the Supreme Court's decision in *McDonald*, the Chicago City Council passed the Responsible Gun Owners Ordinance, containing the catch-22 gun range requirement.

THE CONSTITUTIONAL REVOLUTION THAT WASN'T

The good news is that the Court of Appeals overturned the district court's initial decision in *Ezell*, with one of the appellate judges observing that the Chicago law was nothing more than a "thumbing of the municipal nose at the Supreme Court." The bad news is that the splendid appellate decision in *Ezell* was a rare exception to the generally futile attempts to persuade lower courts to apply the arms-bearing right articulated by the Supreme Court. And that, in a nutshell, is the lesson of the Second Amendment. It is possible to get the Supreme Court to revive long-forgotten constitutional liberties, but the resistance from politicians and lower courts will be fierce.

The Supreme Court rulings in *Heller* and *McDonald* represent hard-won victories of original meaning over decades of misinterpretation. In both cases, the Court rejected the orthodox liberal view that the Second Amendment merely guarantees the "collective right" of state militias to exist, and instead held—oh, miracle of miracles—that the framers actually meant what they said: "The right of *the people* to keep and bear arms shall not be infringed." The Court described the Second Amendment right as encompassing keeping weapons at home for self-defense, as well as "carrying" arms to be prepared for possible "confrontation." Moreover, the Court held that this right is a "fundamental" one that belongs to each and every American, regardless of membership in the military. Unlike the "fundamental" rights invented by activist courts (chapter 5), this one actually appears right in the Constitution's text.

When the Supreme Court says things like that, one might reasonably expect politicians and lower courts to listen. Liberal commentators certainly expected *Heller* and *McDonald* to produce dramatic results; namely, streets soaked in blood. *Washington Post* columnist Colbert King, for example, decried *Heller* as a victory for "D.C. street thugs." In anticipation of the anarchy that the decision would no doubt unleash, King declared that America would need "more body bags." Liberal blogger David Ehrenstein agreed with those dire predictions and, like a good pacifist, called for the murder of Justice Antonin Scalia, the author of the *Heller* opinion. But D.C. did not descend into anarchy; or rather, it did not descend any further into anarchy. The street thugs already had guns. The real issue in *Heller* and other Second Amendment cases is whether law-abiding citizens like Rhonda Ezell can exercise their right to defend themselves.

In the wake of the *McDonald* ruling, Kristen Rand, legislative director of the Violence Policy Center, wailed, "People will die because of this decision." Die? Of boredom, perhaps, while waiting for their gun permit. Chicago still maintains one of the most onerous gun registration regimes in the country, even without the gun range ban. Windy City residents must apply for a permit, and then a registration certificate, and then a "Firearm Owner's Identification Card." And that's just for the privilege of keeping a gun in one's home. Carrying, or "bearing," a gun outside the home is absolutely forbidden. In D.C., the city government responded to *Heller* by enacting an elaborate twelve-step gun permitting process that is estimated to take up to eight weeks to complete.

Virtually no restriction on gun ownership, no matter how burdensome, has been struck down by a court. There have been over four hundred challenges to gun laws since *Heller*, and they have been overwhelmingly rejected, leading the antigun Brady Center to crow that *Heller* was a "hollow victory." While pretending to "apply" the Supreme Court's decisions in *Heller* and *McDonald*, state and federal courts have held that there is no constitutional right to have a gun if:

- You're outside your house, even on your driveway.
- You're under twenty-one.
- Your gun automatically reloads (as most do these days).
- You've ever been convicted of a crime, or indicted, or arrested.

You want a gun in New York City? No problem. Of course, all the above restrictions apply. Plus, you can't have a gun if you have outstanding debts, or if you've ever been fired from a job, or if you have a "poor driving history" (because guns don't kill people, bad drivers with guns do). In fact, I would think twice about applying for a New York gun permit if you've ever had an overdue library book.

WHICH PART OF "SHALL NOT BE INFRINGED" DON'T THEY UNDERSTAND?

Notwithstanding two Supreme Court decisions, America's political class—the ones who know what's best for you—remains oblivious to the original meaning of the Second Amendment. Liberals continue to insist (for reasons I'll examine below) that the amendment confers only a "collective" right for militias to have guns, or, at best, an individual right conditioned on military service. According to those interpretations, the Second Amendment might just permit a National Guardsman to carry a gun; but it is totally irrelevant to an average citizen like Rhonda Ezell, or somebody who innocently thinks that it is still acceptable to hunt or practice marksmanship. It is simply impossible to square that ultranarrow interpretation with the text of the amendment itself.

The heart of the Second Amendment—what lawyers call the "operative clause"—goes like this: "The right of the people to keep and bear arms, shall not be infringed." Like the First Amendment, this clause does not claim to *create* any right. Instead, it assumes the existence of a right and protects it against "infringement." What was that right? It was the individual's "right to keep and bear arms" for self-defense—precisely the right that Rhonda Ezell sought to exercise. That is how the language would have been understood by Congress and the state ratifying conventions that approved the language.

Long before the United States even existed, Americans considered the right to bear arms part of their legal birthright. One of the worst outrages of George III had been his attempt to disarm the colonists—the battles of Lexington and Concord were fought to prevent British forces from confiscating guns and ammunition in those towns. In a series of laws between 1757 and 1763, the crown had authorized its American agents "to seize and remove the Arms" of the colonial militias. And just for good measure, the crown was also allowed to take the "Clothes and Accoutrements" of the militiamen—bearing arms was out, baring arms was in.

In place of local militias, the British sent thousands of regular troops to keep an eye on the colonists. Americans responded to these measures by calling on their countrymen to hurry up and arm themselves. British loyalists called this sedition, but various patriots pointed out that they were merely urging people to exercise their rights. As an anonymous writer noted in the *New York Journal* in 1769, "It is a natural right which the people have reserved to themselves, confirmed by the Bill of Rights, to keep arms for their own defence."

Notice the reference to the Bill of Rights? That's not the U.S. Bill of Rights, which did not yet exist in 1769. Rather, it was the English Bill of Rights of 1689, which declared that all Protestant subjects "may have arms for their defence." That is, self-defense. Not only did the colonists invoke the 1689 Bill of Rights, but many of them cited Sir William Blackstone's *Commentaries on the Laws of England*, which describes "the right of having and using arms for self-preservation and defence" as a vital individual right, essential to safeguarding the three "absolute rights" of Englishmen: personal security, personal liberty, and private property. According to Blackstone, the right to bear arms flowed directly from the "natural right of resistance and self-preservation, when the sanctions of society and laws are found insufficient to restrain the violence of oppression." In plain English: it's your right to keep a gun because the cops may not be around when the burglars break in.

Between 1776 and the ratification of the American Bill of Rights, four states adopted laws protecting the right to bear arms: two of them explicitly included individual use of arms for self-defense. The Pennsylvania Declaration of Rights, for example, proclaims that "the people have a right to bear arms *for the defence of themselves* and the State" (emphasis added). Other states, such as Massachusetts and Delaware, adopted general declarations of the people's right to "defend" life and liberty. As Joyce Lee Malcolm, a leading expert on the Second Amendment, notes, "It is difficult to see how the right to defend one's life could be fully exercised if citizens were deprived of the right to be armed."

The point is that by 1791, the right to bear arms was old hat for Americans. Under natural law, English law, and state law, it was an individual right that grew out of the larger rights of self-preservation and self-defense. Moreover, the Second Amendment was enacted in response to proposals that various states had made when ratifying the Constitution. Not one of those states proposed a federal right to bear arms that would be limited to military purposes. New Hampshire, for example, advocated a right to keep arms for every citizen—not just militiamen—with the only exception being those engaged in "Actual Rebellion." In Pennsylvania, the minority report of the state ratifying convention proposed that the Constitution be amended to protect the "right to bear arms for the defence of themselves and their own State, or the United States, or for the purpose of killing game."

It makes absolutely no sense to think that the ratifiers of the Second Amendment, or any citizen reading that amendment in 1791, would have understood it to create a mere collective right. Why would Americans accept an arms-bearing right weaker than that which they had enjoyed under English law? Weaker than the right already guaranteed by several states? Weaker than what the ratification conventions were calling out for? They wouldn't have accepted it, not for a minute.

Equally important, the Second Amendment safeguards a right belonging to "the people." As we've already seen in chapter 2, "the people" was a term of art in the Constitution and other documents of the founding era. The people were members of the social compact; they elected state and federal representatives, petitioned the government, served as jurors, and so forth. The people comprised all the permanent members of the community, not just those on active military duty. Old men like Ben Franklin, for example, were members of "the people," even if not members of the militia.

Just a decade after the Bill of Rights was ratified, American jurist St. George Tucker commented on the link between the Second Amendment and Blackstone's right of self-preservation and defense. The right to keep and bear arms, declared Tucker, "may be considered as the true palladium of liberty. . . . The right to self-defence is the first law of nature." That sentiment was echoed forty years later by Supreme Court justice Joseph Story, who described the Second Amendment as "the palladium of liberties of a republic." Palladium, I should note, is the English name of the statue of Athena, also known as Pallas, that in Greek mythology protected the city of Troy. Once the palladium was stolen—by Odysseus and Diomedes—Troy was conquered by the Greeks. Granted, that horse-with-the-soldiers-inside thing also helped, but the rhetorical point is that a palladium is all that stands between you and destruction. It wasn't every day that people like Tucker and Story threw around words like *palladium*, and it's not likely they would have used that word to describe a provision that did nothing more than protect the right of militiamen to be armed.

The Second Amendment originally applied only to the federal government, but as the Supreme Court held in *McDonald*, the doctrine of incorporation means that it must also apply to the states by virtue of the Fourteenth Amendment. So we also have to consider the original understanding of the right to bear arms by those who ratified the Fourteenth Amendment. Here again, all the evidence points to an individual right—not a collective right of militias. One of the motivations for the broad language in the Fourteenth Amendment was to strike down Jim Crow–era laws disarming black citizens. The ratifiers of the Fourteenth Amendment understood it to constitutionalize an earlier statute—the Freedmen's Bureau Act of 1866—which guaranteed the "full and equal benefit of all laws and proceedings concerning personal liberty [and] personal security . . . including the constitutional right of bearing arms." In this context, with blacks being terrorized by lynch mobs throughout the Reconstruction South, individual self-defense was at the very core of the right to bear arms. Nobody can seriously suggest that the Fourteenth Amendment was simply intended to safeguard the right of African Americans to join their state militia.

LIBERALS EMBRACE ORIGINALISM, SORT OF

Despite all evidence to the contrary, antigun zealots insist that their narrow reading of the Second Amendment is the true "originalist" reading. Let's pause for a moment to soak up the irony: are there any other guarantees of the Bill of Rights that liberals wish to confine to their 1791 meanings? Not the Eighth Amendment's prohibition on cruel and unusual punishments (chapter 10), which liberals say must "evolve" to secure the good opinion of the "international community." Nor can the establishment clause be read according to original meaning, which would allow direct state aid to churches (chapter 6). And the Fifth Amendment? Professor David Strauss—of *The Living Constitution* fame—suggests that if we stuck to the original meaning of "due process," we'd somehow still have slavery.

When it comes to the right to keep and bear arms, however, liberals suddenly become sticklers for the original text. Well, not the whole text of the Second Amendment, because that operative clause is a little awkward for them. Instead, they focus on the first thirteen words: "A well regulated Militia, being necessary to the security of a free state." That is the preamble, or prefatory clause, of the Second Amendment. According to the traditional anti-gun interpretation, that prefatory clause means that the Second Amendment applies only to militias.

But not even that reading goes far enough for most liberals, since *militia* was a very broad term in 1791: it comprised all males of fighting age. Indeed, state laws generally required all men to keep arms and to know how to use them. Thus liberals rely on the term "well regulated" to mean that the Second Amendment applies only to the militia in active service (because a minuteman just sitting around waiting to be called up for service is not "well regulated"). And some commentators even go so far as to say that the right to bear arms only applies to state militias when specifically called into action by the federal government. Thus, according to the liberal narrative, the framers were simply saying "state militias can have guns."

Well, of course they can. And if that were all the Second Amendment said, it would hardly have been worth the time, especially since Article I of the Constitution had already given Congress authority to "arm" the militias when pressed into federal

duty. But more important, the very premise of the argument—
that the scope of the Second Amendment is only as broad as its
preamble—is shockingly naive. Prefatory clauses are an ancient
device in the law. Lawyers are forever puffing up their documents
with "whereas" clauses and other statements of purpose. But such
clauses have no legal effect—not today, and not in 1791, either.
The leading eighteenth-century court decision on the topic said
quite clearly that "the preamble could not be used to restrict the
effect of the words" of a statute.

Left-wing academics often declare that the preamble to the
Second Amendment is "unique" in the Constitution, as though
that requires us to give it special legal effect. But in fact, the Second Amendment is not unique. Although no other provision in
the federal Bill of Rights has a prefatory clause, many state constitutions of the era did contain such clauses. As UCLA professor
Eugene Volokh explained in a groundbreaking law review article
in 1998, those prefatory clauses were never used to trump the
plain meaning of the operative clauses.

The Pennsylvania Constitution of 1790, for example, states
that "the free communication of thoughts and opinions is one of
the invaluable rights of man; and every citizen may freely speak,
write, and print on any subject, being responsible for the abuse of
that liberty." The same phrase was repeated, almost verbatim, in
six other constitutions of the late eighteenth and early nineteenth
centuries. No sensible person suggests that those clauses empowered the state to suppress speech that did not rise to the level of
"thoughts and opinions."

The New Hampshire Constitution of 1784 guarantees a free
press with the following statement: "The liberty of the Press is essential to the security of freedom in a State; it ought, therefore, to
be inviolably preserved." Notwithstanding the preliminary state-

ment of purpose, no one has suggested that the New Hampshire press is only free to publish material that promotes the "security of freedom in a State."

That's not to deny that there is a *connection* between the prefatory and operative clauses—the framers weren't writing haiku. The prefatory clause is a rhetorical device; it states one purpose for the operative clause—the purpose that was likely to be most persuasive for its intended audience. Remember that the Bill of Rights was drafted to win over reluctant Anti-Federalists. During the ratification debates on the Constitution, Anti-Federalists argued that the federal government might disarm the citizen militia and impose rule by standing army à la George III. In Federalist No. 29, Hamilton tried to allay those fears by emphasizing that a federal army would pose no threat to liberty so long as "there is a large body of citizens . . . who stand ready to defend their own rights and those of their fellow citizens." When such assurances were insufficient, the Second Amendment was adopted to expressly guarantee that the federal government would not have a monopoly on arms.

The maintenance of state militias was the immediate selling point, as it were, for the Second Amendment, but the amendment upholds a much broader right. There's nothing unique about that. As one English judge observed in 1802, "It is nothing unusual in acts . . . for the enacting part to go beyond the preamble; the remedy often extends beyond the mischief which first suggested the necessity of the law." Likewise, the Second Amendment's prefatory clause "does not suggest that preserving the militia was the only reason Americans valued the ancient right," as Justice Scalia stated in *Heller*; "most undoubtedly thought it even more important for self-defense and hunting."

THE TYRANNY OF THE ANTIGUN ELITE

One of the more endearing delusions of the antigun crowd is that the "collective rights" interpretation of the Second Amendment has a long and distinguished pedigree. Just listen to the authoritative voice of six former U.S. attorneys general who, in 1992, wrote a stern letter to the *Washington Post*, telling the great unwashed that "for more than 200 years, the federal courts have unanimously determined that the Second Amendment concerns only the arming of the people in service to an organized state militia; it does not guarantee immediate access to guns for private purposes."

More than two hundred years! Impressive, since the Second Amendment was ratified just 201 years before the letter was written. The obvious implication of the letter is that the Second Amendment had been embroiled in two centuries of nonstop litigation, with gun nuts repeatedly trudging into court only to be reminded by long-suffering judges that only militias have a right to "bear arms." It's a vivid image—and as divorced from reality as one might expect from six superannuated government lawyers.

The truth is that the Second Amendment hardly ever made it to court before the latter half of the twentieth century. Those courts that did consider the Second Amendment, or analogous state provisions, consistently ruled that the amendment protected an *individual* right to have a gun—exactly the opposite of what the former AGs wrote. The first state court to hint at a collective rights interpretation was the Kansas Supreme Court, in a 1905 decision that was ignored for decades thereafter. As for federal courts, it was not until 1935 that a federal judge ruled that the Second Amendment applies only to militias. That judge was Halsted Ritter, who would go on within one year to be convicted and impeached by the Senate on misconduct charges. Before the 1960s, only one other federal court adopted the collective rights theory—the Third Circuit in the case of *United States v. Tot*. Mind you, none of the judges on the *Tot* court could cite any authority to support the collective rights theory, but they at least managed to escape impeachment.

The Supreme Court addressed the meaning of the Second Amendment only once before *Heller*, in the 1939 case of *United States v. Miller*. That decision, however, did not resolve the individual versus collective rights debate. In *Miller*, two mobsters had been indicted of transporting a sawed-off shotgun across state lines, in violation of the National Firearms Act. The mobsters challenged the indictment on constitutional grounds. In a famously muddled opinion, the Court held that the Second Amendment did not protect the right to keep weapons like sawed-off shotguns that were not "used for military or public defense purposes." The Court did not mention whether the defendants were members of, or even eligible for, the militia; rather, it looked exclusively at the type of weapon they were carrying.

There were other problems with *Miller*. For starters, the pro-individual-rights argument was never even presented to the Court. The case was appealed to the Supreme Court by government prosecutors (after they initially lost in the district court), but the defense lawyer refused to file a brief, or even show up for oral argument. Another problem is that the Court's conclusion makes no sense. The logical consequence of the Court's focus on military-type weapons is that the people would have a constitutional right to possess machine guns, bazookas, and shoulder-launched missiles, all of which come in handy for "military or public defense purposes."

But *that*'s not how *Miller* has been used by lower courts.

Beginning in the 1960s, as gun control became fashionable, *Miller* provided the faulty pedigree for dozens of court decisions upholding gun laws on a collective rights basis. Moreover, collective rights was a catchy theory for left-wing intellectuals— "collective" had that irresistible air of gray Soviet uniformity that puts an extra spring in their step. As Cato Institute analyst David Kopel writes, the collective rights theory became "the easy way [for intellectuals] to sneeringly dismiss anybody who raised constitutional objections to gun control."

The Sneerer in Chief of the antigun movement is Garry Wills, a Pulitzer Prize–winning historian who has been called the most outspoken advocate of the collective rights theory. In a highly influential 1995 essay in the *New York Review of Books*, Wills managed to argue both that the Second Amendment "had no real meaning," and that it has lots of meaning—all of it military. Wills condemned conservative legal scholars for taking advantage of the unfortunate fact that the "general public" suffers from a "disposition to believe that the Second Amendment protects gun ownership." Sadly for Wills, the American people seem to have been laboring under that misapprehension for a long time—at least since 1803, when St. George Tucker observed that the Second Amendment allows individuals to exercise "the first law of nature," i.e., self-defense.

Undaunted by history, Wills argued that the Second Amendment applies only to militias; in fact, specifically, only to those militias that are "organized, armed, and disciplined by the federal government." Thus, the thesis of Wills's essay contradicts the very rationale of the Second Amendment, which was to fulfill Hamilton's promise that a "large body of citizens"—comprising the citizen militias—would serve as a counterweight to a federal standing army. In the spirit of intellectual give-and-take, Wills branded those who disagreed with him as "fantasists," "madmen," "deranged," "frivolous," and "wacky."

Touch a nerve, did we, Garry? For all his scholarly pretentions, Wills simply assumes his ultimate conclusion: that the Second Amendment is all about military readiness. Having made that leap, Wills proceeds to ask in ever more petulant tones why conservatives don't understand the "military context" of the amendment. He cannot fathom, for example, why "fanciful" right-wingers fail to appreciate that the word *keep* (as in "keep and bear arms") was understood by the Founders to be a military term. Why, it was just in 1675—a mere 116 years before the Second Amendment was ratified—that an English pamphleteer wrote that the king must not be allowed to "*keep up* a standing army" (italics by Wills). And if that doesn't convince you, consider that "as an English noun, 'keep' meant the permanently holdable part of a castle." Oh, that clinches it!

Wills's argument does lead to some odd interpretations of other constitutional provisions, like Article I, Section 5, which says that "each House [of Congress] shall *keep* a Journal of its Proceedings" (emphasis added). Presumably, Wills thinks that Congress *keeps* a journal so that copies can be hurled at an invading army.

But Wills was a paragon of scholarship compared to Michael Bellesiles, an historian whose 2000 book *Arming America* set out to prove that the framers never intended to protect individual gun ownership, since almost nobody owned a gun in the late eighteenth century. Instead, they relied on things like swords, axes, and sarcasm to defend themselves. The book was an immediate hit with the intellectual elite, winning the Columbia University Bancroft Prize and a glowing *New York Times* review from none other than Garry Wills. It soon came to light, however,

that Bellesiles had simply made up his facts, citing probate records, travel diaries, and other documents that either didn't exist
or flatly contradicted his conclusion. By 2003, Bellesiles had been
obliged to resign from his teaching position at Emory University
and to return the Bancroft Prize money to Columbia.

With advocates like Wills and Bellesiles, it's no wonder that
supporters of collective rights soon saw the writing on the wall. In
1989, left-leaning University of Texas professor Sanford Levinson
published an article conceding the "embarrassing" fact that the
Second Amendment appears to guarantee an individual, not a
collective, right. Throughout the 1990s, more and more liberal
academics abandoned the collective rights theory. By 2000, Harvard's Laurence Tribe had revised his constitutional law treatise
to conclude that the Second Amendment provides "a right . . . on
the part of individuals."

Tribe's change of heart was simply too much for the Ninth
Circuit Court of Appeals—the most liberal appellate court in the
nation—to compute. In a 2002 case, the Ninth Circuit declared
that Professor Tribe had not changed his mind about the Second
Amendment, but that he was simply "stymied by the task of construing the Second Amendment." In that case, *Silveira v. Lockyer*,
the Ninth Circuit proudly upheld the collective rights theory,
while scolding one of the few conservatives on the court, Judge
Alex Kozinski, for "cling[ing] fast to the individual rights view."

OLD WINE IN A NEW BOTTLE

By 2007, every member of the Supreme Court would be "cling-
ing" to the same view as Judge Kozinski. In *Heller*, a D.C. special police officer who worked at the Federal Judicial Center

was denied a permit to keep a handgun at home. Although only five justices held that D.C.'s handgun ban violated the Second Amendment, all nine justices acknowledged that the amendment establishes an individual right; that is, a right that can be individually possessed and enforced. And once again, in *McDonald*, the justices were unanimous in supporting an individual rights interpretation of the Second Amendment, although they disagreed—bitterly—over the scope of that right.

The Supreme Court remains divided on gun rights because a very curious thing has happened to the individual rights interpretation. As soon as the liberal justices conceded the Second Amendment applies to individuals, they and their academic allies rushed to declare that by "individuals," they don't mean ordinary people—certainly not *the* people. Instead, the new orthodoxy became the "militia-conditioned individual right" theory; i.e., that the Second Amendment applies to individuals, but only to the extent that they participate in an organized militia. Unlike the thoroughly discredited collective rights theory (i.e., "only state militias can have guns"), this new interpretation declares that "only individual members of state militias can have guns."

See the difference? Neither can I. The militia-conditioned right is nothing more than the old collective rights theory with lipstick. And virtually all the same tired arguments made by Wills & Co. have been trotted out to support the new and improved version. Thus, advocates of the militia-conditioned right insist that the phrase "bear arms" had an exclusively military meaning at the founding. That would have been news to Jefferson and Madison, who in 1785 cosponsored a bill in the Virginia Assembly that regulated individuals' ability to "bear a gun" for the purposes of killing deer. Wills dismisses this legislation in characteristic fashion because, unlike the Second Amendment, it does not use the word *bear* in a "military context." How does he know that the Second Amendment has a "military context"? Because it contains military words like *bear*. Only a "wacky" person could disagree with that logic.

The fact is that in 1791, just like today, *bear* meant "to carry." The phrase "bear arms" was often used in early America to refer to carrying weapons for personal reasons. Between 1776 and 1820, nine states adopted constitutional provisions guaranteeing individuals the right to "bear arms *in defense of themselves and the State*," or similar formulations. The very first time the Supreme Court mentioned the Second Amendment, it assumed an individual rights interpretation. In the infamous *Dred Scott* case (see chapter 2), Chief Justice Roger Taney argued that if African Americans could gain citizenship, they would have to be afforded "the full liberty . . . to keep and *carry* arms wherever they went" (emphasis added). Taney was not worried about blacks joining the state militia; rather, he was raising the specter of black citizens with an individual right to possess guns.

There is also no doubt, *pace* Wills, that the verb *keep* was not a military term of art in the eighteenth century. To the contrary, "keeping arms" was often specifically used to describe nonmilitary uses. In July 1789 Samuel Nasson, an Anti-Federalist delegate to the Massachusetts ratifying convention, referred to the need to enact an amendment to secure "the right to *keep* arms for Common and Extraordinary Occasions [*sic*] such as to secure ourselves against the wild Beast and also to amuse ourselves by fowling and for our Defense against a common enemy" (emphasis added). In the same year, the pastor Jeremy Belknap described the "right to *keep* arms" as part of the "personal and domestic rights" of "the people" (emphasis added).

Ultimately, the conditional rights theory depends on the losing argument that the preamble of the Second Amendment limits the scope of its operative clause. But in a new twist, some scholars argue that the Second Amendment is a dead letter because the militia referred to in the preamble no longer exists. The original understanding of the militia was codified in the Uniform Militia Act of 1792, which defines the nation's militia as "every free able-bodied white male citizen of the respective States" between the ages of eighteen and forty-five, with certain exceptions. In their 2002 book *The Militia and the Right to Bear Arms*, Columbia professor H. Richard Uviller and Richard Merkel argue that such a militia is extinct, and therefore the "condition" for the individual right to own a gun has vanished. But they overlooked one small fact: federal law still—today—defines "the militia of the United States" as consisting of all able-bodied males between the ages of seventeen and forty-five, with certain exceptions. That law (10 U.S.C. § 311) divides the militia into two classes: the "organized militia," consisting of the National Guard and Naval Militia, and the "unorganized militia," consisting of everyone else. It's true that service in the unorganized militia is pretty easy these days—I myself have never been asked to drill on the village green. Nonetheless, federal law has never ceased to acknowledge the existence of the citizen militia. Thus, even if the Second Amendment applies only to members of the militia, it applies to all able-bodied males of fighting age. And if the government goes that far, but fails to extend the right to women, the handicapped, and the elderly, I daresay that Uncle Sam would have an equal protection/due process lawsuit on its hands. And rightly so: the right to self-defense—the real core of the Second Amendment—ought to apply to all people.

As unconvincing as the militia-conditioned interpretation is, it is the new pet theory of the Supreme Court's liberal bloc.

With just a small change to the Court's membership, it could become the law of the land. It may not matter much, however, since lower courts have been pretty much ignoring *Heller* and *McDonald* anyway. And that is because the Supreme Court needlessly sabotaged gun rights in *Heller*.

OPEN LOOPHOLE, INSERT TRUCK

In his otherwise splendid opinion in *Heller*, Justice Scalia made a most unnecessary remark. He sought to reassure the public that the recognition of an individual right to bear arms should not "cast doubt on longstanding prohibitions on the possession of firearms by felons and the mentally ill, or laws forbidding the carrying of firearms in sensitive places such as schools and government buildings, or laws imposing conditions and qualifications on the commercial sale of arms." And then he threw in a footnote declaring that this list of prohibitions is just a *partial* list of gun regulations that are "presumptively lawful." To be fair, Scalia did specify "longstanding prohibitions," the point being that traditional restrictions on gun ownership—like those going back to the nineteenth century—can help to illustrate the original meaning of the Second Amendment.

Perhaps Scalia believed that readers would take him at his word. He should have known better. In the years since *Heller*, courts have discovered that all sorts of antigun laws are actually "longstanding," no matter how recently enacted. It's been estimated that in 80 percent of the Second Amendment cases since *Heller*, courts have upheld the challenged regulations as examples of Justice Scalia's "presumptively lawful" restrictions.

Take the ban on felons having guns. The longstanding

prohibitions that Justice Scalia was referring to had to do with keeping guns out of the hands of individuals *convicted* of *violent* felonies. But the lower courts have used this example to justify disarming people guilty of nothing worse than nonviolent misdemeanors. In a Wisconsin case, for example, a plumber named Floyd Hopkins was forbidden to carry a gun for three years upon his conviction for misdemeanor theft—the scoundrel had failed to return his rental car at the appointed time. Hopkins was not a career criminal, and he had no violent crimes in his record. But the trial judge decided that Hopkins had an antisocial streak "that, you know, while it is not, you know, who you truly are, it's becoming who you are." Even the Milwaukee DA's office—the prosecution—was embarrassed by the judge's decision: on appeal, the DA recommended that the appellate court reverse the trial judge and lift Hopkins's gun ban. But instead, the Wisconsin Court of Appeals affirmed the trial court's order that Hopkins must be disarmed because he might, someday, "graduate" to violent crimes.

In some places, like New York City, citizens lose the right to bear arms the moment they are indicted, or even arrested. Oddly enough, getting arrested guarantees you all sorts of "rights" that are not mentioned in the Constitution at all—like "Miranda rights"—and yet the black-and-white Second Amendment can't survive, even with the presumption of innocence.

What about "conditions and qualifications on the commercial sale of arms"? That sounds reasonable. Based on that loophole, the District of Columbia persuaded the federal Court of Appeals to bless its draconian post-*Heller* law, under which those who survive the twelve-step registration process are required to keep their guns unloaded and either disassembled or locked up, except when there is a threat of "immediate harm" to the homeowner (because that's just when you want to start assembling your gun).

The district also banned an entire category of weapons—semi-automatic rifles, which it refers to as "assault weapons." The "assault weapon" label is a nifty rhetorical device, meant to conjure up images of Rambo-like goons rappeling off the side of your house to get to your daughter's bedroom. But in reality, most guns sold now are "semi-automatic," which merely means that they reload automatically. They are not machine guns; they fire only one shot with each pull of the trigger. But a majority of the D.C. Circuit Court of Appeals blessed the assault weapons hysteria, conveniently ignoring the fact that in *Heller* the Supreme Court had struck down a ban on semi-automatic handguns—a type of gun much more likely to be used in an assault than the difficult-to-conceal rifles labeled as "assault weapons."

Well, okay, but who can argue with laws banning guns from "sensitive places" like schools? Or, to be more precise, any place within a thousand feet of a school, which is the federally mandated "Gun-Free School Zone." As you may recall from chapter 3, that law was struck down by the Supreme Court in *Lopez* because it exceeded Congress's enumerated powers. In response, Congress promptly reenacted the law, this time specifying that the ban applies only to "firearms in . . . interstate commerce," and with that cosmetic change, the law has been upheld. So if you can find a gun that was manufactured entirely within your state (including all component parts and ammunition), you might be able to evade the federal Gun-Free School Zone law. But then again, maybe not. In 2006 the Ninth Circuit Court of Appeals upheld the federal firearms conviction of a man who had "machined and assembled" a machine gun in his own home and never carried it across state lines. Although the Court initially held that federal law could not reach that far under the commerce clause, it reversed itself after the Supreme Court's decision in *Raich*, the medical marijuana case (see chapter 3). Citing *Raich*, the Ninth Circuit held that Congress could ban the possession of *home-made* machine guns because if everybody started making their own machine guns, it would "substantially affect interstate commerce in machineguns." In any event, even if you're not covered by federal law, you're probably subject to a similar state or local law. Wisconsin and California, for example, have thousand-foot laws. So do many cities, such as Aurora, Illinois, which forbids any weapon—even pepper spray—within a thousand feet of any school or university. Good news for criminals looking to prey on young coeds.

According to the Brady Center to Prevent Handgun Violence, the entire District of Columbia is a sensitive place "in light of the . . . assassination attempt of Rep. Gabrielle Giffords" in 2010. But the attempted assassination didn't take place in D.C., it happened in Giffords's district—at a supermarket near Tucson, Arizona. Presumably the Brady Center considers any place where a congressman might visit—i.e., any populated area—to be sensitive.

The "sensitive places" rationale has been applied to airports, national parks, and any place "where large numbers of people, often strangers (and including children), congregate for recreational, educational, and expressive activities." As one scholar put it, under such reasoning, "sensitive places" could include "restaurants, movie theaters, university campuses, public transportation, stadiums, playgrounds, shopping or commercial districts, parking lots, and potentially even sidewalks in densely populated areas."

Or your driveway. In 2008 a California appellate court

upheld a conviction for possessing a gun on a private driveway (*People v. Yarbrough*). In its sweeping decision, the court held that the entire "area in front of a home"—your front yard as well as your driveway—falls within the "historical tradition" of banning guns from "sensitive places."

THE HOUSE-TRAINED SECOND AMENDMENT

As court after court chips away at the Second Amendment, the right to bear arms has proven to be little more than a right to keep a disassembled, unloaded gun in a locked box in the attic, and pray that your next intruder is unusually patient. No fewer than ten state and federal courts have refused to recognize a right to possess a gun *anywhere* outside the four corners of one's own home.

Only one appellate court, in Puerto Rico, has held that the Second Amendment protects the right to bear arms outside the home. Meanwhile, judges on the mainland refuse to do so. The ostensible reason for this is that both *Heller* and *McDonald* involved plaintiffs who sought the right to keep a gun at home for self-defense; thus, it would be presumptuous for lower courts to recognize any right beyond that. The Maryland Supreme Court, for example, declared that if the U.S. Supreme Court meant to uphold a right to carry guns outside the house, "it will need to say so more plainly."

Hard to see, actually, how the Supreme Court could have been any plainer. In *Heller*, the Court declared that the phrase "bear arms" was originally understood to mean the "carrying [of weapons] for a particular purpose—confrontation," and that the term includes to "wear, bear, or carry . . . upon the person or in the clothing, or in a pocket." Now, let's see: Where would one "carry" a gun? According to the lower courts, the Supreme Court was referring only to the right to carry a gun from the kitchen to the living room.

It's a preposterous idea. A citizen reading the Bill of Rights in 1791 would have had no reason to insert an implicit at-home limitation in the right to bear arms, particularly since the next two amendments contain explicit at-home limitations: the Third Amendment (soldiers may not "be quartered in any house" in time of peace), and the Fourth Amendment (protecting the "right of the people to be secure in their . . . houses"). When the framers wanted to limit a right to the home, they knew how to do so—and every sensible person reading the Second Amendment knew it.

Even Justice Scalia's throwaway line in *Heller* that the Second Amendment permits "laws forbidding the carrying of firearms in sensitive places" necessarily implies that the Second Amendment protects the right to carry in *non*sensitive places. In *McDonald*, the Court described the Second Amendment as protecting "a personal right to keep and bear arms for lawful purposes, most notably for self defense within the home." There again, if at-home gun possession is the "most notable" example of the Second Amendment right, then one assumes that there are other, slightly *less* notable ways to exercise that right.

But why spoil the party for antigun zealots? They are delighted with the concept that the Second Amendment "protects a limited right to possess handguns in the home for self-defense," as the Brady Center described it. Granted, it's a little odd: having spent four decades lecturing us that the Second Amendment applies only to soldiers on the field of battle, the gun control lobby is now busy proclaiming that it applies only to citizens inside their homes. But then, logic never was their strong suit.

If the central component of the Second Amendment is self-defense, as the Supreme Court said in both *Heller* and *McDonald*, then it obviously applies outside the home. There are places in this world—dark alleys, parking garages, deserted parks—where the people have every right to desire extra protection. And with good reason: approximately two-thirds of all rapes and sexual assaults occur outside the victim's home. But in states like Maryland, you have no right to carry a gun until it's too late—literally. Under Maryland law, ordinary citizens can have a permit to carry a gun only if they can provide evidence of "recent threats, robberies, and/or assaults," complete with "notarized statements from witnesses." In other words, you can't have a gun until after you're attacked (assuming you survive the attack), and even then, only if your assailant has the decency to strike in front of witnesses willing to sign an affidavit. In one case, a Maryland appellate court held that a community activist who had received various threats was not eligible for a carry permit because he had not been physically assaulted—yet. The court pointed out that if mere threats could justify the right to bear arms, then "each person could decide for himself or herself that he or she was in danger." Imagine that.

BEWARE THE BALANCING TEST

The ultimate fate of the right to bear arms may depend on the answer to a question that the Supreme Court never asked, namely: What standard should lower courts use to evaluate gun regulations?

Most lower courts have used the tools of strict scrutiny and intermediate scrutiny to restrict the right upheld in *Heller* and

McDonald. As we've already seen in the context of free speech and free exercise of religion, those concepts allow judges to balance away any individual right, provided the government can come up with a good reason to infringe the right. How good is really good? Under strict scrutiny, the reason must be "compelling," whereas intermediate scrutiny demands only an "important" reason. In practice, individual judges can use those vacuous words to impose their own ideas about gun regulation.

The Supreme Court, wisely, did not ask lower courts to use a balancing test to decide whether government can infringe the right to keep and bear arms. Not once in *Heller* or *McDonald* did the Supreme Court say that gun restrictions should be subject to strict, intermediate, or any other sort of scrutiny. In fact, the Court was clear in both cases that lower courts should apply the Second Amendment according to "text, history, and tradition." Constitutional rights, said Justice Scalia, "are enshrined with the scope they were understood to have when the people adopted them." Restrictions on gun ownership, therefore, are not judged by "balancing," but rather by asking whether the restriction is an example of a "longstanding" regulation that might have existed in 1791 or 1868 (when the Fourteenth Amendment was ratified). Indeed, Scalia went so far as to point out that the Second Amendment "is the very product of an interest balancing by the people," and that judges don't get to come up with a new balance.

Defying logic, lower courts appear to assume that the Supreme Court was silently inviting them to balance Second Amendment rights. Even in *Ezell*, although the Seventh Circuit Court of Appeals reached the right result, it did so by articulating a complicated balancing test, roughly equivalent to the intermediate scrutiny test that has done so much to erode freedom of speech (see chapter 6). For most courts, the use of any balancing test is fatal to gun rights. Because the ostensible goal of gun restrictions is to save lives, it is easy for courts to declare that the government has a "compelling" or "important" reason to trample on individual rights.

It was not until 2011, when DC's post-*Heller* gun law made it to the Court of Appeals, that a lone dissenting judge, Brett Kavanaugh, made what should have been the obvious point: the Supreme Court's failure to set forth a balancing test in *Heller* and *McDonald* was intentional. The Supreme Court's invocation of "text, history, and tradition" was not a bit of color commentary—it is the method of interpretation mandated by the Court. But lower courts resist "text, history, and tradition" as an interpretive method—and openly defy the Supreme Court— because "text, history, and tradition" is less empowering for judges, and it tends toward conservative conclusions. Moreover, Living Constitution judges and scholars object to the hard work of originalism—remember Professor David Strauss's lament in chapter 1 that deciphering original meaning is a "brutally hard" task? In *McDonald*, Justice Scalia conceded that "historical analysis can be difficult; it sometimes requires resolving threshold questions and making nuanced judgments about which evidence to consult and how to interpret it. I will stipulate to that."

But just because something is hard doesn't mean it's not worth the extra effort. Sometimes originalism is tough, but we're dealing with the supreme law of the land. Get over it.

CHAPTER NINE

LIFE, LIBERTY, AND THAT OTHER THING

Property Rights Declare Bankruptcy

No State shall . . . pass any . . . Law Impairing the Obligation of Contract.

—ARTICLE I, SECTION 10

No person shall . . . be deprived of life, liberty, or property, without due process of law; nor shall private property be taken for public use, without just compensation.

—FIFTH AMENDMENT

No State shall make or enforce any law which shall abridge the privileges or immunities of citizens of the United States.

—FOURTEENTH AMENDMENT

AT 4:30 A.M. ON APRIL 20, 2011, Amish farmer Daniel Allgyer went outside to milk his cows. A few minutes later, three cars pulled up to his property, breaking the predawn peace of rural Pennsylvania. Five armed men emerged from the cars and began walking toward the house where Allgyer's wife and children were sleeping.

Allgyer rushed out of the barn and exclaimed, "What art thou doing?"—or words to that effect—to which the men deadpanned, "A routine inspection." The men then proceeded to rummage around Allgyer's barn, as well as the coolers and freezers used to store dairy products. As it turns out, four of the men were federal agents (two gun-toting U.S. marshals and two Food and Drug Administration agents); the fifth was a Pennsylvania state trooper. By the time the posse drove away from the farm, Allgyer's children were asking their mother, "Is Daddy going to jail?" Not yet—but he might, as a result of the shocking discovery the agents made that morning.

They found *milk*—never underestimate the investigative powers of the federal government. To be precise, they found unpasteurized milk. For that is what Allgyer produced at his Rainbow Acres Farm, and sold to enthusiastic consumers. There was no fraud or deception about the milk; to the contrary, devotees of unpasteurized, or "raw," milk sought out Rainbow Acres from as far afield as Maryland and the District of Columbia. The problem was that federal law prohibits selling, or even transporting, raw milk across state lines.

The raid on Rainbow Acres was actually the culmination of a yearlong sting operation in which undercover FDA agents posed as out-of-state consumers looking to score raw milk. When Allgyer agreed to sell them the illicit substance—and in jugs that lacked government-approved labeling, no less—the feds knew they had their man. It was only a matter of time before they would get the proper warrants to search the farm. Immediately after the search, the FDA filed a ten-page complaint against Allgyer in federal court. In February 2012, Allgyer and his wife finally threw in the towel, deciding to shut down Rainbow Acres rather than try to battle the federal government.

A country in which government harassment of a peaceful dairy farmer is passed off as "routine" is not one that respects "life, liberty, and property." If those words mean anything, they should, at a minimum, encompass the right of a citizen to feed his family by selling to willing adults a product that is so safe for human consumption that it is dispensed in vending machines in the nanny states of Europe. In the United States, however, Congress protects large dairy producers by regulating niche competitors out of the market.

In February 2010 a farmers' advocacy group sued the FDA, challenging the federal raw milk regulations as a violation of the due process rights of farmers and their customers. The FDA, of course, considers the suit to be frivolous, and it may well be that the courts will agree. Heaven knows why—it's not as though the courts have been shy about interpreting the due process clauses in other contexts. As we saw in chapter 5, the Supreme Court long ago developed the doctrine of "substantive due process," under which it has concocted innumerable "liberty interests" deemed worthy of constitutional protection: the right to contraception, abortion, sodomy, and even the right to grow one's hair as long as one desires, without the fear of government condemnation. In 1999, for example, the Supreme Court described the "freedom to loiter" as a fundamental right to be protected against encroachment by dastardly antivagrancy laws (*Chicago v. Morales*).

Under the Living Constitution, idleness is a fundamental right; but good hard work? That's optional. In fact, the deck is stacked against property and rights relating to property. Normally, when a law infringes individual rights—even bogus liberty interests like the freedom to loiter—courts presume that the law is invalid unless the government can come up with a "compelling" justification. But when it comes to property rights, the presumption is reversed. Courts will uphold any government interference with private property as long as they can find some "rational basis" to support the law. Today, Americans still engage in productive economic activity, of course, but only at the sufferance of big government.

THE ORIGINAL TEA PARTY

The Founders had a very different view of property rights. The Boston Tea Party of 1773 was in fact a protest against the same type of special interest legislation represented by today's federal milk regulations. The Tea Act of 1773 gave the East India Company the exclusive right to ship tea to the colonies and to sell tea in America through its agents. The effect of this law was to put American shippers and tea sellers out of business.

Had the colonists reacted like Supreme Court justices—assuming that Parliament must have had a "rational basis" for the Tea Act—we might still be British subjects. Instead, they had the decency and good sense to dress up like Mohawk warriors and dump 342 chests of tea into the harbor. This splendid act of defiance galvanized the colonial resistance and accelerated the inevitable clash with the mother country.

The fact that the colonists thought they had a legitimate gripe against Parliament is itself noteworthy. What rights had Parliament violated? There was no U.S. Constitution; no Bill of Rights; not even a Declaration of Independence as of 1773. But the American colonists believed that they already possessed inalienable property rights. The eighteenth-century view was that property rights existed independent of any particular government. They were embedded in both natural rights and the English common law.

When the framers wrote the Constitution, they did not consider it necessary to sprinkle the word *property* throughout the document because, as the Cato Institute's Roger Pilon explains, they "simply assumed the existence of such rights—because the common law, grounded in property, was the background for all they did." In fact, for the Founders, all rights were considered a type of property. That is the origin of the term *entitlements*—the very word reflects the old idea that one has title to rights in the same way one has title to a house.

The framers protected property rights primarily by creating a central government with little power to interfere with private property. Article I of the Constitution sets forth the powers of the federal government, which are "few and defined" and mainly focused on "war, peace, negotiation, and foreign commerce," as Madison observed in Federalist No. 45. The power of the states, by contrast, would extend to "*all* the objects which, in the ordinary course of affairs, concern the lives, liberties, and *properties* of the people" (emphasis added). The federal government would scarcely have any jurisdiction over private transactions, except for a power to regulate interstate commerce—a power that the Founders viewed as a fairly narrow one (see chapter 3).

The framers did provide some protection of property rights against the states. Most notably, Article I, Section 10 of the Constitution prohibits the states from making laws "impairing the Obligation of Contracts." (There is no equivalent prohibition against federal laws impairing contracts. At the time it was thought that the federal government lacked power to invade private contract rights.) Less obvious to modern eyes, but more significant at the founding, is the following sweeping guarantee: "The Citizens of each State shall be entitled to all Privileges and Immunities of Citizens in the several States" (Article IV, Section 2). The language of "privileges and immunities" was nothing new—it was drawn from earlier governing documents going back to the Charter of Virginia of 1606. The phrase was understood to encompass the inalienable "natural" rights of man as well as "positive" rights; that is, the legal privileges traditionally granted by statute. The privileges and immunities clause, therefore, guaranteed a basic level of individual rights throughout the Union. In Federalist No. 80, Alexander Hamilton described the clause as "fundamental" and even as the "basis of the Union."

The Bill of Rights, ratified two years after the Constitution, articulated some of the rights that were understood to be reflected in the privileges and immunities clause. Nobody imagined that those amendments created any new rights; rather, they simply acknowledged certain preexisting rights. Indeed, the challenge confronting Madison and other framers of the Bill of Rights was capturing the whole bundle of common-law rights in a finite set of amendments. The solution was the Ninth Amendment, which states that "the enumeration in the Constitution, of certain rights, shall not be construed to deny or disparage others retained by the people." In other words, the Bill of Rights is great, but it doesn't repeal the privileges and immunities clause, or the broader common-law rights of Americans.

THE RIGHT TO EARN AN HONEST LIVING

At the heart of a citizen's "privileges and immunities" is the right to earn an honest living. Without it, other rights tend to lose their meaning, which is why English common law has protected the right to earn a living since the Magna Carta. The immediate predecessor of the privileges and immunities clause was a similar provision in the Articles of Confederation, which explicitly included "all the privileges of trade and commerce."

Sir Edward Coke, the English jurist considered a great authority by founding-era lawyers, observed that "at common law, no man could be prohibited from working at any lawful trade, for the law abhors idleness." Of course, when the government declares an entire profession, say, prostitution, to be illegal, then the right to practice a "lawful trade" won't do you any good. But democratically elected governments rarely prohibit a profession outright. Instead, they use licensing schemes, regulations, and monopoly privileges to cut off the trade from all but a favored few. But all such stratagems were anathema to the traditional right to earn a living. Madison himself would argue, not long after the Bill of Rights was ratified, that "no just government will . . . deny to part of its citizens that free use of their faculties, and free choice of their occupations, which . . . constitute their property in the general sense." If those are things that every "just government" must respect, are they not "Privileges and Immunities of the Citizens in the several States?"

The original answer was "Yes." In 1823, Justice Bushrod Washington (nephew of George), held that the privileges and immunities clause protected such "fundamental" rights as "the right to acquire and possess property of every kind"—and Washington wasn't talking about the right to apply for an NEA grant. In those days, the way one acquired property was through working. Lest there be any doubt, Washington went on to explain that the clause guarantees the right of a citizen of one state to reside in any other state for such purposes as "trade, agriculture, [and] professional pursuits." That decision—in the case of *Corfield v. Coryell*—remained the leading interpretation of the term *privileges and immunities* up to the Civil War.

Unfortunately, the Article IV clause was interpreted as merely an antidiscrimination provision; meaning only that if a state provides this or that right to its own citizens, then it must extend the same right to visitors. For example, if South Carolina required in-state residents to obtain a $25 license before engaging in offshore commercial fishing, it could not discriminate against nonresidents by charging them an unreasonably higher licensing fee of $2,500 to engage in the same activity (*Toomer v. Witsell*). But cases subsequent to *Corfield* suggested that the clause did not require states to recognize any particular privilege or immunity. Thus, if South Carolina decided to charge *every* commercial fisherman $2,500 to pursue a livelihood—or if it simply chose to outlaw commercial fishing altogether—courts would be hard pressed to find that the Article IV provision was violated.

After the Civil War, when Congress wanted to guarantee the rights of the former slaves, it used the language of privileges and immunities. The first section of the Fourteenth Amendment provides that "no state shall . . . abridge the privileges or immunities of citizens of the United States."* The new clause was meant to fix the overly narrow interpretation of the original privileges and immunities clause as a mere antidiscrimination rule. The new provision would make it clear that the Constitution requires states to respect *all* privileges and immunities uniformly for all "citizens of the United States." Admittedly, this is one of those phrases that requires originalists to do some hard work. There

---

* The clause in the Fourteenth Amendment is known as the privileges *or* immunities clause, as distinct from the original Constitution's privileges *and* immunities clause.

is no infallible way to identify every right subsumed within the phrase "privileges or immunities," but there is a reliable guide: common-law rights, as embodied in case law and as (partly) codified in the Bill of Rights. Whatever ambiguities might exist around the edges, there can be little doubt that the Fourteenth Amendment prohibits states from depriving the people of such basic liberties as the right to vote, to own property, to bear arms, to engage in freedom of speech and assembly, and, notably, to earn an honest living.

The principal author of the Fourteenth Amendment, Ohio congressman John Bingham, recognized that privileges and immunities included "the liberty . . . to work in an honest calling . . . and to be secure in the fruits of your labor." That is what emancipation was all about: no man is a slave if he owns his own labor. Moreover, although the Fourteenth Amendment was motivated by the need to protect ex-slaves, its language is not limited to them. By its terms, the Fourteenth Amendment protects *all* Americans against state laws that infringe on fundamental rights.

BUTCHERING THE CONSTITUTION

It was a great idea—while it lasted. In 1873, just five years after the Fourteenth Amendment was ratified, the Supreme Court rendered the privileges or immunities clause virtually meaningless. In a decision known as the *Slaughterhouse Cases* (plural because there were originally six related lawsuits), the Court was asked to consider an 1869 Louisiana law that gave a single company the exclusive right to slaughter cattle in the New Orleans area. The independent butchers who had been put out of business sued, arguing that the state had violated the Fourteenth Amendment by abridging their privileges and immunities; specifically, the right "to labor freely in an honest avocation," as their lawyer put it.

From an originalist point of view, the butchers' argument was irrefutable. One of the surest ways for government to violate the right to earn an honest living is to create a monopoly. That was what the British Parliament had done by granting the East India Company exclusive rights to import and market tea. Monopolies were contrary to common law, but unfortunately, Parliament had the power to override the common law. The privileges and immunities clauses were understood to constitutionalize common-law property rights, thus putting them beyond the reach of politicians.

But the Supreme Court upheld the Louisiana monopoly law. A majority of the justices, it seems, just did not like the Fourteenth Amendment: they thought it went too far in interfering with states' rights. And so, in the tradition of judicial activism, they decided to rewrite it. In a clumsy attempt to rationalize the decision, Justice Samuel F. Miller declared that the privileges or immunities clause protects only an esoteric set of rights of "national citizenship" like "protection . . . on the high seas," while leaving "nearly every civil right" at the mercy of state governments. Rarely has a Supreme Court decision been so completely and obviously wrong. The *whole point* of the Fourteenth Amendment was to put "nearly every civil right" under a federal guarantee. In any event, the Louisiana butchers had no desire to slaughter cattle on the high seas, so they were out of luck. And so were future generations of working men and women, because the Court has never overturned the *Slaughterhouse Cases*. Chalk up another victory for *stare decisis* (see chapter 5).

Slaughterhouse does not stir up a lot of outrage on the Left, perhaps because butchers, as a class, are of little concern to your average socially responsible, vegan community organizer. Little do they know—apparently—that the rationale in *Slaughterhouse* was immediately put to use by the Court to uphold sexist laws. The very next decision announced by the Supreme Court held that Illinois had the right to exclude females from the legal profession. A woman named Myra Bradwell had apprenticed in her husband's law office and passed the bar examination, but was denied a law license solely on account of her sex. When her case reached the Supreme Court, she argued that the state had abridged her privileges and immunities. The Court rejected her case in a few paragraphs. "The opinion just delivered in *The Slaughterhouse Cases*," said the Court, "renders elaborate argument . . . unnecessary." Bradwell would not receive her law license until 1892, nineteen years later.

Slaughterhouse also made the world safe for anticompetitive laws. With no need to worry about pesky privileges or immunities, state legislators wasted no time creating monopolies and oligopolies for their political allies. The late nineteenth century saw a dramatic increase in occupational licensing schemes—not just lawyers and doctors (for whom there is a public safety argument for licensing) but now everyone from barbers to horseshoers would be required to obtain a license from the state. The legacy of that era persists to this day, in the form of an economy riddled with barriers to entrepreneurs. By 2005, an estimated 20 percent of the U.S. workforce was covered by state licensing laws, in addition to federal and local regulations.

In Mississippi, for example, a woman who wanted to start a business teaching others how to do African-style hair braiding was told that the requisite license required 3,200 hours of classes; not one of which, incidentally, had anything to do with hair braiding. In Colorado, the Public Utilities Commission allowed only three taxi companies to operate in the state over a period of fifty years. When a group of minority businessmen tried to break the stranglehold, they were shut down by a federal court that held that the Constitution does not create "a substantive right to pursue one's lawful occupation or profession."

THE LOCH NER MONSTER

With the death of privileges and immunities, judges with a free-market bent transferred economic liberties to the due process clauses of the Fifth and Fourteenth Amendments. Those clauses do mention liberty and property, and in those days before the invention of penumbral emanations judges felt the need to anchor their arguments in some piece of text. As we saw in chapter 5, Chief Justice Roger Taney pioneered the argument in his *Dred Scott* decision, asserting that a federal law that purported to deprive a man of his slave "could hardly be dignified with the name due process of law." Two of the dissenting justices in *Slaughter-house* picked up on that theme, arguing that if the pursuit of lawful employment is not a privilege or immunity, then it is part of the "liberty" protected by the due process clause.

By 1897 a unanimous Supreme Court announced that the due process clause protects "liberty of contract," and specifically the right "to pursue any livelihood or avocation, and for that purpose to enter into all contracts." In that case (*Allgeyer v. Louisiana*—no relation to the Amish farmer Allgyer), the Court struck down a state law that imposed fines on people who entered into insurance contracts with companies that hadn't complied with the onerous requirements of Louisiana law. In other words, the legislature was trying to shield its local insurance market, much as it had protected its favorite abattoir some years earlier.

The Supreme Court reached the right result (striking down the law), but for the wrong reason. By using the due process clause to enforce the right to earn a living, the Court ignored the original meaning of the text, which was understood to protect the common-law *procedural* rights of defendants (see chapter 5). The word *liberty* in that clause conveyed nothing more than freedom of movement—the sense of being "at liberty"—which is the very basic liberty that you lose when the state locks you in the slammer without a fair trial. The term "due process of law" has nothing to do with the substance of legislation; it reaches only procedure and processes.

Nonetheless, *Allgeyer* launched the doctrine of economic due process, a theory most famously identified with the Supreme Court's 1905 decision in *Lochner v. New York*. In that case, the Court overturned a New York law setting maximum working hours for all bakery employees. Once again, the Court construed the Fourteenth Amendment as protecting the individual's "power to contract in relation to his own labor." For the next three decades, federal and state courts struck down scores of laws that they thought went too far in restricting economic liberty.

But why stop there? Once the due process clause became a source of "substantive"—as distinct from "procedural"—rights, judges could use it to enforce any rights that struck their fancy. By 1923 the Supreme Court was inserting noneconomic liberties into the Fourteenth Amendment, such as a parent's right to direct his child's education (*Meyer v. Nebraska*). And that, in a nutshell, is the problem with judicial activism, even in a good cause. By ignoring the original meaning of the due process clause, the Supreme Court opened the door for the full-blown doctrine of substantive due process, the prime vehicle for liberal judicial activism (see chapter 5). In 1905, substantive due process was all about contract rights. By 1973, it was all about abortion on demand.

The economic part of substantive due process ended abruptly in 1937, when the Supreme Court—now packed with FDR appointees—overturned *Lochner* in a case called *West Coast Hotel v. Parrish*. Actually, *Lochner* was not merely overturned; it was consigned to the innermost circle of hell. The political and academic boosters of the New Deal needed a scapegoat, and *Lochner* was a convenient target. Until 1980, praise for *Lochner* was unheard of; even today, it is an extreme minority viewpoint. Rather, the conventional wisdom holds that the "*Lochner* era" of laissez-faire judicial decisions somehow—the details aren't important—precipitated the Great Depression. In 1992, Republican-appointed justices O'Connor, Souter, and Kennedy praised the *West Coast* decision for putting an end to the "Lochner era cases" that "rested on fundamentally false assumptions about the capacity of a relatively unregulated market to satisfy minimal levels of human welfare."

Of course. If only New York bakers had shorter hours, the Depression could have been avoided. The reality is that *Lochner*, like *Allgeyer*, reached the right result, but on the wrong basis: the Court should have relied on the privileges or immunities clause rather than the due process clause. The New York law—ostensibly passed as a health measure—was a pretext to protect established bakers from their we-try-harder competition. It also had the effect of depriving workers the opportunity to seek upward mobility by working longer hours.

GOT RIGHTS?

The year after *West Coast* killed economic due process, the Supreme Court drove the nail into the coffin with its decision in

United States v. Carolene Products. In that case, Carolene Products had been criminally indicted for selling Milnut, a combination of skimmed milk and coconut oil. That may not sound appealing, but it hardly sounds criminal. In fact, Milnut was perfectly safe to drink and had the virtue of being cheaper than ordinary milk—not a trivial consideration during the Depression. But Congress had made it a crime to sell "filled milk," that is, skim milk combined with any nondairy fat or oil. Like the anti–raw milk regulations at issue in Dan Allgyer's case, the Filled Milk Act was a blatant attempt to protect established dairies from competition. Carolene challenged the Filled Milk Act on due process grounds, but the Supreme Court upheld the law.

It's no use crying over filled milk, I know, but *Carolene* did more than simply deprive consumers of choice. The Supreme Court set up a basic dichotomy that survives to this day. On the one hand, the Court signaled that it would closely scrutinize laws that appear to infringe on the guarantees of the Bill of Rights (or other, unspecified rights of "discrete and insular minorities")—this is the "strict scrutiny" we've already seen in the context of the First Amendment. On the other hand, the *Carolene* Court stated that laws involving economic rights would not merit strict scrutiny. Rather, legislation affecting ordinary commercial transactions would never be struck down so long as the court could find some rational basis for upholding the law—in *Carolene Products*, the laughably false contention that Milnut was dangerous for human consumption because it had allegedly been "stripped of elements essential to the maintenance of health." Mind you, skimmed milk itself wasn't outlawed — just the competitive product, skimmed milk filled with additional fats and oils.

The federal prohibition against filled milk, as well as a law against "filled cheese" (cheese laced with vegetable oil), lasted until the mid-1970s. Similarly, long-standing state laws against margarine survived into the 1960s. Even today, *Carolene Products* remains a useful weapon for traditional agribusiness looking to justify new varieties of protectionist legislation. So long as there is a rational basis, legislators will have a free hand to outlaw products that threaten entrenched interests. And it needn't be a rational basis actually articulated by the legislators; courts have, on countless occasions, conjured up their own rational basis on the legislature's behalf. Who knows how many choices are being withheld from consumers? Or how many small farmers and niche businesses are being denied the right to sell nontoxic products in the marketplace?

THE GOVERNMENT GIVETH, AND GIVETH SOME MORE

Once the right to earn an honest living had been effectively destroyed, the next logical step in the decline of civilization was to create a constitutional right *not* to work; that is, a constitutional right to receive a welfare check. Franklin Roosevelt proved himself up to the challenge. In his 1944 State of the Union address, FDR proposed what he modestly referred to as the "Second Bill of Rights"—including such goodies as the right to a "useful and remunerative job," if you want one. And if you don't, you still get "a decent home," "adequate medical care," "the opportunity to . . . enjoy good health," and freedom from all "economic fears." Such rights would apply to every American. Well, perhaps not the thousands of Japanese Americans whom FDR had recently sent off to concentration camps (a move upheld by the Supreme Court in 1944's *Korematsu v. United States*).

The arrogance of FDR's proposal really was astonishing. Now that his own Court appointees had eviscerated the ancient inalienable rights of working, contracting, and accumulating property, FDR had repackaged these concepts as gifts from a benevolent government. The formula proved irresistible to the United Nations, where it was essentially adopted as Article 25 of the Universal Declaration of Human Rights.

In America, however, the Second Bill of Rights never made it into the Constitution, although it came close. In the 1960s, the Supreme Court rendered a series of decisions culminating in *Goldberg v. Kelly* (1970), which held that welfare checks constituted property under the Fourteenth Amendment. Thus, a state could not reduce existing welfare benefits without affording affected recipients "due process of law."

TWO CHEERS FOR RICHARD NIXON

Not long after *Goldberg*, the Court began to backtrack, thanks to some (relatively) conservative justices appointed by Richard Nixon. In *Dandridge v. Williams*, the Court upheld a Maryland law capping welfare benefits at $250 a month, regardless of family size. Chief Justice Warren Burger cleverly pointed out that the welfare limits were "economic legislation" and thus could be upheld under the lax rational basis test of *Carolene Products*.

By 1975, "the whole idea of minimum welfare guarantees had become implausible," laments liberal professor (and Obama regulatory czar) Cass Sunstein in his book *The Second Bill of Rights*. Sunstein, whom we last saw defending the administrative state in chapter 4, has outlined a plan to get welfare rights into the Constitution. Not by amendment, mind you—those are *so*

Article V—but simply by a little creative "interpretation" of the Fourteenth Amendment. After all, constitutional rights are not "rigid rules," but rather "general principles capable of growth and change." Sunstein argues that it would be perfectly legitimate for the Supreme Court to insert FDR's welfare rights into the Constitution, because such a decision would not "stretch the document" any further than a slew of other activist decisions. There's a novel defense of judicial activism: everybody's doing it.

Sunstein is hardly alone in the world of legal academia. Berkeley professor Goodwin Liu sounded the same themes in his 2008 article "Rethinking Constitutional Welfare Rights." Like Sunstein, Liu believes that constitutional welfare rights should be enacted by an enlightened judiciary. According to Liu, who would go on to be nominated (unsuccessfully) for a federal judgeship by President Obama, judges have a duty to decide precisely when Americans' "collective values" have converged around the idea of such rights. Funny, I thought that's what elections were for.

GANGSTER GOVERNMENT

The Constitution no longer protects the right to enter into contracts. But what about the sanctity of existing contracts? In Federalist No. 44, Madison wrote that "laws impairing the obligation of contract are contrary to the first principles of the social compact, and to every principle of sound legislation." As we've already seen, the framers expressly prohibited the states from enacting laws "impairing the Obligation of Contracts" (Article I, Section 10).

The prohibition against impairing contracts is so clear that for many years courts actually enforced it. In 1810, for example, the Supreme Court invoked that section to prevent Georgia from rescinding land grants. Nine years later the Court cited the same section to block New Hampshire from retroactively changing the charter of Dartmouth College. The framers seem to have assumed, however, that the federal government would never interfere with private contracts, since it lacked the power to do so. Big mistake. Consider the Chrysler bankruptcy.

In the spring of 2009, as Chrysler teetered on the brink of insolvency, President Obama's auto czar, Steven Rattner, orchestrated a bankruptcy reorganization of the carmaker. At the time, a number of hedge funds held secured debt in Chrysler, making them "senior creditors." But under Rattner's plan, the hedge funds would get 29 cents on the dollar for their debt, while the United Auto Workers union (UAW)—an unsecured creditor—would get 50 cents on the dollar, giving it control over the company.

The Rattner plan was theft. Under bankruptcy law, senior creditors like the hedge funds are entitled to be paid in full before any money flows to junior creditors like the UAW. Those are the terms of the deal when you buy senior debt—hence, the "senior" denomination. The Supreme Court had decided in 1935 that any impairment of a secured party's interest in collateral violates Fifth Amendment property rights (*Louisville Joint Stock Bank v. Radford*). That decision, in turn, became a bedrock doctrine of bankruptcy law that had a "substantial impact" on the current Bankruptcy Code, according to a 1983 *Harvard Law Review* article by James Steven Rogers, a noted authority on commercial law. The Constitution and Bankruptcy Code, however, were brushed aside in the Obama administration's haste to reward a political ally. Over the years, the UAW had donated some $25 million to Democratic candidates, and it was only fitting to reward that sort of loyalty with a majority equity interest in Chrysler.

One of Chrysler's senior creditors, Perella Weinberg Partners, briefly tried to rally opposition to the administration's kleptocratic plan. The president immediately took to the airwaves to denounce the hedge funds as "speculators" who wanted to destroy Chrysler—through the clever ruse of lending it millions of dollars. Privately, the White House had an even blunter message for Perella Weinberg: *Nice hedge fund you got there. Shame if anything happened to it.* Perella Weinberg's lawyer later revealed that Rattner himself had directly threatened the fund, vowing to use the White House's influence with the media to destroy the fund's reputation. Not surprisingly, Perella Weinberg caved in.

In a May 5, 2009, column in the *Washington Examiner*, Michael Barone aptly called the Obama administration's tactics in the Chrysler bankruptcy "Gangster Government," a theme explored in greater depth by David Freddoso in his book *Gangster Government*. For our purposes, the episode is relevant because it was made possible by a Living Constitution philosophy. If the Obama administration had believed the Constitution to embody fixed principles, it could not have displayed the sort of contempt for property rights that it did.

In fact, the administration also revealed its dislike of constitutional checks and balances. In his cheerful memoir of expropriating the car industry, *Overhaul*, Rattner would comment that "the auto rescue succeeded in no small part because we did not have to deal with Congress." Like his intellectual forebear, Woodrow Wilson, Rattner has no patience for constitutional formalities that get in the way of efficient "administration." Indeed, if Congress fails "to get its act together," says Rattner, "we should explore alternatives." Alternatives, that is, to the hopelessly outdated idea of representative government. Who needs elections when you're the auto czar?

IT'S A WONDERFUL LIFE—FOR DEBTORS

In the wake of Hurricane Andrew, the Florida legislature passed a statute barring insurance companies from canceling, or refusing to renew, homeowner's insurance policies. The obvious purpose was to prevent insurers from pulling out of the Florida market, or parts of it. But wait, this was a state (Florida), and so it was covered by Article I's express prohibition against laws impairing the obligation of contracts, right? Apparently not: the Eleventh Circuit Court of Appeals upheld the law in 1998 because "courts properly defer to legislative judgment." In 2005 the Louisiana legislature would pass a similar law to protect victims of Hurricane Katrina—at the expense of insurers. And once again, the legislation was upheld by the courts.

Never mind what the Constitution says. Private contracts have been at the mercy of state legislatures since the 1934 Supreme Court decision in *Home Building & Loan Association v. Blaisdell*. The facts of *Blaisdell* are sort of like the old Jimmy Stewart movie *It's a Wonderful Life*. Just like in the movie, a bad guy was trying to destroy a modest building and loan association that was struggling to survive the Depression. In the movie, the bad guy is Old Man Potter, but in *Blaisdell*, it was the state of Minnesota. The state had passed a law forbidding lenders from foreclosing on defaulting borrowers, and giving the deadbeats the right to stay in their homes at a below-market "rent." Notwithstanding the text of Article I, Section 10, the Supreme Court held that Minnesota could go ahead and impair contracts all day long if they thought it was necessary to deal with an "economic emergency." And that is where the resemblance to the movie ends, for there was no guardian angel to save the building and loan.

The "emergency" rationale of *Blaisdell* was preposterous.

When the Constitution was ratified, everyone understood that "the contracts clause had the specific purpose of abolishing debtor-relief legislation," according to historian Woody Holton. That sort of legislation had proliferated before 1787, and was always justified by some economic emergency or another. The purpose of the contracts clause was to stop the states from penalizing creditors for every economic downturn. That purpose is also reflected by the context of the contracts clause: it is grouped together with other creditors' rights, such as the right to insist on payment in "gold and silver Coin"—another dead letter, incidentally.

After *Blaisdell*, legislatures got into the business of rewriting contracts to suit their policy agendas—or their reelection strategies. And even though the destruction of contract rights is theft, and even though the Constitution prohibits it, the Supreme Court has "bent over backwards" to validate statutes that impaired contracts, according to Robert Levy and William Mellor's classic study of judicial activism, *The Dirty Dozen*. In time, the "emergency" doctrine was further watered down to a multifactor balancing test—one of our red flags of judicial activism (see chapter 5). In deciding whether states can destroy vested contract rights, courts will consider:

1. Whether the impairment is "substantial"
2. Whether the state has a "significant and legitimate public purpose"
3. Whether the impairment is "reasonable"

Lord, give me strength. This is the fate of property under the Living Constitution. If you want to loiter and collect welfare, liberal courts will defend your rights to the hilt. After all, each new ward of the state serves to aggrandize government and its various rent seekers. But if you want to engage in private, productive activity, your rights are tentative, subject to any regulation—prospective or retroactive—that meets the barest test of rationality. Next thing you know, the state will simply come and confiscate your property. Oh, wait . . .

TAKE MY HOUSE, PLEASE

Actually, the government can seize your house—most often, to build a road or some other useful public article. Everyone knows that; it's the power of eminent domain. Eminent domain is a constitutionally sanctioned governmental activity that requires only that the taking be for a public use and that the property owner be justly compensated for his or her loss. What you may not know is that the state can also take your house and just give it to somebody else who might generate more tax revenue than you. For that is precisely what the Supreme Court held in *Kelo v. City of New London*.

The *Kelo* case began in 1998 when pharmaceutical giant Pfizer announced the development of a research facility near the working-class Fort Trumbull section of New London, Connecticut. Inspired by this windfall, an unelected branch of the city government, the New London Development Council, hatched a grandiose plan to create a ninety-acre business park adjacent to the Pfizer facility. There would be a hotel, conference center, offices—the works.

Everyone was delighted. Well, everyone except the existing residents of Fort Trumbull, who were unceremoniously informed that their homes would be destroyed to roll out the red carpet for

Pfizer. Seven of the homeowners, led by Susette Kelo, challenged the seizure of their houses.

New London took the position that it was merely exercising its power of eminent domain, recognized by the Fifth Amendment's takings clause: "nor shall private property be taken for public use, without just compensation." The clause must mean that government *can* take private property as long as it provides "just compensation," which New London was offering. True, but New London's argument ignored the significance of the words "for public use." Under the Fifth Amendment, property may be seized only for public use. Like other provisions of the Bill of Rights, the takings clause was "incorporated" against the states via the Fourteenth Amendment (see chapter 5).

Kelo lost in the Supreme Court. A majority of the justices upheld New London's right to destroy private houses and give the land to private developers. The majority opinion, written by the liberal justice John Paul Stevens, argued that the "more natural" interpretation of "public use" is really "public purpose," and private development such as the New London office park can serve a "public purpose."

Stevens's interpretation of the takings clause is "more natural" only if shredding the Constitution is what comes naturally to you. At the time the Bill of Rights was ratified, the term "public use" was well understood to refer to projects that would, in fact, be used by the general public: roads, canals, bridges, and the like. Such public works would either be owned directly by the government or by a private person acting as a public utility; for example, water-powered mills that, in early America, were legally required to serve the public.

Moreover, in the founding era, not every "public use" would justify a government taking, but only those uses that were deemed to be "necessary." The Bill of Rights was adopted at a time when various state constitutions, as well as the influential Northwest Ordinance, spelled out the "necessity" or "public exigency" threshold for the exercise of eminent domain. It hardly seems likely that those who ratified the Fifth Amendment would have understood it to give the federal government an easier standard for seizing property than that which applied to many states.

In 1798—just seven years after the Bill of Rights was ratified—Supreme Court justice Samuel Chase wrote that the Supreme Court would be prepared to overturn "a law that takes property from A and gives it to B," because such a law would be "a flagrant abuse of legislative power . . . against all reason and justice." Somewhere between 1798 and 2005, a "flagrant abuse" became a "public purpose." How?

The most important precursor to *Kelo* was the 1954 Supreme Court decision in *Berman v. Parker*, which involved a District of Columbia plan to seize private property and resell it to private developers in the name of combating "blight." It was all in the name of "urban renewal," which, as Justice Clarence Thomas would later point out, was a euphemism for "negro removal." Over 97 percent of the people forced out of their homes by the D.C. plan were black. But the liberal Warren Court—those heroes of *Brown v. Board of Education*—upheld the plan. Once again, the Court abdicated its duty to protect property rights on the grounds that it must "defer" to the government's rationale for seizing private land. If the D.C. government (together with Congress) says that eliminating "blight" is a "public use" of property, then their say-so is "well nigh conclusive," said the Court.

This judicial deference is curious, to say the least. The same Warren Court would go on to hold that the police deserve no deference at all when conducting a search. And in *Goldberg v.*

Kelly, the Court applied its least deferential standard—strict scrutiny—against any government attempt to reduce an existing welfare entitlement. But if the government simply decides to take your house? No problem—key's under the mat.

After *Berman*, states and cities suddenly discovered blight all over the place. In fact, any plot of land with untapped economic potential turned out to be blighted. In 1981 the Michigan Supreme Court upheld a Detroit plan to condemn an entire neighborhood and give the land to General Motors. The neighborhood was not blighted in any normal sense of the word; it just happened to stand in the way of a GM plant. That decision, *Poletown Neighborhood Council v. City of Detroit*, was finally overturned in 2004 when the Michigan Supreme Court came to its senses and admitted that *Poletown* was a "radical departure" from the Constitution. The Court decisively rejected the notion that "a private entity's pursuit of profit was a 'public use' for constitutional takings purposes."

Unfortunately, the Michigan Court's epiphany had no impact on the U.S. Supreme Court, which decided *Kelo* one year later. Instead, the Court reached back to *Berman* as proof of "our longstanding policy of deference to legislative judgments in the field." In this case, the legislature—well, an unelected board of technocrats, actually—had decided that the office park would create public benefits, which meant that it was a "public purpose," which was basically, just about, if you squint, the same as "public use." What business was it of the U.S. Supreme Court to impose its interpretation of the Fifth Amendment on the constitutional scholars of New London?

In her rousing dissent in *Kelo*, Justice Sandra Day O'Connor warned of the implications of the majority's decision: "Nothing is to prevent the state from replacing any Motel 6 with a Ritz-

Carlton, any home with a shopping center, or any farm with a factory." She was right. As Levy and Mellor report in *The Dirty Dozen*, *Kelo* "opened the floodgates of abuse." In the first year after the decision, local governments moved to forcibly transfer over 5,700 properties from one private party to another private party. The only bright spot is that *Kelo* created its own backlash: a wave of legislation in many states to provide greater protection against eminent domain abuse than currently afforded under the Living Constitution. But if you're not lucky enough to live in one of those states, keep an eye out for bulldozers.

LET THEM PITCH TENTS

Susette Kelo and her neighbors got a raw deal, but it could have been worse. At least New London conceded that it had an obligation to provide "just compensation." Millions of Americans, however, endure government "takings" without any compensation at all. The government can, by law or regulatory action, destroy the economic value of property overnight. As a matter of original meaning, such government invasions of property should also be considered "takings."

Consider the case of David Lucas. In 1986 Lucas paid $975,000 for two beachfront lots on the Isle of Palms in South Carolina with the intention of building houses on the properties. Two years after he bought the land, the South Carolina legislature passed a law banning any "permanent habitable structures" on coastal property like Lucas's. Lucas sued the state, and in 1992 the Supreme Court wisely held that Lucas had suffered a constitutional "taking." Even though the state had not literally seized the property, the result was the same, since Lucas was forced to sacrifice "all economically beneficial use of the property," as Justice Scalia wrote for the majority.

But *Lucas* was just one skirmish in the long-running war over "regulatory takings"—a war in which the Living Constitution crowd will not go down easily. After all, if government actually had to respect property rights when adopting regulations, where would we be? In a dissenting opinion, Justice Blackmun nicely summarized the liberal bloc's indifference to property when he argued that Lucas had not lost the value of his property because he was still free "to picnic, swim, camp in a tent, or live . . . in a moveable trailer." As a statement of judicial arrogance, it's hard to top that—a life-tenured justice telling the guy who lost his $1 million investment to go pitch a tent on the beach.

Blackmun rejected the whole notion of regulatory takings, arguing that the Fifth Amendment's takings clause was meant to apply only to "direct, physical takings." Over the next few years, there was an onslaught of law review articles by professors anxious to prove that Blackmun's "direct, physical takings" theory has some basis in the text. It doesn't. To the contrary, Blackmun's version of originalism wrongly assumes the Founders had a first-grader's view of "property" as consisting of nothing more than possession: if the state does not physically take away your toy, but only prevents you from playing with it, then it's still yours and you've lost nothing. But the men who drafted and ratified the Fifth Amendment were well aware that the law treated property as a bundle of rights. The leading authority of the day, Sir William Blackstone, summarized the "absolute right" of property as consisting in "free use, enjoyment, and disposal . . . without any control or diminution" (*Commentaries on the Laws of England*, book I, chapter 1).

I repeat: "without any . . . diminution." For the Founders,

any deprivation of "use" or "enjoyment" was a deprivation of property. Or to put it more bluntly, as Coke had done centuries earlier, "What is land but the profits thereof?" In 1792, just one year after ratification of the Bill of Rights, Madison published an essay arguing that it is equally wrong for government to indirectly violate property rights as it is to directly take property.

Liberal scholars have argued that the original meaning of the takings clause could not have embraced regulations because, in the late eighteenth century, Americans were already subject to various land-use regulations. Professor John Hart, for example, cites early American "fish passage" laws that compelled dam owners to modify their dams to allow fish to pass upstream, but did not offer compensation to the dam owners.

But those laws were *state* laws, and the Fifth Amendment did not apply to the states until long after the Fourteenth Amendment was ratified in 1868. In any event, a number of states did strike down fish passage laws—New York in 1819, Virginia in 1828—on the grounds that such laws "invaded private rights," as one court put it. Even in the absence of a state-level takings clause, early American courts recognized the distinction between mere regulation—for example, to prevent nuisances—and "invasions" of property in which private property owners were required to surrender some part of their land for a perceived public benefit. In 1827 the New York Supreme Court declared that "the line between . . . a clear invasion of right on the one hand and regulations not lessening the value of the right . . . must be distinctly marked."

As long ago as 1871, the Supreme Court acknowledged that property can be "taken" without a "direct, physical" seizure. In *Pumpelly v. Green Bay Co.*, a landowner challenged a Wisconsin law authorizing the building of a dam that ended up flooding his property. The defendant innocently argued that there had been no taking, since Pumpelly still had all of his land; it just happened to be under water. But the court rejected that ridiculous contention. As Justice Miller wrote, it would be "a very curious and unsatisfactory result" if the state could evade the just compensation requirement of the Fifth Amendment simply because it had not taken property "in the narrowest sense of the word."

The Court reached a similar conclusion in 1922, when it held that a Pennsylvania statute had effectively "taken" property from the Pennsylvania Coal Company by making it economically unviable to work some of its mines. Oliver Wendell Holmes observed that "while property may be regulated to a certain extent, if regulation goes too far it will be recognized as a taking." It is fashionable nowadays for law professors to cite this statement as the origin of regulatory takings, so that they may pass it off as an invention of the idiosyncratic Holmes. But as we've seen, Holmes was drawing on a rich tradition of constitutional and common-law precedents.

The Supreme Court's earlier clear thinking on takings has been tarnished—blighted, one might say—by a 1978 decision that allowed New York City to cancel the building of an office tower atop Grand Central Station, thus destroying $150 million of property rights belonging to the Penn Central Railroad. The Court replaced the literal Fifth Amendment with a multifactor balancing test that would weigh the "character of the taking," the interference with "investment-backed expectations," and the economic impact on "the parcel as a whole," among other malleable factors. Given the Court's tendency to defer to the government when mere property is at stake, tests like that will always tilt in favor of the state.

That's why *Lucas* was an important step in the opposite direction. Unfortunately, later decisions have tried to keep the *Lucas* rationale as narrow as possible. In 2002, for example, the Supreme Court held that a regulatory invasion of property must last forever to qualify as a taking. In that case (*Tahoe-Sierra Preservation Council v. Tahoe Regional Planning Agency*), the Court held that a twenty-year moratorium on building around Lake Tahoe's perimeter did not amount to a taking because the property owners would get their rights back—eventually. In fact, fifty-five of the lot owners died just waiting for the Supreme Court's decision.

Under the original meaning of the takings clause, many more regulatory actions would require "just compensation." Not only would this be good for the rule of law—like any enforcement of original meaning—but it would provide a much-needed restraint on overreaching officials in states and cities across the country.

Like those in Half Moon Bay, California. In 2000, the government of that upscale beach resort halted a planned development of eighty-three homes on the pretense of protecting "wetlands." Except that the only reason the land was wet to begin with was a botched storm drain system installed by—you guessed it—the city government. And even while the city was prohibiting the property owner from developing his land, it also assessed him nearly $1 million to maintain the pristine "wetlands." After much litigation, a federal court awarded the property owner nearly $38 million in compensation because the property had been taken—just as surely as if the city had directly and physically seized the land. Half Moon Bay ultimately negotiated its liability down to $18 million, but even that amount required the city to fire nineteen employees and take on debt obligations stretching thirty years into the future. But, hey, the city wanted wetlands—and it got them.

CHAPTER TEN

CRUEL AND UNUSUAL

The Supreme Court Outsources the Constitution

Excessive bail shall not be required, nor excessive fines imposed, nor cruel and unusual punishments inflicted.

—Eighth Amendment

On the evening of September 8, 1993, seventeen-year-old Christopher Simmons and a friend broke into Shirley Crook's home near St. Louis, tied her up with duct tape and electrical wire, drove her to a nearby bridge, and threw her off, alive and conscious. She was found dead in the Meramec River the next afternoon.

This was no crime of passion or burglary gone wrong; it was plain, old-fashioned premeditated murder. Simmons had planned the killing well in advance, and had described his plans in detail to various friends. He even encouraged his friends to join in the crime, assuring them that, as juveniles, they would "get away with it."

As it would turn out, Simmons had a point. Even though he later confessed to the crime, and even though the jury recommended that Simmons receive the death penalty, the Supreme Court held that it would be unconstitutional to execute him. In fact, the Court held that it would be "cruel and unusual" to execute any juvenile, even depraved murderers, because it would offend "decency" to kill a lad of tender years. Or rather, a lad who had been of tender years when the crime was committed. By the time the Court got around to saying all this, Simmons was twenty-nine.

The 2005 decision in *Roper v. Simmons*, declaring that the Eighth Amendment prohibits the death penalty for juvenile murderers, came as a surprise to some people. Just fifteen years earlier, the Court had reached exactly the opposite conclusion, holding that the juvenile death penalty is *not* "cruel and unusual." But in *Simmons* the Court decided, as Justice Antonin Scalia mockingly observed, "that the meaning of our Constitution has changed over the past fifteen years—not, mind you, that this Court's decision fifteen years ago was *wrong*, but that the Constitution has *changed*." That is what happens when you replace the real Constitution with a Living Constitution.

The majority in *Simmons* claimed simply to be following an emerging "national consensus" against the juvenile death penalty—as though the meaning of the Constitution's text depends on the latest Gallup poll. But there was no "national consensus" in reality. As of 2005, the juvenile death penalty was outlawed in just eighteen states, only four of which had actually changed their laws during the preceding fifteen years. What really motivated the Court was not a national consensus, but an alleged international one. The Court's crucial finding—the crescendo of its opinion—was that "the opinion of the world community" was overwhelmingly against the juvenile death penalty. And therefore the Constitution would have to bend under the "weight" of foreign sensibilities. It was, no doubt, a great comfort to Shirley Crook's husband, Steve, to know that the cold-blooded murderer of his wife would receive the maximum punishment allowed by the United Nations.

Simmons is proof positive that the Supreme Court's Eighth Amendment jurisprudence has gone seriously off the rails. How far? Consider this: in May 2011, a majority of the justices held that the overcrowded conditions in California prisons were so "cruel and unusual" that it was necessary to release 46,000 convicted felons onto the streets. Better to endanger law-abiding citizens, it seems, than to force criminals to double up in cells.

THE OUTER LIMITS OF CRUELTY

The tragedy of cases like *Simmons* is that the Court could have— should have—reached a different result by sticking to the plain meaning of the text. This isn't rocket science. The entire text of the Eighth Amendment consists of sixteen words, and only a few of those words require any degree of interpretation.

For example: the amendment prohibits "cruel and unusual punishments." Without knowing anything about the Founders, it should be obvious that a punishment has to be both cruel *and* unusual to violate the Eighth Amendment. But even that minimum level of fidelity to the text is too much for some justices. In 1968, Justice Harry Blackmun wrote that "cruel *and* unusual" really means "cruel *or* unusual," because "we would not want to place ourselves in the position of condoning punishment which is shown to be only 'cruel' but not 'unusual,' or vice versa" (*Jackson v. Bishop*).

Heaven forbid! Naturally, one sympathizes with the plight

of a Supreme Court justice being "place[d] . . . in the position" of adhering to each and every word of the Constitution. Changing *and* to *or* is a prime example of the kind of activism that Justice Black warned about in his *Griswold v. Connecticut* dissent. As you'll recall from chapter 5, Black observed that substituting "crucial words" of a constitutional provision is "one of the most effective ways of diluting or expanding a constitutionally guaranteed right."

Most Supreme Court justices are not so transparent as Blackmun was in *Jackson v. Bishop*. More often, they simply ignore the bit about "unusual" and focus on the prohibition against cruelty, which, as we will see, has allowed the Supreme Court to develop the meaningless "evolving standards of decency" test for Eighth Amendment cases.

By skipping over "unusual," however, the Court misses the very essence of the Eighth Amendment's original meaning. The prohibition against cruel and unusual punishments was copied almost verbatim from the English Bill of Rights of 1689, in which Parliament had laid down certain limits on the Crown's power. Although the Founders were in some senses revolutionary, when it came to rights, they were profoundly conservative. They considered the historic English liberties to be an essential part of their birthright, and they aimed to keep them. It is no coincidence that the first ten amendments to the Constitution were labeled the "Bill of Rights."

"Unusual" comes from the Latin *usus*, or "usage." In the context of the English guarantee against "cruel and unusual" punishments, the word *unusual* meant "contrary to long usage"— and "long usage" was defined by the common law. Whereas "unusual" might count as a vague compliment today—"she was wearing really *unusual* earrings"—back then, it had the invariably negative connotation of "unlawful." That is how the word would have been understood by those who ratified the Bill of Rights.

Like other parts of the Bill of Rights, the Eighth Amendment was a direct response to Anti-Federalist fears that Congress would use its powers to overturn the common law. In expressing those fears, the Anti-Federalists regularly used "unusual" as a shorthand for "contrary to common law." In the Virginia ratifying convention, for example, Patrick Henry argued that without common-law restraints, the federal government would engage in a series of "new and unusual experiments." George Mason also complained that nothing in the Constitution guaranteed "the benefit of the common law" and, therefore, "Congress may . . . inflict unusual and severe punishments." Likewise, Massachusetts ratifier Abraham Holmes demanded some mechanism to prevent Congress from "*inventing* the most cruel and *un-heard* of punishments" (emphasis added).

The Eighth Amendment, then, sets an outer limit on the level of cruelty in criminal punishments: that which the common law allowed in 1791 is acceptable. Congress cannot invent new (i.e., unusual) punishments that exceed common-law severity. As law professor John Stinneford explained in his widely cited 2008 article, "The Original Meaning of 'Unusual,'" the Eighth Amendment is properly understood as a safeguard against "cruel innovation."

LEND ME AN EAR

How cruel must an innovation be to violate the Eighth Amendment? The original answer was: pretty darn cruel. By today's standards, the threshold for cruelty was high in 1791. Although many of the Founders probably shared Sir William Blackstone's enthusiasm for the "humanity" of the common law, English and American law allowed for things like whipping and branding, and mandated the death penalty for hundreds of crimes. Traitors could be disemboweled.

Harsh, yes. But remember: the Eighth Amendment does not *require* government to inflict any of those penalties. It just says that the government cannot go beyond that. For the first century after ratification of the Bill of Rights, that was an uncontroversial proposition. An 1832 treatise on the "Rights of an American Citizen," for example, explains that the Eighth Amendment prohibits "barbarous and cruel punishments," such as "breaking on the wheel, flaying alive, rending asunder with horses." According to an 1840 text, the amendment prohibits "the rack or the stake, or any of those horrid modes of torture." As late as 1890, the U.S. Supreme Court described the Eighth Amendment narrowly as prohibiting only those punishments involving "torture or lingering death." As examples, the Court cited crucifixion and burning at the stake.

In 1789 Representative Samuel Livermore expressed reservations about the then-proposed Eighth Amendment in terms that give us some idea of founding-era attitudes about punishment. "It is sometimes necessary," said Livermore, "to hang a man, villains often deserve whipping and perhaps having their ears cut off; but are we, in future, to be prevented from inflicting these punishments because they are cruel?"

My, how things have changed. Under the Living Constitution, *cruel* can be—and is—redefined every day. Not surprisingly, prisoners have flooded the courts with frivolous lawsuits, claiming all manner of cruelty. Federal courts have had to grapple with allegations of cruel and unusual punishments involving such horrors as:

- Being forced to miss the NFL playoffs
- Having a blood sample taken (based on the refreshingly originalist argument that "vampires were feared and vilified" by the Founding Fathers)
- Living in Iowa (as a condition of parole)
- Exposure to secondhand smoke

No, wait—that last one wasn't a frivolous lawsuit, it was a Supreme Court decision. In 1993, the Court held that a prisoner who was exposed to "environmental tobacco smoke" from other inmates—it's not as though the guards were blowing smoke in his face—had suffered cruel and unusual punishment (*Helling v. McKinney*). Congressman Livermore, I'm afraid that cutting off ears is out of the question.

THE EVOLVING CONSTITUTION

The Eighth Amendment is unique among constitutional provisions in that lower courts are literally forbidden from even trying to apply the original meaning of the text. Instead, the Supreme Court has commanded that judges must draw the meaning of "cruel and unusual," not from anything the framers wrote, but from "the evolving standards of decency that mark the progress of a maturing society."

That command came, not surprisingly, from the Warren Court. In *Trop v. Dulles* (1958), the Court struck down a section of the Military Code that imposed "denationalization"—

forfeiture of citizenship—for those guilty of wartime desertion. Warren and three of his colleagues held that depriving a deserter of his passport was cruel and unusual, even though the same deserter could have legally been hanged. There was also the slight problem that similar provisions had been on the books since the Civil War, which is why Warren had to invent the "evolving standards" test. Essentially, Warren made the modest claim that he had a more "evolved" sense of decency than Abraham Lincoln, who had not objected to the denationalization law.

Trop bore the hallmarks of judicial activism (see chapter 5). There was the ritual denial that the Court was making up the law. As the Court maintained, the decision was not a matter of "personal preferences," but rather was a heroic attempt "to defend the Constitution." There was the usual over-the-top rhetoric— not just the "evolving standards" bit, but also the proclamation that the Eighth Amendment is based on "nothing less than the dignity of man." And there was a new element: the invocation of foreign law to explain the meaning of the U.S. Constitution. "The civilized nations of the world," said Warren, "are in virtual unanimity that statelessness is not to be imposed as punishment for crime."

All of this was a bit too much—*de Trop*, as it were—for Felix Frankfurter, a fervent New Dealer who came to be regarded as a conservative on the Warren Court. In his dissenting opinion, Frankfurter pointed out that desertion had been a capital offense since 1776. "Is constitutional dialectic so empty of reason," Frankfurter asked, "that it can be seriously urged that loss of citizenship is a fate worse than death?"

Even though the evolving standards test attracted only four votes of the *Trop* Court—a plurality, not a majority—it has become, by dint of repetition, a bedrock principle of Eighth

Amendment jurisprudence. For penal law, that has indeed been a fate worse than death.

THE WAR AGAINST CAPITAL PUNISHMENT

Perhaps the most visible result of the "evolving standards" nonsense is the perennial campaign of left-wing lawyers and judges to have the death penalty declared unconstitutional—not just as applied to minors, as in *Simmons*, but in all cases. In 2002 a federal district judge in New York struck down the federal death penalty under a combination of the Fifth and Eighth Amendments. Mixing and matching his constitutional provisions— why not?—Judge Jed Rakoff held that the Eighth Amendment's "evolving standards" must also be applied to the due process clause of the Fifth Amendment. Predictably, the *New York Times* heralded the decision as "cogent" and "powerful." The Second Circuit Court of Appeals, thankfully, thought otherwise.

Reasonable minds can differ about the wisdom of the death penalty. There are valid policy arguments against it: death *is* irrevocable, and convicted criminals *are* sometimes exonerated long after the fact. But the place to air those concerns is in the legislature, not the Supreme Court. The argument that the Constitution categorically forbids capital punishment is ridiculous, as a quick glance at the text will reveal. The Fifth Amendment, for example, contemplates the death penalty in three different places: "No person shall be held to answer for a *capital* . . . crime, unless on a presentment or indictment of a Grand Jury, . . . nor shall any person be subject for the same offence to be twice put in jeopardy of *life* or limb; . . . nor be deprived of *life*, liberty, or property, without due process of law" (emphasis added).

The text assumes that the federal government can create "capital crimes"—that is, crimes punishable by death—so long as the prosecutors proceed by indictment. It assumes that a person can be put in "jeopardy of life" for an offense, just not twice ("jeopardy of limb," too—perhaps Congressman Livermore had a hand in that). And it also assumes that a person can be "deprived of life," provided due process is observed. Nobody reading those words could have concluded that the Constitution categorically prohibits capital punishment.

The Constitution's section on treason (Article III, Section 3) implicitly recognizes the death penalty. It allows Congress to define the punishment for treason, with limitations relating to "corruption of blood" and "forfeiture," which were consequences that the common law allowed to be visited upon the *heirs* of a traitor. The penalty that common law imposed upon the offender himself—death—is not ruled out. In his 1833 *Commentaries on the Constitution*, Supreme Court justice Joseph Story described this provision as clarifying that treason was not *"exclusively* punishable with death" (emphasis added).

The same Congress that proposed the Eighth Amendment also passed the Act of April 30, 1790, which created various capital offenses, including running off with "goods or merchandise to the value of fifty dollars." For 180 years, the Supreme Court refused to hold the death penalty unconstitutional. As late as 1971, the Court rejected a constitutional challenge to California's death penalty statute (*McGautha v. California*).

In 1972, however, something—the Constitution, or society, or decency, or whatever—*evolved*. In *Furman v. Georgia*, the Court struck down a death penalty statute for the very first time. Technically, the decision invalidated only those statutes—like Georgia's—that gave judges and juries too much discretion in deciding when to impose the death penalty. But the practical effect was to overturn every death penalty law on the books. That was exactly what the Court's most liberal justices—William Brennan and Thurgood Marshall—wanted. They each wrote separate opinions arguing that the death penalty should be declared per se unconstitutional.

If you don't lie awake at night worrying about a Supreme Court filled with liberal activists, then read those concurring opinions in *Furman*. Justice Brennan asserted that the death penalty is wrong because it violates four principles—principles that appear to have come from a random assortment of fortune cookies ("Punishment must not be degrading," "The state must not arbitrarily inflict a severe punishment"). Certainly, his principles had no basis in the text. In fact, Brennan said almost nothing about original meaning, except to note that the debates on the Eighth Amendment show "no indication . . . that a special exception was to be made for death." In other words, because nobody made the point—obvious in 1791—that the Constitution permits capital punishment, we are left with nothing but Justice Brennan's principles to guide us.

As for Justice Marshall, he said even less about the text, merely observing that the "elasticity" of the Eighth Amendment presents the Court with a "danger of too little or too much self-restraint." It takes a certain chutzpah for a Supreme Court justice to warn his colleagues about exercising too much self-restraint.

Georgia and other states reacted to *Furman* by changing their death penalty laws. If too much discretion was the problem, the states would do away with discretion. The legislatures rewrote the laws to define certain classes of crime for which the death penalty was mandatory. Voilà! No discretion whatsoever. From the standpoint of original meaning, such statutes were perfectly constitutional. There's no evidence that the Eighth Amendment was understood to eliminate mandatory sentences; to the contrary, mandatory death sentence laws were common in the states at the time of the Bill of Rights. But when the post-*Furman* statutes were challenged, the Supreme Court struck them down because—I'm not making this up—they didn't give juries enough discretion.

Beginning to sense a pattern? Think of it as the Goldilocks approach to the Eighth Amendment. The states can't give juries too much discretion or too little discretion—it has to be "just right." All the while, the Court continued to insist that it was not going along with Justice Brennan's desire to ban the death penalty altogether. In *Gregg v. Georgia* (1976), a fractured Supreme Court just barely held that the death penalty does not *necessarily* violate the Eighth Amendment.

But Brennan was winning the war. His "principles" were endorsed by three justices in *Gregg*, which was enough for later opinions to treat them as settled law. Most notorious was the principle that the Eighth Amendment requires the death penalty to be proportionate to the crime. That may sound innocuous, but "proportionality review" is just a fancy way of allowing judges to second-guess the policy judgments of legislatures. Who's to say when a punishment is proportionate to the crime? One could say, for example, that juveniles, due to their immaturity, can never be as culpable as adults; ergo, it is disproportionate to subject them to a grown-up punishment like the death penalty. That, in fact, was the logic of *Simmons*.

The justification for proportionality goes something like this. The Eighth Amendment prohibits "excessive" punishments, and *excessive* is a code word for "disproportionate." Actually, the amendment says no such thing. It does prohibit excessive "bail" and excessive "fines." Having used the word *excessive* twice in a row, the framers would hardly have objected to using it a third time if all they wanted to do was prohibit excessive punishments. But they chose to use different words: they prohibited only those punishments that are "cruel and unusual."

Likewise, if the framers wanted to require that punishments be proportionate, they had a perfectly good word for that: proportionate. Several of the early state constitutions did require proportionality. The Pennsylvania constitution, for example, provided that punishments should be "in general more proportionate to the crimes." New Hampshire mandated that "all penalties ought to be proportional to the nature of the offense." South Carolina's constitution said much the same thing. I could go on—but the point is that the framers had plenty of examples of proportionality provisions before them. In other areas, they borrowed freely from state constitutions. They chose not to do so here.

DEATH IS DIFFERENT . . .

Not even Brennan, it seems, really believed that proportionality review was required by the Constitution. If he did, he would presumably have insisted on a rule of proportionality in all Eighth Amendment cases. But he and other liberal justices insisted that proportionality applied only to death penalty cases, because the "penalty of death is different in kind from any other punishment," as the plurality said in *Gregg*. Liberal judges have repeated this phrase, and variations thereof, so often, that it is known to constitutional lawyers as the "death is different" doctrine.

"Death is different"—when combined with the "evolving standards" mantra—has empowered the Court's liberals to achieve incrementally what they failed to get in *Furman*—the abolition of the death penalty. Today, the death penalty has been considered unconstitutional when applied in a wide variety of situations, including when:

- The crime is anything other than murder, including rape of a child.
- The crime is murder, but without torture or aggravated battery.
- The crime is "felony murder"—meaning a death that occurs in the course of and in furtherance of the commission of a felony, such as when a security guard is shot during the course of a bank robbery.
- The defendant is a minor.
- The defendant has even mild mental retardation.
- The death sentence is mandatory.
- The method of execution presents a "substantial risk of severe pain."

Other than that, the justices have no problem with the death penalty. Certainly they would never go so far as to prohibit it.

The point, again, is not that the death penalty is invariably good policy. But it is constitutional. So long as death is not carried out by some method of "cruel innovation" that involves "torture or a lingering death," it does not violate the Eighth Amendment. The Constitution leaves such decisions about life and death to elected legislatures and the citizens who sit on juries—not to shifting coalitions of judges on the Supreme Court.

. . . OR MAYBE IT'S NOT SO DIFFERENT

The promise that "death is different" lasted less than a decade. By 1980, left-leaning justices had decided that life sentences are also "different." In *Rummel v. Estelle*, the Court considered the constitutionality of Texas's habitual offender statute, which mandated a life sentence for any person convicted of three felonies. Although five justices voted to uphold the statute, four dissenters argued that "proportionality review" must not be limited to capital cases—never mind that stuff about "death is different"—because, in the words of Justice Lewis Powell, "we are construing a living Constitution." Are we ever!

As a concession to the dissenting justices, the majority in *Rummel* added a footnote conceding that they might extend "proportionality" beyond the death penalty in an extreme case; if, for example, "a legislature made overtime parking a felony punishable by life imprisonment." Big mistake. Within three years, that footnote would be cited as evidence that proportionality was "deeply rooted" in constitutional law—not just in death penalty cases, but in all cases. The other evidence of the deeply rooted nature of proportionality was a 1910 case decided under the constitution of the Philippines. Based on such persuasive precedents, a slightly "evolved" majority of the Court overturned a life sentence in circumstances indistinguishable from *Rummel*.

By 2010 the Court had moved beyond overturning individual sentences. In *Graham v. Florida*, the Court held that life without parole could never be imposed on a juvenile offender, except possibly juvenile murderers. Because of the diminished culpability of minors—the reasoning of *Simmons*—the Court declared that it would be "disproportionate" to subject them to life imprisonment. So much for "death is different."

AS THE CONSENSUS TURNS

The Court's liberals and their accomplices claim that their Eighth Amendment decisions are based on objective factors, rather than policy preferences.

How does one "objectively" determine the evolving standards of decency? In theory, the Court looks for evidence of a national consensus for or against a particular punishment. In practice, however, the notion of a consensus is fairly flexible—as we saw in *Simmons*, a change in four states over a fifteen-year period was regarded as a veritable groundswell against the juvenile death penalty. In 2008 the Court declared that there was a national consensus against executing people who rape children, even though two years earlier, Congress had passed a law prescribing the death penalty for child rape. But then, what does Congress know about national consensus?

In 2002, the Court threw out the death sentence for a "mildly mentally retarded man" who had robbed a local airman and then killed him, execution-style. The Court perceived a national consensus against executing the mentally retarded based on laws in eighteen states, only seven of which actually contained absolute prohibitions. Not surprisingly, the lower courts have since been flooded with appeals from prisoners who have suddenly been diagnosed as retarded.

In the 2010 *Graham* case, the Court found a national consensus against life sentences for juvenile offenders. Which was more than a little odd, since thirty-seven states, the District of Columbia, and the federal government itself all had laws authorizing life-without-parole sentences for minors, even for non-homicide crimes. Shockingly—there's no other word for it—the Court disregarded those laws because the majority of justices were not convinced that the legislators had given the issue their "full legislative consideration." Besides, said the Court, "there are measures of consensus other than legislation."

The reality behind all of these cases, as in *Simmons*, is that the majority was desperately trying to conform to an international consensus, not a national one. In each case, the justices wearily trudge through the evidence of national consensus as though completing an unpleasant chore, but then come alive when they get to the part about international law. In *Graham*, for example, the Court boasted that it regularly looks "beyond our Nation's borders" to interpret the Eighth Amendment and, therefore, was proud to join "the global consensus against the sentencing practice in question."

The main support for this "global consensus" was Article 37 of the UN Convention on the Rights of the Child, which had also been cited by the *Simmons* majority. The Supreme Court places great weight on that convention despite, or perhaps because of, the fact that the president and Senate of the United States have refused to ratify it. One has to wonder about the mental processes by which judges can convince themselves that an international treaty that had been rejected by the people's elected representatives is a better barometer of evolving standards than the laws actually passed by those representatives. And remember, this was a decision from the supposedly archconservative Roberts Court.

Having established that international opinion is "not irrelevant," as the Court gamely put it in 1982, there is no chance that the justices will retreat from using foreign and international law. For one thing, it greatly increases the scope of a judge's discretion—as Justice Scalia often notes—because the judge can pick and choose among international authorities to arrive at any particular conclusion. There's always some court in the world that will agree with you. In *Knight v. Florida*, for example, Justice Stephen Breyer cited a decision of the Supreme Court of Zimbabwe as authority for the proposition that a delay in carrying out the death penalty violates the United States Constitution. That would be the same Zimbabwe, incidentally, that has been ruled by the same man since 1980, and which is a regular target of groups such as Amnesty International and Human Rights Watch.

In *Lawrence v. Texas*, a majority of the Supreme Court pointed to European law as proof of an international consensus against laws prohibiting homosexuality. Had they consulted the laws of Latin American nations or the Muslim world, they might have detected a very different consensus. And how come the Court's liberals appear unfazed by the fact that the United States is one of only six countries that allows abortion on demand up to the point of viability?

DELIBERATE INDIFFERENCE—TO THE CONSTITUTION

Because of the Court's Eighth Amendment activism, the people and their elected representatives have lost the power to determine when a punishment fits the crime. Any punishment—capital or custodial—must conform to the Court's multiple, overlapping precedents, and even then, it's liable to be struck down if it contravenes, say, Ugandan law.

The states have also lost the ability to run their own prison systems. In fact, most Eighth Amendment litigation these days has nothing to do with the severity of any particular sentence.

Instead, most of the action has to do with allegedly "cruel and unusual" conditions within prisons. In 2008, prisoners filed 54,796 lawsuits nationwide, up from 40,000 in 1995, despite the passage of a federal law creating various procedural hurdles for litigious inmates. Many, perhaps most, of these cases allege Eighth Amendment claims against their jailkeepers.

Having said that, one could hardly object to the volume of Eighth Amendment cases if even a fraction of them were meritorious. But they are not. They can't be, for the simple reason that the Eighth Amendment has nothing to do with the conditions of a particular prisoner's confinement. The amendment prohibits only "punishments" that are cruel and unusual. A "punishment" is a "fine, penalty, or confinement inflicted upon a person by . . . sentence of a court," as *Black's Law Dictionary* puts it.

Incarceration for twenty years is a punishment. A prison policy that all inmates shall get twenty minutes of exercise per week is not. That is how "punishment" was understood by those who wrote and ratified the Eighth Amendment. Two leading law dictionaries of the founding era defined *punishment* as "the penalty of transgressing the laws." For nearly two centuries after ratification of the Bill of Rights, the Supreme Court never hinted that the Eighth Amendment dictated anything about the relative hardships of prison life.

All of that changed in 1976, when the Court asserted that prison officials could violate the Eighth Amendment if they exhibit "deliberate indifference to the serious medical needs of prisoners" (*Estelle v. Gamble*). Technically, this was not a binding statement of law because the Court actually rejected the particular claim at issue—inadequate treatment of a back injury. Nonetheless, the "deliberate indifference" standard was immediately treated as the law of the land. And the list of impermissible deprivations quickly grew. By 1981, the Court would declare that indifference to "the minimal civilized measure of life's necessities" amounts to cruel and unusual punishment (*Rhodes v. Chapman*).

"Life's necessities" is, to say the least, a flexible concept. Who can blame the prisoner who claimed that watching the NFL playoffs is one of those necessities? One method to restrict the scope of prison litigation is to require some showing of actual injury, which is, after all, a traditional element of "standing" to sue. For a while, that's what the Court did. At first, inmates had to prove that the deliberate indifference of prison officials resulted in "significant injury." But in the 1992 case of *Hudson v. McMillan*, which involved a single beating by a prison guard resulting in only minor injuries, the Court held that the Eighth Amendment is violated by any "unnecessary" infliction of pain. The very next year, the Court decided *Helling v. McKinney*—the secondhand smoke case—in which an "unnecessary risk" of injury was enough to violate the Constitution.

I don't mean to suggest that prisons are free to mistreat inmates; they aren't. Prisoners can, and often do, bring legitimate grievances under prison rules, state law, or federal statutes. There's no need to distort the Constitution to buttress such prisoner complaints. As Justice Thomas pointed out in his dissent in *Helling*, the Eighth Amendment was simply not intended to serve as a national prison code. But that is what it has become as judges try to determine what risks are "necessary" within each prison.

Which brings us back to the tsunami of prisoner lawsuits. For if the courts are empowered to make up a national prison code as they go along, why on earth shouldn't an inmate roll the dice on a lawsuit? Encouragement may come from decisions like that of a federal judge in Oregon who upheld a convicted murderer's complaint about being served "Nutraloaf"—a bland but perfectly nutritious food loaf sometimes served to prisoners who can't be trusted with utensils. Such culinary degradations violated not only the Eighth Amendment but also the Fourteenth, because, rather paradoxically, prisoners have a "liberty interest" in a "normal prison diet" (*LeMaire v. Maass*). Granted, the *LeMaire* decision was eventually overturned by the Ninth Circuit, but only over a vigorous dissent by Judge John Noonan, who urged that serving "unpalatable food" constitutes cruel and unusual punishment. Many inmates, it would seem, agree with Noonan. Among the thousands of prisoner rights cases are those complaining of the ingredients in the pancake syrup, the size of the portions, the use of reconstituted milk, the absence of fruit juice, and the monotony of cheese sandwiches.

GET OUT OF JAIL FREE

The expansion of prisoners' "rights" does not simply mean that individual convicts receive a little more comfort than they might otherwise get. If that were the worst of it, there would be little to complain about.

What makes Eighth Amendment litigation so destructive is a separate development in constitutional law: the rise of the equitable decree. As we saw in chapter 5, the 1970s school-busing cases led to a radical reinvention of the federal judiciary's "equity" jurisdiction. Originally understood as a limited power to craft narrow remedies, equity turned into a blank check for courts to usurp control over schools, hospitals, and other institutions. The means for achieving this was the use of "structural injunctions," that is, highly detailed orders that would have to be implemented, over a course of months or years, under the supervision of a federal judge.

In 1978, the Supreme Court approved the use of these new-found equitable powers to "correct" prison conditions of confinement that violate the "evolving standards of decency." Within three years, prisons or entire prison systems in twenty-four states had been declared unconstitutional and subject to some measure of judicial micromanagement.

There is no better illustration of a judiciary run amok than the Supreme Court's May 23, 2011, ruling in *Brown v. Plata*. That was the case I mentioned at the beginning of the chapter, in which the Court upheld a structural injunction requiring California to release 46,000 prisoners for the sake of remedying an Eighth Amendment violation.

What was the Eighth Amendment violation? It wasn't overcrowding in and of itself, but the fact that overcrowding created a "risk"—remember the *Helling* passive smoke case?—that prisoners *might* receive inadequate medical and mental health care. As recently as 1996, the Supreme Court had rejected the same argument, holding that an inmate cannot claim a constitutional violation "simply on the ground that the prison medical facilities were inadequate" (*Lewis v. Casey*). But that was then. By 2011, the Eighth Amendment had "evolved." Another landmark decision for the reactionary Roberts Court.

But even assuming that the California prisons have inadequate medical facilities, the remedy is bizarre. According to a majority of the Supreme Court, the lower court's order to release 46,000 prisoners within two years was "narrowly drawn"— perhaps because the court could have released even more prisoners. But why release any? Faced with an overburdened health care system, California could have hired more doctors, or built more prisons, or even brought back flogging as an alternative to prison (except that the Supreme Court banned flogging in 1968). The notion that releasing tens of thousands of prisoners is the most "narrow" solution to the problem at hand is nonsensical.

It takes a particular brand of arrogance to think that prisons will never improve without judicial intervention. In reality, public-spirited citizens and politicians have responded to problems in the prison system throughout history. Before the Eighth Amendment even existed, Philadelphia Quakers had established the Walnut Street Jail, which, according to historian Larry Sullivan, included such innovations as "prison industries . . . health care and educational opportunities [and] religious services." Later prison reform movements had an enormous impact in America during the nineteenth and early twentieth centuries—all before anyone imagined that the Eighth Amendment contained its own penal code. The operation of prisons is indeed a very serious matter, which is exactly why it should not be left to judges.

CHAPTER ELEVEN

FEDERALISM

The Forgotten Tenth Amendment

The powers not delegated to the United States by the Constitution, nor prohibited by it to the States, are reserved to
the States, respectively, or to the people.

—TENTH AMENDMENT

IN 1994 JOHN RAPANOS, a property developer in Michigan,
was arrested for having work done on a parcel of land without
the necessary permits. Rapanos had hired contractors to excavate
some sand and place it in a ditch—all on his property—but he
had neglected to seek approval from the authorities.

What sort of trumped-up gang of government busybodies
insists on a permit just to move some sand around? The local
zoning board? County commissioner? State agency? Actually, it
was the federal Environmental Protection Agency, or EPA. That
the federal government took *any* interest in Mr. Rapanos's sand
is astonishing. Look all you want in the Constitution, even in the
"penumbra," you won't find any hint that the federal government
is empowered to regulate local land use. And because that power
is not delegated to the federal government, it is retained by the
states. Federalism—a notion inherent in the Constitution, but

made explicit in the Tenth Amendment—demands that states remain sovereign within all areas not surrendered to the federal government. Even today, most people assume that zoning decisions are made by state and local authorities, not by Washington agencies.

LAND = WATER

The EPA's argument was very simple: Rapanos had violated the federal Clean Water Act by discharging a "pollutant" (which can include sand) into "navigable waters." There's another clue that something was seriously amiss in this case. The Rapanos property is twenty miles away from the nearest navigable water; in fact, the property has no standing water at all. But the federal bureaucracy, under pressure to use the Clean Water Act to save "wetlands," had redefined the term "navigable waters" to include any land with a "hydrological" connection to navigable waters. What that means is that the act would extend to any place that might, occasionally, contain water that might, theoretically, work its way into the general water system. Ergo, when Mr. Rapanos placed dry sand in a dry ditch he was polluting America's navigable waters—and to do that, you need a permit from the Army Corps of Engineers, which jointly administers the Clean Water Act along with the EPA.

Under this new definition of "navigable waters"—dreamed up by federal bureaucrats—the fate of tens of thousands of development projects depended not on local decision-makers, but on the Army Corps of Engineers. With veto power over any use of land that might be wet, or even damp, for just a few days of the year, the corps became the zoning board for the United States, usurping a function that had always belonged to the states. Under the EPA's logic, small puddles and backed-up sinks could be a matter of federal jurisdiction. Did your kid wet the bed? Don't change the sheets without consulting the Army Corps.

If you think I'm joking, consider the consequences of *not* getting Army Corps permission. In 1993, Ocie and Carey Mills, a father-and-son team of do-it-yourselfers, were sent to prison for twenty-one months for placing "clean fill dirt on a plot of subdivided dry land" (as the judge put it) without a permit. In the Rapanos case, the government asked for a sentence of sixty-three months—*more than five years*—for failure to get a permit. The trial judge flatly refused to put a man behind bars for "mov[ing] some sand." The government appealed, and the case was ultimately settled.

BE CLEAR WHEN YOU VIOLATE THE CONSTITUTION

In the meantime, however, the government also filed a civil case against John Rapanos that made it all the way to the Supreme Court. In a 2006 decision, the high court rejected the expansive definition of "navigable waters" that had turned the Army Corps "into a *de facto* regulator of immense stretches of intrastate land," as Justice Antonin Scalia described it. Scalia pointed out that the Clean Water Act expressly recognizes that states have the "primary" responsibility for land-use decisions—a clear sign that Congress meant to respect state sovereignty. So far, so good. But then the Court went on to say that Congress could take over local zoning decisions if it really wanted to. In fact, the Court stated that Congress could intrude upon *any* area of traditional state authority, so long as it makes its intention "clear" in the legislation.

The so-called clear statement rule turns federalism into a charade: if Congress can destroy states' rights with "clear" legislation, there are no limits to federal power. Remember that state sovereignty is not just a slogan; it is protected by the Bill of Rights. The Tenth Amendment guarantees that the states and the people retain all powers not delegated to the central government. Early commentators understood the Tenth Amendment to be an important reservation of sovereign powers to the states. But somehow, the Tenth Amendment has ended up as a sort of poor relation among constitutional rights. No other guarantee of the Bill of Rights can be overruled by a clear statement. Just imagine the outcry if the Supreme Court declared that Congress could go ahead and abridge freedom of speech so long as it did so with "clear" legislation.

According to one school of thought, it's too late to revive the original understanding of federalism in which states enjoy real autonomy. Better to embrace the typical Washington view—aptly caricatured by Justice Sandra Day O'Connor—of states as "regional offices [or] administrative agencies of the Federal Government." Why not consolidate everything into one big federal apparatus so that we have, say, a Department of Nebraska right alongside the Departments of Defense and Commerce?

The reason is that federalism still matters. Not because it protects states, but because it protects *individual* liberty. The framers sought to promote freedom by diffusing government power. First, they divided power between state and federal governments, and then they required separation of powers at the federal level and (indirectly) at the state level, by guaranteeing to each state a "republican" form of government (Article IV, Section 4).

This combination of federalism and separation of powers creates "a double security . . . to the rights of the people," as James Madison wrote in Federalist No. 51. In the early nineteenth century, for example, it was the states that led the resistance to the Fugitive Slave Act, a federal law that required state magistrates to cooperate in returning runaway slaves to their owners. In response to an 1826 Pennsylvania law prohibiting the removal of slaves from the commonwealth, the Supreme Court held that states retained the authority to stop their own judges from enforcing the Fugitive Slave Act (even though they could not block federal judges from doing so).

For the first 150 years of the Republic, give or take, the division of power between state and federal governments was wildly successful. British historian Lord Acton wrote that the American principle of federalism was responsible for producing "a community more powerful, more prosperous, more intelligent, and more free than any other the world has seen." But Acton died in 1902, a few decades before federalism entered its long death spiral. The later emergence of an omnipotent federal government has had exactly the effect on individual liberty that Acton and Madison would have predicted. Just ask John Rapanos, Ocie Mills, or any of the thousands of men and women languishing in jail for violation of "federal crimes" of dubious constitutionality. And beyond prisons, millions of Americans suffer the consequences of rampant centralization, whether it's a federal housing policy that turns local property bubbles into national meltdowns, or a one-size-fits-all health care mandate.

Even supposed conservatives often ignore the Tenth Amendment. The Defense of Marriage Act (DOMA), passed by a Republican Congress in 1996—and willingly signed by Democrat Bill Clinton—deprived states of their traditional power to define

marriage within their own borders. In 2010 a federal judge in
Massachusetts struck down the part of DOMA that interferes
with states' rights to recognize same-sex marriages as a violation
of the Tenth Amendment. Liberals didn't know what to do with
themselves: gay marriage—good; but Tenth Amendment—bad.
The Obama administration itself took directly contradictory positions in the space of one month. In January 2011, the Obama
Department of Justice submitted a brief arguing for a reversal
of that decision, but then abruptly declared in February that
DOMA was, in fact, unconstitutional. Although the president's
decision appears to have been motivated by political calculation
(unless the Living Constitution actually evolved within a four-
week period), he reached the right result. The definition of marriage is a matter of state, not federal, law.

Another "conservative" assault on federalism came with the
2005 REAL ID Act, promoted by the George W. Bush administration and passed by a Republican Congress. Billed as a Home-
land Security measure, the law tells states how to make driver's
licenses and nondriver identification cards: a traditional state
function if ever there was one. On the bright side, REAL ID has
managed to unite Left and Right: at least twenty-five states of all
ideological stripes have passed legislation to resist implementation of REAL ID.

WHAT DOES THE TENTH AMENDMENT
PROTECT?

Boosters of federal power pay lip service to states' rights, but they
argue that such rights must yield to the supremacy clause of Article VI, which states that "this Constitution, and the Laws of

the United States which shall be made in Pursuance thereof . . . shall be the supreme law of the land." But that argument is based on a fallacy; namely, that every law passed by Congress is "supreme." Under the supremacy clause, however, a law is "supreme" only if made "in Pursuance" of the Constitution—including the enumerated powers of Article I. A law that asserts powers not delegated to the federal government is no more "supreme" than a law establishing a national religion—or DOMA.

The Tenth Amendment was originally understood to make this point crystal clear. The main obstacle to ratification of the Constitution was the Anti-Federalist fear that a "supreme" federal government would eventually wipe out the states as autonomous entities. The main text of the Constitution contains a number of safeguards to prevent that from happening. First, the federal government was granted only limited powers. Second, the Senate was originally elected by the legislatures of the states, and senators "were considered ambassadors of their state governments," according to George Mason law professor Todd Zywicki. It was understood that senators would be on guard against legislation that would strip power away from their electors. Moreover, the fact that the Senate's assent was required for treaties and appointments meant that the states originally had tremendous leverage over the federal government (the Seventeenth Amendment changed that, as I discuss below).

The state ratifying conventions, however, were not satisfied with those structural features. Seven of the conventions demanded an amendment that would expressly protect the sovereign powers of the states—a demand that was ultimately met by the Tenth Amendment. Liberals often denigrate the Tenth Amendment as being merely "declaratory," as though that detracts from its validity. Much of the Constitution is declaratory of truths that the

Founders considered obvious. Madison, for example, thought the Bill of Rights "may be deemed unnecessary" because such rights were already safeguarded. Hamilton described both the necessary and proper clause and the supremacy clause as "declaratory." The Constitution declares many things. It does so to remove any doubt.

The sovereign power retained by the states is known as the "police power"—that's "police" as in the ancient Greek *polis* (city-state)—and includes things like regulation of public health and safety. Even before the Tenth Amendment was proposed, the Constitution was properly understood to leave the states with complete power to pass and enforce laws touching on "the lives, liberties, and properties of the people, and the internal order, improvement, and prosperity of the State," as Madison observed in Federalist No. 45. The Tenth Amendment, however, protected the states against any construction of the Constitution that would deprive them of "the authority of preserving order, of enforcing moral duties and restraining vice within their own territories," as Thomas Jefferson wrote in 1823.

The key point is that the Constitution does not grant police powers to the states. It doesn't have to. The states—which existed before the federal government—already had those powers, and they never agreed to relinquish them. In happier times, the Supreme Court observed that the states' police power "exists independently of [the Constitution] by reason of its never having been surrendered by the states to the General Government" (*House v. Mayes*, 1910). Yes, Congress can make laws to carry out the enumerated powers of Article I, but when it comes to everything else—zoning, family law, public health and safety, etc.—the states remain "supreme." At least, that was the original idea.

POLICE POWER VS. SANCTUARY NATION

In 2010 the Arizona legislature passed a law that used the traditional police powers of the state to do something that the federal government was failing to do: enforce the immigration laws. The law (SB 1070) adds state penalties to certain violations of federal immigration law. It also requires police to do an immigration check on people whom they arrest—provided they have a reasonable suspicion that the person is in the country illegally.

Arizona had good cause to pass SB 1070. It's been estimated that half of all illegal aliens entering the United States come through Arizona's porous border. Illegal aliens comprise 6 percent of Arizona's population and 7.4 percent of its workforce. Many of the aliens crossing into Arizona are simply desperate for work, but others are hardened criminals. The Mexico/Arizona border zone is so dangerous that large areas of state parkland are now off-limits to law-abiding citizens. Criminal aliens make up a whopping 17 percent of Arizona's prison population. All in all, the State spends hundreds of millions of taxpayer dollars each year to provide prison cells and social services for people who would not be in the country at all if the federal government had done its job. If a state does not retain enough "police power" to deal with a crisis of that magnitude, then the Tenth Amendment is a dead letter.

The Obama administration took a different view. Just before SB 1070 was due to take effect, the administration persuaded a federal judge to block four sections of the law, including the mandatory immigration check of arrestees. That decision was later upheld by the Ninth Circuit Court of Appeals. In a nutshell, the Ninth Circuit said that those four sections of SB 1070 are preempted by federal law, which is "supreme" under Article VI.

The Ninth Circuit was dead wrong. The sole *constitutional* basis for preempting the Arizona law is Congress's power to "establish an uniform Rule of Naturalization" (Article I, Section 8). That means only Congress can set the rules for who should be admitted to the United States, and under what conditions they can remain. Granted, an individual state cannot make a law that conflicts with the "uniform rule" set by Congress. But states can make laws that affect aliens, including laws that make life more difficult for illegal aliens. In 1976, for example, the Supreme Court upheld a California law prohibiting companies from knowingly employing illegal aliens. Such a law, said the Court, was a "mainstream" example of the state's "police power" (*DeCanas v. Bica*).

The Supreme Court has even recognized the power of states to expel undesirable aliens—a power that comes much closer to impinging on Congress's power to set a "uniform rule." In *New York v. Miln* (1837), the Court blessed a state law that allowed New York City's mayor to deny entry to any would-be immigrant whom he thought likely to become a public burden. The Court held that such a law was an entirely appropriate exercise of "the power to regulate internal police" in light of the fact that New York is "more than any other city in the Union" exposed to the risk of having to pay for the maintenance of poor immigrants. "It is the duty of the State," said the Court, "to protect its citizens from this evil." Substitute Arizona for New York, and you have the very rationale for SB 1070.

When it suits their purposes, liberals believe that states have autonomy over immigration matters. If they didn't, there would be no justification for "sanctuary cities," that is, cities that enact policies to block enforcement of federal immigration law. As of 2007, over thirty major American cities had adopted such policies. There are even sanctuary states, like Alaska and Oregon. In 2011, Democrats in the California State Assembly passed a bill giving county officials the ability to opt out of a mandatory program of information sharing with federal immigration authorities. The bill stalled in the state senate, but it may not matter, since most of California's major cities already have sanctuary policies.

Unlike the sanctuary laws that liberals adore, nothing about the Arizona law actually conflicts with federal law. To the contrary, SB 1070 penalizes only behavior that already violates federal law. Moreover, the primary federal immigration statute, the Immigration and Nationality Act (INA), specifically provides for the kind of federal-state cooperation that the Arizona law advances. The INA requires, for example, that federal authorities "shall respond" to state and local requests to verify the immigration status of any person. It also empowers state and local officials to arrest previously deported felons who have reentered the country illegally. In short, when the federal government fails to make use of its immigration law, states are entitled to borrow it for a while.

So where was the conflict? The Ninth Circuit found that the Arizona law would undermine not the INA, but the executive branch's "policies" and "objectives." The St. Thomas More Law Center put it more bluntly: the law was "pre-empted by an executive policy of *non-enforcement* of federal law" (emphasis added). That policy of non-enforcement is so extreme that the Obama administration originally attempted to block every single section of SB 1070, even the part that prohibits "sanctuary cities" within the state. From the Obama point of view, cities have the right to *block* federal immigration law, but states cannot *enforce* it. Only the Living Constitution could produce such a bizarre result.

In a June 2012 ruling, the Supreme Court largely agreed with the Ninth Circuit's decision. The Court upheld only one of the four provisions struck down by the Ninth Circuit, suggesting that states retain little autonomy to exercise their police powers in ways that conflict with White House policy.

THE CLAUSE THAT NEVER SLEEPS

Not only are state laws preempted by existing federal laws and executive branch policies, but they are even trumped by *hypothetical* federal laws. Welcome to the land of the dormant commerce clause.

You'll recall the real commerce clause (Article I, Section 8). It empowers Congress to "regulate Commerce . . . among the several States." When Congress exercises that power, its laws are "supreme" under Article VI and, therefore, preempt any state law to the contrary. But in cases going back to the nineteenth century, federal courts have asserted the power to strike down any state law that "unjustifiably" burdens interstate commerce "even if Congress has yet to act in the area concerned," as the Supreme Court explained in 1994. Literally, courts can undo democratically enacted state laws simply because Congress might, someday, pass a law to the contrary.

This doctrine is known as the "dormant" or "negative" commerce clause. The clause does not appear in the Constitution's text, but since when has that stopped a federal court? The dormant commerce clause is a tool for judges to impose their own policy choices. Whether one law clashes with another law is a question for judges to decide. But how can a judge determine whether a particular regulation "unjustifiably" burdens commerce? In a democracy, the people are supposed to make those decisions. That might just be why the framers did not include a dormant commerce clause in Article I.

DON'T MAKE A FEDERAL CASE OUT OF IT

Power abhors a vacuum. As state sovereignty shrinks, federal power inevitably grows. The enumerated powers of Article I and the reserved powers of the Tenth Amendment are two sides of the same coin. Every time Congress is allowed to expand its jurisdiction under the commerce or general welfare clauses, fewer and fewer powers are "reserved to the States . . . or to the people."

Consider health care: a prime example, one would think, of an area where the states reign supreme, given their inherent police power over public health and safety. The 2010 Affordable Care Act (ACA), however, abolishes this traditional area of state autonomy by imposing a federal mandate that citizens purchase health insurance policies that conform to rigid standards. As Judge James Graham of the Sixth Circuit put it, the "ultimate issue" in the litigation challenging ACA is this: "Does the notion of federalism still have vitality?" Graham voted to strike down the law because "it intrudes on both the States and the people," and it "feels very much like the general police power that the Tenth Amendment reserves to the States and the people." Graham, however, was in the minority. A majority of the Sixth Circuit upheld the law, as the Supreme Court would later do, stating that the Tenth Amendment "adds nothing" to the analysis.

The Founders would be surprised—some might even mutter an oath—to learn that the Tenth Amendment has "nothing" to do with a federal law that grabs power from the states. What was the point of reserving powers to the states if not to restrain the federal Leviathan? It is true—as vigilant liberals always point out—that the Tenth Amendment limits the federal government to those powers "delegated" by the Constitution, rather than those powers "expressly delegated," which had been the wording in the analogous section of the Articles of Confederation. The omission was deliberate. On three occasions, Congress refused to add the word *expressly* to the text of what became the Tenth Amendment. That snippet of drafting history sends even the most ardent Living Constitution fans into paroxysms of originalist joy. Look, they exult, the framers gave Congress *implied powers.*

Implied powers, yes, but in a very limited sense. Nobody in 1791 would have thought that the omission of the word *expressly* was meant to open up new vistas of social engineering for Congress. Rather, *expressly* was left out of the Tenth Amendment for the same reason that the necessary and proper clause was inserted in Article I: to clarify that Congress could exercise narrow powers that were "incidental" to its enumerated powers. As we saw in chapter 3, the Founders viewed the federal government as the agent of the people, with the same fiduciary duties as a private sector agent. That meant that the government had to be kept on a short leash to make sure that it didn't stray from its delegated powers. But at the same time, the government had to have enough power to do things like collecting taxes and raising armies.

Under the Articles of Confederation, Congress was confined to the powers "expressly delegated"—a phrase that had been interpreted so strictly as to prevent Congress from exercising even perfunctory powers, like granting passports, despite the fact that passports were obviously "incidental" to the Congress's powers over defense and foreign affairs. Even John Marshall, one of the most fervent nationalizers (along with Hamilton) of the founding era, agreed that the omission of the word *expressly* was simply meant to avoid the "embarrassments" suffered under the Articles of Confederation. In *McCulloch v. Maryland*, Marshall held that state sovereignty need not yield to every power dreamed up by Congress, but only those congressional measures that are "plainly adapted" means for carrying out a "legitimate" constitutional end.

In the nineteenth century, Congress made relatively few attempts to encroach on the states' turf (remember: senators were chosen by state legislatures). One such effort, an attempt by Congress in the 1860s to impose a tax on state judicial officers, was beaten back by the Supreme Court. There was no dispute that Congress had the power to levy taxes; Article I says so. But to use Chief Justice Marshall's test from *McCulloch*, the "means" chosen by Congress have to be consistent with "the letter and spirit of the Constitution"—including the Tenth Amendment. In *Collector v. Day* (1870), the Supreme Court held that imposing a tax on state officials was not a proper exercise of Congress's taxing power. The Court treated the Tenth Amendment as a "rule of interpretation" that Congress's powers should be construed as to leave the states' sovereign powers "unaltered and unimpaired," except where they were expressly surrendered to the federal government. The same philosophy animated the Court's decision in *Hammer v. Dagenhart* (1918) that a federal statute to regulate child labor was an unconstitutional invasion of state police powers.

The first sustained attack on the Tenth Amendment came with the New Deal. One of the early products of the New Deal Congress was the National Industrial Recovery Act, which gave the force of federal law to "codes of fair competition" drawn up by industry groups and encompassing everything from working conditions to the price and quality of goods sold—even if the goods were sold intrastate. In *A.L.A. Schechter Poultry Corp. v. United States*, lawyers from the National Recovery Administration sought to put some Brooklyn-based chicken butchers in jail for violating the "Live Poultry Code." The butchers were convicted, but the Supreme Court overturned the convictions in 1935, holding that the act exceeded Congress's enumerated powers. The government's lawyers had tried to play the Depression card. In times of "national crisis," they argued, the federal government has to be able to intervene in local affairs. Nonsense, said the Court: "Such assertions of extraconstitutional authority were anticipated and precluded by the Tenth Amendment." After the case was finished, Justice Louis Brandeis—a famously "progressive" jurist—told the Roosevelt administration's lawyers that the Court's decision was "the end of this business of centralization. . . . I want you to go back and tell the President we're not going to let this government centralize everything."

Roosevelt, however, outlasted Brandeis. Indeed, his administration lasted longer than anyone expected, given that every previous president had followed George Washington's example of a two-term maximum. FDR was elected to four consecutive terms (a result now prohibited by the Twenty-Second Amendment). By 1941, Brandeis was off the bench and the Supreme Court was now dominated by FDR appointees and those who had been cowed by the president's court-packing scheme (chapter 3). This more compliant Court decreed in *United States v. Darby* (1941) that the Tenth Amendment is "but a truism" that does not in any way limit the scope of Congress's powers.

In *Darby*, the Court upheld the Fair Labor Standards Act of

1938 (FLSA), which imposed uniform wage and hour standards throughout the United States, with violators barred from selling goods across state lines. Before then, the relationship between employer and employee had been strictly a matter of state law. In allowing Congress to dictate the terms of strictly intrastate employment contracts, the Court claimed to be following in the tradition of Marshall's opinion in *McCulloch*, which distinguished between constitutional "ends," which must be expressly enumerated, and "means," which can be implied. But the Court got its ends and means backward. The Court asserted that the "end" of the FLSA was "excluding [certain goods] from interstate commerce" and that the federal takeover of employment law was simply a means to that end. Nobody in his right mind thought that the *goal* of the FLSA was to exclude items from interstate commerce. The goal was to set national wage and hour standards, and the threat of being excluded from interstate commerce was simply the means to coerce obedience.

Before *Darby*, the Tenth Amendment had been understood to reinforce a system in which the state and federal governments had equal autonomy within their respective spheres. Courts were prepared to protect either side from encroachment by the other. This was a concept sometimes referred to as dual federalism. But after *Darby*, dual federalism ground to a halt. In 1952 political scientist Edward Corwin observed that dual federalism was no longer "capable of delimiting national legislative power." The catchphrase of the New Deal was "cooperative federalism," which Corwin (himself a former adviser to FDR) described as a "short expression for a constantly increasing concentration of power at Washington in the stimulation and supervision of local policies."

With Supreme Court justices who can't tell their ends from their elbows, the federal government continues to grow. It has be-

come commonplace for Congress to assume extraordinary powers dressed up as the "means" to exercise some faraway, tangen-
tially related constitutional "end." Be it regulation of homegrown
wheat or of homegrown pot, as we saw in chapter 3, the Supreme
Court has allowed Congress to ride roughshod over the states.

TRADITIONAL GOVERNMENT FUNCTIONS

Even when Congress is legitimately acting within its enumerated powers, it cannot pass absolutely any law—only those that
are necessary *and proper*. Or, as Chief Justice Marshall put it,
Congress can pursue a "legitimate" end only through means that
are consistent with the "letter and spirit" of the Constitution.
Congress cannot, for example, prohibit interstate trade in newspapers, since that would abridge freedom of the press.

What if Congress tried to exercise its commerce power by
requiring a state to move the location of its capital? Such a law
would certainly have a big effect on interstate commerce, but
would it be proper? The Supreme Court, contemplating such a
hypothetical situation, said that it clearly would not be (*Coyle
v. Oklahoma*, 1911). Nothing in the Constitution explicitly says
that the states should be able to control the location of their capi-
tals. But then, what's left of the Tenth Amendment, and the related concepts of federalism and state sovereignty, if states don't
have some basic freedom to order their own affairs?

The issue of whether states have some essential core of sovereignty has played out in a couple of Supreme Court decisions
involving our old friend the FLSA. The original statute—the one
upheld in *Darby*—was bad enough, but it at least exempted state
and local governments, in recognition that there was something

fishy about Congress dictating personnel policies to supposedly sovereign state governments. In 1974, however, Congress did away with those concessions to the states. When the issue reached the Supreme Court in 1976, the Court held that Congress had exceeded its constitutional powers—specifically, it had violated the Tenth Amendment (*National League of Cities v. Usery*). Assuming that the FLSA was within Congress's power in the first place, the statute impaired an important "attribute of state sovereignty," namely, the power to set wages for state employees. The Court held that the Tenth Amendment forbids any legislation that would take away the states' freedom "to structure integral operations of traditional government functions."

Given the Court's track record, the *Usery* decision was a huge victory for states' rights—and for original meaning. Even Archibald Cox, a liberal scholar and former Watergate special prosecutor, conceded that the *Usery* decision "is almost surely consistent with the original conception of the federal union and might not have surprised any constitutional scholar prior to the 1930s."

Of course, one would expect the Supreme Court's liberals to show *Usery* the same *stare decisis* veneration that they afford to cases like *Roe v. Wade*. Or perhaps not. It took less than a decade for the Court's liberal bloc, led by Justice Harry Blackmun, to overturn *Usery*. In 1985 the Court held that Congress was perfectly entitled to impose the FLSA on municipal transit workers (*Garcia v. San Antonio Metropolitan Transit Authority*). The Court's main rationale for junking *Usery* was that judges were having a hard time defining the scope of "traditional government functions."

And so, to spare judges the trouble of grappling with the Tenth Amendment, the *Garcia* Court declared that the judiciary would no longer enforce *any* limits on federal power vis-à-vis the states. If states felt threatened by federal power, they would have to seek protection in the "procedural safeguards" of the political system. Except that the one and only "procedural safeguard" to protect states at the federal level—the election of senators by state legislatures—had been abolished by the Seventeenth Amendment in 1913. Not that the justices had anything against the states. "Of course," wrote Justice Blackmun for the majority, "we continue to recognize that the States occupy a special and specific position in our constitutional system." Sure, they make license plates.

Compared to *Garcia*, the "clear statement" rule—with which we began the chapter—was actually a step in the right direction. The rule was first articulated by Justice O'Connor as a way to get around Garcia without actually overturning it, which she presumably did not have the votes to do. In *Gregory v. Ashcroft* (1991), a group of Missouri judges sued the governor, complaining that the state's mandatory retirement for judges at age seventy violated the federal Age Discrimination in Employment Act. It was not completely clear whether the act applied to judges in the first place, since it exempted state government appointees "on the policymaking level." But the judges argued that the act applied to them on the theory that judges "do not make policy"—wishful thinking, unfortunately. In any event, the Court pointed out that states have always been able to control their own judicial branches without federal interference, and Congress would have to be very clear if it wanted to alter the usual balance between states and the federal government.

MASTER AND COMMANDER

Although the clear statement rule falls far short of original meaning, it has allowed the Court, in cases like *Rapanos*, to stop the executive branch from exploiting congressional ambiguity to grab power from the states. But what happens when there is no ambiguity? What happens when Congress *is* completely clear about its intention to abridge states' rights? The answer, unfortunately, is that Congress can do almost anything it wants. But the Court has at least drawn a line in the sand with the so-called anti-commandeering principle.

The anti-commandeering principle holds that Congress may not hijack the legislative or administrative machinery of a state by forcing the state to adopt or administer regulatory programs designed in Washington. The doctrine emerged in a 1992 case (*New York v. United States*) in which the Court struck down a federal law that gave states two options for dealing with radioactive waste: either (1) take ownership of all the waste generated within the state's borders, or (2) regulate the waste according to Congress's instructions. How could this be commandeering—protested the government—we gave states a choice! The problem is that it was a choice between two options that Congress had no power to foist upon states. It was as though Congress gave states a "choice" between banning smoking and withdrawing from the Electoral College.

The majority opinion in *New York*—written by Justice O'Connor—rested on firmly originalist grounds. The Constitution does not create a system in which federal laws are to be administered by the states. To the contrary, the Philadelphia delegates decisively rejected the so-called New Jersey Plan, which would have required federal laws "to be carried into execution by the judiciary and executive officers of the respective States." The New Jersey Plan had a major problem: it continued the flawed arrangement that existed under the Articles of Confederation, in which Congress was left having to beg or coerce the states to implement national laws.

The government made the same argument that FDR's men had made in *Schechter Poultry*—that a national "crisis" (this time, radioactive waste rather than the Depression) demanded federal intervention in state affairs. But O'Connor rejected the argument, wisely pointing out that "the Constitution protects us from our own best intentions. It divides power . . . precisely so that we may resist the temptation to concentrate power in one location as an expedient solution to the crisis of the day."

In a later decision, the Court also struck down parts of the Brady Handgun Violence Prevention Act that required local law enforcement officials to conduct background checks on prospective gun purchasers (*Printz v. United States*, 1997). Just as Congress cannot force states to adopt particular internal policies, it also cannot "commandeer" state employees to administer federal laws. Again, the majority cited founding-era evidence that the Constitution does not authorize the federal government to act through the states. In Federalist No. 36, for example, Hamilton suggested that the federal government may attract the services of state officers— but only by paying them higher wages ("an accumulation of their emoluments," as he delicately put it). In dissent, the liberal justice Stephen Breyer did not present any contrary evidence of original understanding, but he did point out that federations such as Switzerland, Germany, and the European Union all act through their member states. All in a day's work for a justice who looks to the Supreme Court of Zimbabwe for guidance (see chapter 10).

GENEROUS, TO A FAULT

The anti-commandeering principle, unfortunately, covers only extreme cases. There is more than one way to coerce a state, and the most common method is not "commandeering" but bribery. I don't literally mean envelope-under-the-table bribery, but then, there's no need for skullduggery when federal grants are to be had.

In 2007 federal grants accounted for 28.7 percent of all state revenues. By 2010—after the Obama administration's "stimulus" legislation (the American Recovery and Reinvestment Act)—the percentage had risen to 35.5 percent, or $553 billion. Back in 1947, the total was $1.4 billion, and that was after all the New Deal programs had been implemented. Today, politicians at all levels are addicted to federal grants. For congressmen, they fund pork-barrel projects back home; for state officials, they plug perennial budget gaps.

But there's a catch. Congress doesn't just give away money. Virtually all federal grants are "conditional"; that is, they require the receiving state to adopt some particular policy designed in Washington. Is that commandeering? Of course it is. The "whole point" of conditional grants, according to law professor Ilya Somin, is to "give state governments an incentive to implement policies they would not adopt of their own independent volition."

"Incentive" is putting it mildly. What politician in his right mind turns down "free" money? Since state taxpayers are contributing to the federal treasury, any state that refuses to accept a grant is "in effect subsidizing its competitors," as Somin points out. To call conditional grants "voluntary" is like calling Social Security voluntary: you have to pay into the system your whole life, but you're free to turn down the benefits. Or look at it this way: Would Pennsylvania and other states have dared to resist the Fugitive Slave Act if they depended on Washington for a third of their revenues?

Nothing in the Constitution authorizes the federal government to kill the states with kindness. Congress has no power to underwrite state treasuries. Even the power to provide for the "General Welfare" (Article I, Section 8) is no help, since it was understood that the *general* welfare meant *national* welfare, and not individual state budgets. In fact, at the Philadelphia convention, a proposal was made to empower the federal government to pay "the debts . . . of the several States"—a proposal that would have been completely unnecessary if anyone thought that the general welfare clause already covered federal subsidies to states. And the delegates rejected that proposal. Later on, when the federal government did "assume" the states' debts, it was the result of a grand political bargain. Nobody suggested that the move was authorized by the general welfare clause.

No court has ever stopped Congress from coercing the states with money, but occasionally presidents have. In 1854 President Franklin Pierce—that sadly overlooked New Englander—vetoed a bill that would have granted ten million acres of land to the states on the condition that the income from the land be used to care for the "indigent insane." It was a "worthy" object, Pierce wrote in his veto message, but Congress simply had no authority to deal with "idiocy." None of the enumerated powers "touches the subject," he wrote. With amazing foresight, Pierce predicted that the natural temptation of states to accept federal largesse would end up turning them into "humble suppliants for the bounty of the Federal Government, reversing their true relations to the Union."

Nowadays, the federal government has no qualms about dealing with idiocy; in fact, it's something of a specialty. Congress has used its power of the purse to force states to adopt innumerable policies, including "Buy American" rules, historic preservation standards, and specific eligibility requirements for unemployment benefits. Congress even passed an amendment to its 2009 stimulus legislation that changed each state's internal budget process, giving legislatures new powers to override their governors.

The path for all this nonsense was cleared by the Supreme Court's 1937 decision in *Charles Steward Machine Co. v. Davis*. That case involved a New Deal program that forced states to set up unemployment compensation schemes according to federal specifications. As long as a state obeyed the mandate, companies within the state would get a 90 percent refund on certain federal taxes; if the state refused, companies would get nothing back. In a five-to-four decision—what liberals call a "razor-thin" majority when they don't like the outcome—the Court rejected the contention that the unemployment program was coercive. The dissenting justices correctly saw it as an unconstitutional invasion of state sovereignty, but they were one vote shy.

Thanks to conditional grants, a twenty-year-old marine on break from his or her duties cannot legally order a beer in any state. Any state that sets a drinking age lower than twenty-one loses every penny of its federal highway funding. That result was upheld by the Supreme Court in 1987 in *South Dakota v. Dole*. The *Dole* Court said that Congress had the power to dictate drinking age policies to states under the general welfare clause because such a condition was "not . . . unrelated" to the federal interest in highway funding. The drinking age is "not unrelated" to federal highways, according to the Court, because it affects the number of drunk drivers. Just try to follow the logic: because Congress has the power to create interstate highways (itself a dubious conclusion), it also has an interest in reducing drunk driving, and, therefore, it can require states to adopt any policy that might reduce drunk driving, even indirectly. Presumably the feds could mandate exactly what Breathalyzers state troopers use. For all I know, they do.

The *Dole* Court did concede that federal "inducements" could become so heavy-handed that at some point "pressure turns into compulsion"—and compulsion would be unconstitutional. That point, however, remains purely hypothetical. To date, not a single court has struck down a conditional federal grant program on the compulsion principle of *Dole*. In 2011 Chief Judge Joel Dubina of the Eleventh Circuit declared it a "mystery" why so many federal courts have "cast aside" their duty to apply the compulsion principle.

In 2012, the Supreme Court finally applied the compulsion principle. In its otherwise disastrous decision upholding the Affordable Care Act, the Court held that Congress had attempted to coerce the states to agree to a massive expansion of their Medicaid programs—swelling the Medicaid population by an estimated 17 million individuals by 2017. States stand to have to pay for part of the fees and all of the administrative expenses caused by this expansion. But if a state refuses to implement the new policy, it will lose every penny of its Medicaid funding. That, said the Court, went too far.

But we cannot rely on judicial vigilance for enforcement of the Tenth Amendment. The dominant idea in the courts remains the *Garcia* concept that states must rely on "procedural safeguards" to protect their sovereignty. So be it: the long-term solution to federal coercion is to restore the safeguard that was abolished in 1913 with the adoption of the Seventeenth Amendment. Before the Seventeenth Amendment, "the now widespread Washington practice of commandeering the States . . . would have been unthinkable," according to Professor Zywicki. Repealing the Seventeenth Amendment would restore the Senate as the guardian of states' rights.

It is, unfortunately, highly unlikely that two-thirds of both Houses of Congress would agree to any amendment that would threaten federal hegemony. To repeal the Seventeenth Amendment—or to make other changes to rein in Washington—the people must resort to the other method that the Constitution provides for making amendments: a national convention. As luck would have it, that is the topic of the next chapter.

CHAPTER TWELVE

COME THE
REVOLUTION

Time for a New Convention

On the Application of the Legislatures of two-thirds of
the several States, [Congress] shall call a Convention for
proposing Amendments.

—ARTICLE V

LIEUTENANT HIROO ONODA WAS THE last officer of the Imperial Japanese Army to lay down his arms after the end of
World War II. He finally gave up the fight in March 1974. For
nearly thirty years, Onoda had conducted guerrilla operations
against the locals on Lubang Island in the Philippines, dismissing reports of Japanese surrender as enemy propaganda. When
he was finally discovered hiding out in the jungle, Onoda explained that he was still awaiting orders from the imperial high
command.

If you're an originalist, you might feel a little bit like Lieutenant Onoda: doggedly fighting a war that was lost years ago.
The mainstream pundits, at any rate, will do their best to convince you that you're just as deluded as poor old Onoda-san if

you insist on fidelity to a document that is, like the Japanese emperor, essentially symbolic.

But there is no need for us to surrender. Not yet, anyhow. It is still possible for the forces of limited government and state sovereignty to win. It is still possible to awaken the power of property rights and other dormant liberties. It is, in short, possible to bring back the spirit of the Founders' Constitution—the Naked Constitution.

How? Not by asking the three branches of the federal government to reform themselves, that's for sure. Originalists should, of course, try to elect constitutional conservatives to the White House and Congress, and then press them to appoint originalist judges to the bench. But we know from experience that such a strategy will only change things at the margins. Conservative judges are excessively devoted to the concept of *stare decisis* (see chapter 5), meaning that it's too late to expect the courts to restrict the federal government to its enumerated powers. The Supreme Court could not even bring itself to strike down the Obama health care law; it's not likely to disturb the precedents that have turned the commerce clause into a blank check for Congress. Nor has the Court shown any appetite for restoring the state/federal balance of power in any meaningful way.

Congress is worse. Even the most conservative politicians give in to the temptations of big government. Under the "compassionate conservatism" of President George W. Bush, government spending skyrocketed, including an expansion of Medicare and increased federal meddling in education (not one of the enumerated powers). In the 2012 Republican presidential primaries, Congressman Ron Paul—a self-proclaimed libertarian—found himself having to defend his long-standing support of pork-barrel "earmarks."

HOPE AND CHANGE—THE
CONSTITUTIONAL WAY

Paradoxically, the best way to save the Constitution is to change it—very carefully, and without any help from Congress, thank you very much. Article V of the Constitution provides two methods for amending the document. One is what I call the congressional method: Congress proposes an amendment by a two-thirds vote of both Houses, and then the states ratify it, if three-fourths of the states agree. That is the method that has been used for all twenty-seven of the existing amendments.

But what if Congress is the problem? The congressional method won't help. The framers foresaw this and provided an alternative process for making amendments: what I call the "convention method." Under the convention method, if two-thirds of the state legislatures request a "Convention for proposing Amendments," then Congress "shall" summon such a convention. "Nothing in this particular is left to discretion," as Alexander Hamilton explained in Federalist No. 85: if the states request a convention, the Congress is "obliged" to call one. If the convention succeeds in proposing amendments, then ratification works the same as in the congressional method; that is, three-fourths of the states must agree to the amendments before they take effect.

The original meaning of the convention method is clear: it was understood as a safety valve that would allow the states to bring about change when Congress was too lazy, or too corrupt, to do so. At the Rhode Island ratifying convention, delegate William Barton said that the convention proviso "ought to be written in Letters of Gold," since it afforded states a "fair opportunity" to rein in the central government.

If there is one thing that both Left and Right agree on, it

is that Congress is too lazy, or corrupt, or both, to bring about real reform. In his book *Republic, Lost*, Professor Larry Lessig—a liberal whose views on executive power I criticize in chapter 4—explains that he agrees with members of the Tea Party "about certain fundamentals: that it is a republic we have inherited; that it ought to be responsive to 'the People alone'; that this one is not." Because of this Left-Right convergence, Lessig argues that the time has come for an Article V convention.

In recent years, organizations have sprung up across America to advocate a convention: ConventionUSA.org, CallAConvention.org, Friends of the Article V Convention (foavc.org), and so on. These groups are attracting supporters among liberals, conservatives, and independents. In September 2011, Harvard Law School held a conference on the feasibility of an Article V convention—cohosted by Lessig and Mark Meckler, the cofounder of the Tea Party Patriots. Many in the Occupy Wall Street movement are also pushing for an Article V convention.

The various boosters of an Article V convention may not share the same ultimate goals, but that's the beauty of it: they don't have to. As Lessig observes, people across the ideological spectrum can "agree on the need for a convention without agreeing on the particular proposals that a convention should recommend." More and more, people are agreeing on the need for a convention because the traditional method of amending the Constitution—the congressional method—won't produce changes to the way Congress does business. Two-thirds of both Houses will never agree to revoke privileges that the members currently enjoy. But the people can.

The potential remedies vary. For many liberals, the answer to corruption in politics is to enact a campaign finance amendment. For me—and other conservatives—the best way to reduce government corruption is to reduce government power ("Power corrupts," as Lord Acton observed) by reinforcing constitutional restraints. Give Congress less money to redistribute and fewer sinecures to dish out, and there will be less graft.

AMENDMENTS FIT FOR A NAKED CONSTITUTION

What kind of amendments might put the Naked Constitution back in action? At first blush, it seems like all we have to do is clarify the magnificent language that is already there. As long ago as 1832, the Georgia legislature proposed a convention that would, among other things, revise Article I so that the enumerated powers of the federal government could be "more distinctly defined." More recently, Professor Glenn Harlan Reynolds half-jokingly suggested that we strengthen the Ninth and Tenth Amendments by adding the phrase: *"And we really mean it!"*

No question, it would be nice to add a little oomph to some of the framers' provisions. We could, for example, explicitly protect the right to earn an honest living, or explicitly protect private property against regulatory takings, even though, as I have argued, both concepts are already embedded in the original meaning of the text. Some interpretive provisions might make sense. But the problem with mere wordsmithing is that activist courts can twist any descriptive phrase to suit their purposes. Even with Reynolds's emphatic "And we really mean it!" we'd be back where we started in a few short years.

What's needed is structural change; that is, amendments that will embed constitutional principles into the very workings of government. I do not mean to suggest that the Constitution binds us only at the level of abstract principles—an argument often advanced by Living Constitution scholars. To the contrary, every word of the Constitution is binding, right down to concrete phrases like "commerce . . . among the several States." But since there is little chance of getting most judges and politicians to adhere to original meaning, the next best thing is to change the constitutional structure in a way that produces results as close as possible to the Founders' vision.

Most of the amendments ratified by the congressional method have been structural, but they have tended to tip the balance of power in favor of Washington. The Sixteenth Amendment, for example, gave Congress vast new resources by authorizing a national income tax, and then the Seventeenth Amendment deprived the state legislatures of any direct voice in how all that money was to be spent. Restoring the constitutional balance is a vital task, and there are a variety of possible means to achieve this. The specifics, of course, would be up to the convention. But since you're asking, here are my personal favorites:

A balanced budget

According to a 2011 CNN poll, 74 percent of Americans favor a constitutional amendment to require a balanced federal budget—a level of support that has been fairly consistent for years. Most state constitutions already mandate balanced budgets. The problem with the states, however, is that they tend to balance their budgets with massive cash infusions from Washington (see chapter 11). A balanced budget amendment would dramatically change the landscape at both the federal and state levels. It's hard to imagine any single amendment that would be more effective at forcing the federal government to trim down to something resembling the enumerated powers (chapter 3).

The Repeal Amendment

Championed by Georgetown University professor Randy Barnett, this is one of the most interesting proposals in recent years. Under the amendment—which at least some members of Congress have endorsed—any federal law or regulation could be repealed by a vote of the legislatures of two-thirds of the states. The Repeal Amendment would help to strengthen federalism (see chapter 11), and to rein in the administrative state (see chapter 4), since it allows for the repeal of regulations as well as statutes.

The House of Repeal

A more amusing, though perhaps less likely, variant on the Repeal Amendment, the House of Repeal has been suggested by Professor Reynolds, based on a concept first articulated by science fiction author Robert Heinlein. The basic idea is to create a new chamber of Congress whose sole function would be to repeal laws. As Reynolds explains, such a chamber would finally "give *someone* in the federal government an incentive to give us *less* law rather than more."

The line-item veto

This amendment would empower a president to veto particular congressional appropriations—perhaps only if the budget is out of balance. It is another tool to enforce limited government, but it also addresses the tendency of Congress to undermine the "unitary executive" (chapter 4). The president could surgically remove legislative provisions that create or fund "independent" bureaucratic fiefdoms beyond his control.

Presidential control of the executive

A more direct way to restore the unitary executive is to use the amendment process to overturn cases like *Humphrey's Execu-*

tor and *Morrison v. Olson* (see chapter 4). Such an amendment would provide that the heads of all departments, agencies, and similar bodies charged with executing the law can be removed "at will" by the president. No more lifetime sinecures for unaccountable bureaucrats.

Term limits

We have term limits for the president; why not for members of Congress? Various proposals have been made, but a good example is the amendment introduced in 2011 by Senator Jim De-Mint: it would limit House members to three terms and senators to two. Once upon a time, it was quite common for citizens to spend some time in Congress and then return to the private sector. Today, Congress is a career. To stay in power, you have to get that new light rail project in your district, which means—fair's fair—you have to support the pet projects of the other 534 members. The longer congressmen stay inside the Beltway, the less receptive they are to the idea of putting limits on federal power. There's academic research to show this—such as the 1991 study by James Payne, *The Culture of Spending*—but it's also obvious to anyone who listens to a long-serving politician. In the summer of 2010, for example, Representative Pete Stark, a forty-year veteran of the House, told a town hall meeting that "the federal Government can do most anything in this country." And to Stark, that was a *good* thing.

Getting rid of the Seventeenth Amendment

The arguments for this proposal are summarized in the previous chapter. In short, the Seventeenth Amendment requires that senators be elected by popular vote rather than by the state legislatures. The amendment was ratified in 1913 with the best of intentions, but nobody foresaw that the federal government would usurp the powers that traditionally belonged to the states. In recent decades, the Supreme Court has generally refused to enforce the Tenth Amendment, taking the position that the states must fend for themselves in the political process. But unfortunately, states have no direct role in the federal political process. Repealing the Seventeenth Amendment would cure that. To those who argue that it would be "undemocratic" to have senators chosen by legislatures, I say: get over it. The Senate is inherently undemocratic: Delaware has as many votes in the Senate as California. That's not a bad thing. As law professor Todd Zywicki has written, the Constitution "did not create a democracy; it established a constitutional republic. Its goal was to preserve liberty, not to maximize popular sovereignty. . . . The framers provided that the power of various political actors would derive from different sources."

AND THAT'S JUST FOR STARTERS. There are other proposals worth considering. A "human life amendment," for example, would make a future *Roe v. Wade* impossible. But such an amendment—like proposed amendments to define marriage or protect the flag—would involve changing original meaning, not restoring it. As I argue in chapter 2, the Founders did not consider the unborn to be constitutional persons. To be sure, there are legitimate reasons to change the meaning of *person* in the Fifth and Fourteenth Amendments, and an amendment (not an activist decision) is the right way to go about it. On the other hand, a human life amendment would mean that abortion would remain a federal, rather than state, issue. It would be nice to have a national convention, rather than nine unelected justices, debate these issues.

IT'S NEVER BEEN DONE—OR MAYBE IT HAS

To pull off an Article V convention, there would have to be applications from thirty-four states, which is a tall order, but not as tall as you might think. The fact that there has never been an Article V convention may reflect congressional resistance more than a lack of demand from the states. It has been estimated that since 1789, there have been over seven hundred Article V applications from state legislatures. I say "estimated" because Congress has never kept track of incoming convention applications. As Lincoln Caplan observed in his 1988 book *Constitutional Brinksmanship*, "there exists no official catalogue of the applications adopted by the states." The catalogue still doesn't exist.

According to some, Congress has already abdicated its duty to call a convention. In 1929 Senator John J. Blaine presented a joint resolution of the Wisconsin legislature, pointing out that thirty-five states—more than two-thirds—had filed Article V applications with Congress. The resolution was referred to the Senate Judiciary Committee and never heard from again.

By the early 1980s, thirty-two states had applied for a convention to consider a balanced budget amendment. That was two states shy of the magic thirty-four, but there's more to the story. In a 1990 law review article, federal judge Bruce Van Sickle pointed out that a total of forty-six states had applied for an Article V convention for various purposes (including balanced budget), but none of the applications objected to combining two or more topics in the same convention. On top of that, there were seventeen outstanding Article V applications that did not specify any agenda at all. Nowhere in Article V is there any suggestion that a convention must be limited to a single topic; to the contrary, the text refers to a convention for proposing "amendments"—plural.

If Congress receives applications from two-thirds of the states for a convention, with some of the applications citing topic A and some citing topic B, wouldn't it make sense to call a convention to consider topics A *and* B? That was Judge Van Sickle's conclusion; he argued that Congress was under a "present duty" to call a convention.

Congress, evidently, felt otherwise. The ruling assumption in Washington in the 1980s was that there was no obligation to call a convention unless thirty-four states passed nearly identical balanced budget applications. When the states got close to that number, Congress moved to short-circuit the process by passing the Gramm-Rudman-Hollings Act of 1985, which required that the federal budget be balanced by 1991. To anyone who thinks that a mere congressional statute can take the place of a constitutional amendment, one has to ask: How's that Gramm-Rudman thing working out for you? Not very well. The bill was partially overturned by the Supreme Court in 1986, then amended by Congress, and ultimately repealed. Apart from a brief period in the late 1990s, deficit spending has continued to grow.

Given this sorry history, perhaps the first thing an Article V convention should do is fix Article V itself—by removing Congress as the gatekeeper for future amendments. In a January 2012 policy analysis for the Cato Institute, law professor Michael Rappaport persuasively advocated reforming Article V to allow two-thirds of the states to propose a constitutional amendment, which could then be directly ratified by three-fourths of the states, without having to wait for Congress to call a convention. As Rappaport points out, with Congress's decisive role in the current scheme, it is "virtually impossible" to limit the federal government in ways that Congress opposes.

BIPARTISAN FEARMONGERING

Congress is not the only institution that fears an Article V convention. Supporters of the status quo will always "campaign furiously" against such a project, as Goldwater Institute fellow Rob Natelson observed in a detailed study of the convention method. Structural change is a bother: it throws into question the whole cozy world of federal entitlements, corporate welfare, and state grants. One hardly knows whom to bribe. Whenever there is serious talk of an Article V convention, therefore, a raft of familiar arguments get trotted out.

One argument, already mentioned, is that all Article V applications must specify the same topic. Nonsense. Another is that Article V applications grow stale after a certain, unspecified number of years. Indeed, at least one law professor claimed (in 1963) that Article V itself had grown stale—the failure of Congress to call a convention meant that the convention proviso is "no longer of any effect." But there's nothing in Article V that puts an expiration date on state applications, or on the convention method itself. There's no time limit on amendments proposed by the *congressional* method. The Twenty-Seventh Amendment was ratified 203 years after it was first proposed by Congress.

The most common—and most ridiculous—argument against an Article V convention is that it would become a "runaway convention." The "runaway" trope begins with the idea that the convention would exceed its mandate; that is, even if Congress calls a convention, say, to consider a balanced budget amendment, the convention might decide to consider a campaign finance amendment as well. That much I'll concede. In fact, Congress should *not* be able to control the agenda of an Article V convention. The whole point of such a convention is to give the people a forum to consider constitutional changes without congressional control. The delegates to such a convention would be the direct representatives of the people; they should set their own agenda.

But somehow, the prospect of a convention setting its own agenda leads extremists on both Left and Right to concoct a nightmare scenario in which an Article V convention could somehow impose all sorts of wacky amendments. During the balanced budget debate of the 1980s, Arthur J. Goldberg, a liberal former Supreme Court justice, warned that an Article V convention would be a "runaway convention" that could "mak[e] wholesale changes to our Constitution and Bill of Rights." The whole process, said Goldberg, is "an uncharted and volatile course shrouded in legal, political and procedural difficulties." Using much the same rhetoric, Phyllis Schlafly, founder of the conservative Eagle Forum, predicted that an Article V convention would take us "along a road our nation has never traveled before," leading to "constitutional chaos, controversy, and confrontation." Good alliteration, Phyllis, but bad logic. Remember, a convention would have no power to make any changes to the Constitution; all it could do is *propose* amendments. The proposals would not become part of the Constitution unless ratified by three-fourths of the states; in other words, thirty-eight states. Any proposal that could win approval by both houses of thirty-eight state legislatures would have to be compelling. As Professor Lessig argues, it would have to be "an incredible proposal" that could "cut across both Left and Right."

And yet I suspect there is a lingering fear that an Article V convention could somehow find a way to get around the ratification process and foist its wishes on an unwilling public. Granted, a situation in which a small group of powerful men and women can change the Constitution without the requisite formalities is a terrifying prospect. It is also a perfect description of the status quo. We *already* suffer from a runaway Congress and runaway courts. A runaway convention is the least of our worries.

MOST AMERICANS—EVEN THOSE WHO DON'T consider themselves originalists—think that the Founding Fathers were onto a good thing, and that our country has deviated from their original design. Despite that popular feeling, federal officials consistently ignore the Constitution because there are powerful incentives to do so. We can't change human nature, but we can change incentives through structural amendments. That is what an Article V convention can achieve.

There are plenty of ways to support an Article V convention, if you're so inclined. The convention applications have to come from the states, so you can start by asking your state legislators to sign an Article V pledge, i.e., a promise to support an Article V application. If they refuse, see if their opponents will sign the pledge at election time. You can also join any of the groups I mentioned earlier.

Conditions have never been so favorable to an Article V convention. Until recently, the convention movement was led almost exclusively by conservatives, often motivated by a desire to undo the extreme rulings of the Warren Court. Liberals saw no need for a convention—why go to the trouble of amending the Constitution when activist courts can do it for you? But now that the Supreme Court has become somewhat more conservative (everything is relative), liberals recognize that they cannot necessarily depend on the judiciary to do their bidding. As I noted at the beginning of this book, it has always been a fallacy to think that the Living Constitution is invariably a "progressive" tool. If you invite judges to rewrite the Constitution, more than a few alleged conservatives will accept the invitation.

That's not to say that all liberals see the need for an Article V convention, even now. Many, perhaps most, of the mainstream professors and pundits continue to believe in the power of courts and Congress to change the Constitution by fiat—the people be damned. These voices of conventional wisdom delight in portraying originalists as hopeless fanatics—latter-day Lieutenant Onodas.

But maybe *we're* not the ones who are deluded. As more and more people agree on the need to return to constitutional first principles, perhaps it is the defenders of the status quo who most resemble Onoda: grimly fighting a rearguard action against inexorable change. The only difference is that instead of Onoda's all-powerful emperor, today's holdouts have pledged eternal loyalty to the Great Living Constitution. But as you and I both know, that particular emperor has no clothes.

ACKNOWLEDGMENTS

Let me start by thanking my friends and colleagues at Ricochet.com, especially co-founders Rob Long and Peter Robinson. Although I have been writing about law for many years, it was only on Ricochet that I found my voice, as well as a community that is endlessly supportive and thought-provoking. My fellow contributors, including professors Richard Epstein and John Yoo, keep me on my toes, while editor Diane Ellis is always ready with help and suggestions.

For ideas, inspiration, and assistance with my related Constitution podcasts, thanks go to Scott Immergut, Ed Whelan, James Poulos, Joe Escalante, K. D. Lee, Victor Davis Hanson, Randy Barnett, Paul Rahe, Eugene Volokh, Walter Olson, Andrew Klavan, Piero Tozzi, James Delingpole, Paul Sherman, and Bob McNamara.

I am grateful for the outstanding work of my two research assistants, Michael Miller and Kathleen Hunker. These are two first-rate legal minds, and I am sure you will be hearing more from them in the future.

Throughout this journey, my intrepid agent, Geri Thoma, has been a friend, sounding board, strategist, and cheerleader. At HarperCollins, it's been my great fortune to have Adam Bellow as an editor. A gentleman and a scholar, Adam has been my guide from the smallest detail to the big-picture items. Also at

HarperCollins, editor Kate Whitenight has been consistently patient and astute in the face of my countless questions, while copy editor Miranda Ottewell wielded a discerning pencil.

For their support and encouragement—even when they vehemently disagree with me—I am thankful to have such loyal friends as Bart Aronson and Mila Zain, Cole Aronson, Jonah Aronson, Arne and Debra Christensen, Zachary Karabell and Nicole Alger, Robert Lieberman and Lauren Osborne, Murdock Martin, Tim Naftali, Gideon Rose and Sheri Berman, Dan Staley, Erik and Ann Tozzi, Alexi Worth and Erika Belsey Worth, Arshad and Ann Stock Zakaria, Fareed and Paula Zakaria, George Zanjani and Jennifer Simon, and Jonathan Zasloff.

I'm thankful for the enthusiastic support of parents and siblings, and for the moments of pure joy provided by my two children, Cecilia and Fiona. But most of all, I am eternally grateful to my wife, Kathleen, whose wisdom, advice, and encouragement make everything possible.

SELECT BIBLIOGRAPHY

Works Cited or Consulted Throughout

Blackstone, William, Sir. *Commentaries on the Laws of England.* Oxford, 1765–1769. In *The Avalon Project at Yale Law School.* http://avalon.law.yale.edu/subject_menus/blackstone.asp.

Bork, Robert. *The Tempting of America: The Political Seduction of the Law.* New York: Free Press, 1990.

Constitution of the United States. http://www.house.gov/house/Constitution/Constitution.html.

Farrand, Max, ed. *The Records of the Federal Convention of 1787,* rev. ed. 1966. http://memory.loc.gov/ammem/amlaw/lwfr.html.

Fisher, Sydney George. *The Evolution of the Constitution.* Philadelphia: Lippincott, 1897.

Johnson, Samuel. *A Dictionary of the English Language.* 6th ed. London, 1785. http://openlibrary.org/books/OL7029571M/A_dictionary_of_the_English_language.

Kurland, Philip B., and Ralph Lerner, eds. *The Founders' Constitution.* Chicago: Univ. of Chicago Press, 1987. http://press-pubs.uchicago.edu/founders/.

Levy, Robert, and William Mellor. *The Dirty Dozen: How Twelve Supreme Court Cases Radically Expanded Government and Eroded Freedom.* New York: Sentinel, 2008.

Rossiter, Clinton, ed. *The Federalist Papers*. New York: Mentor, 1999.

Rutland, Robert Allen. *The Birth of the Bill of Rights, 1776–1791*. Chapel Hill: Univ. of North Carolina Press, 1955.

Tucker, St. George. *Blackstone's Commentaries: With Notes of Reference to the Constitution and Laws of the Federal Government of the United States and of the Commonwealth of Virginia*. 5 vols. Philadelphia, 1803. Reprint, South Hackensack, NJ: Rothman Reprints, 1969.

Woods, Thomas E., and Kevin R. C. Gutzman. *Who Killed the Constitution?: The Fate of American Liberty from World War I to George W. Bush*. New York: Crown Forum, 2008.

Chapter One: Is Homework Constitutional?

Berger, Raoul. *Federalism: The Founders' Design*. Norman: Univ. of Oklahoma Press, 1987.

Brest, Paul. "The Misconceived Quest for the Original Understanding." *Boston University Law Review* 60 (1980), 204.

Corwin, Edward S. *The Twilight of the Supreme Court*. New Haven: Yale Univ. Press, 1934. Reprint, Hamden, CT: Archon 1970.

Strauss, David. *The Living Constitution*. New York: Oxford University Press, 2010.

Tribe, Laurence, and Michael Dorf. *On Reading the Constitution*. Cambridge, MA: Harvard Univ. Press, 1991.

Wilson, Woodrow. "What Is Progress?" In *The New Freedom*. 2nd ed. New York: Doubleday, Page & Company, 1921.

Chapter Two: We the People

Adams, Willi Paul. *The First American Constitutions*. Lanham, MD: Madison House, 2001.

Amar, Akhil Reed. *America's Constitution: A Biography*. New York: Random House, 2006.

Amar, Akhil Reed, and Alan Hirsch. *For the People: What the Constitution Really Says About Your Rights*. New York: Simon & Schuster, 1998.

Eastman, John. "From Feudalism to Consent: Rethinking Birthright Citizenship." Heritage Foundation Legal Memorandum No. 18, March 30, 2006.

Smith, Mark W. *Disrobed: The New Battle Plan to Break the Left's Stranglehold on the Courts*. New York: Crown Forum, 2006.

Stockman, Farah. "Lawyers Make Huge Pro Bono Effort for Guantánamo Bay Detainees." *New York Times*, July 2, 2008.

Tribe, Laurence. "Ten Lessons Our Constitutional Experience Can Teach Us About the Puzzle of Animal Rights: The Work of Steven M. Wise." *Animal Law* 7 (2001), 1.

Wise, Steven M. *Rattling the Cage: Toward Legal Rights for Animals*. New York: Perseus Books, 2000.

Chapter Three: Congress

Barnett, Randy. *Restoring the Lost Constitution*. Princeton, NJ: Princeton Univ. Press, 2004.

——. "The Original Meaning of the Commerce Clause." *Univ. of Chicago Law Review* 68 (2001), 101.

Comeback America Initiative. "Fiscal Facts Presentation." http://www.tcaii.org/UploadedFiles/PresentationNotesFinal.pdf.

DiLorenzo, Thomas. *Hamilton's Curse*. New York: Crown Forum, 2008.

Lash, Kurt T. "Resolution VI: The Virginia Plan and Authority to Resolve 'Collective Action Problems' Under Article I, Section 8." Illinois Public Law and Legal Theory Research Papers Series No. 10-40, August 2011.

Lieberman, Jethro. *The Evolving Constitution*. New York: Random House, 1992.

Natelson, Robert. "The Agency Law Origins of the Necessary and Proper Clause." *Case Western Reserve Law Review* 55 (2004), 243.

Rossiter, Clinton. *Alexander Hamilton and the Constitution*. New York: Harcourt, Brace & World, 1964.

Walker, David M. *Comeback America: Turning the Country Around and Restoring Fiscal Responsibility*. New York: Random House, 2010.

Will, George. *Restoration: Congress, Term Limits, and the Recovery of Deliberative Democracy*. New York: Free Press, 1992.

Chapter Four: The President

Bader, Hans. "Free Enterprise Fund v. PCAOB: Narrow Separation-of-Powers Ruling Illustrates That the Supreme Court Is Not 'Pro-Business.'" *Cato Supreme Court Review* (September 16, 2010), 269.

Beckstead, Brad. "Small Audit Firm Prevails Over Big Government" (Press Release). February 22, 2010. http://www. becksteadwatts .com.

Belz, Herman. *A Living Constitution or a Fundamental Law*. New York: Rowman & Littlefield, 1998.

Buckley, James. *Freedom at Risk*. New York: Encounter Books, 2010.

Calabresi, Steven, and Saikrishna Prakash. "The President's Power to Execute the Laws." *Yale Law Journal* 104 (1994), 541.

Calabresi, Steven, and Christopher Yoo. *The Unitary Executive: Presidential Power from Washington to Bush*. New Haven, CT: Yale Univ. Press, 2008.

Coglianese, Cary. "Presidential Control of Administrative Agencies: A Debate over Law or Politics?" *Univ. of Pennsylvania Journal of Constitutional Law* 12 (2010), 637.

Delahunty, Robert, and John Yoo. "Making War." *Cornell Law Review* 93 (2007–8), 123.

Epstein, Richard. "Executive Power, the Commander in Chief, and the Militia Clause." *Hofstra Law Review* 34 (2005–6), 317.

———. "Why the Modern Administrative State Is Inconsistent with the Rule of Law." *New York Univ. Journal of Law and Liberty* 3 (2008), 491.

Hardin, Charles M. *Presidential Power and Accountability: Toward a New Constitution*. Chicago: Univ. of Chicago Press, 1974.

Lessig, Lawrence, and Cass Sunstein. "The President and the Administration." *Columbia Law Review* 94 (1994), 2.

Olson, Theodore. "The Impetuous Vortex: Congressional Erosion of Presidential Authority." In *The Fettered Presidency*, edited by L. Gordon Crovitz and Jeremy Rabkin, 225–44. Washington, DC: American Enterprise Institute for Public Policy Research, 1989.

Prakash, Saikrishna. "The Essential Meaning of Executive Power." *Univ. of Illinois Law Review* 3 (2003), 701.

———. "Unleashing the Dogs of War: What the Constitution Means by 'Declare War.'" *Cornell Law Review* 93 (2007–8), 45.

Savage, Charlie. "Barack Obama's Q&A." *Boston Globe*, December 20, 2007. http://www.boston.com/news/politics/2008/specials/CandidateQA/ObamaQA/.

Schlesinger, Arthur M. *The Imperial Presidency*. 2nd ed. Boston: Houghton Mifflin, 1973.

Taft, William Howard. *Our Chief Magistrate and His Powers*, 2nd ed. New York: Columbia Univ. Press, 1925.

Wilson, Woodrow. "The Study of Administration." *Political Science Quarterly* 2 (June 1887), 197. http://www.jstor.org/stable/2139277.

Wood, Gordon. *The Creation of the American Republic, 1776–1787*. Williamsburg, VA: Omohundro Institute, 1969.

Yoo, John. "The President's Constitutional Authority to Conduct Military Operations Against Terrorists and Nations Supporting Them." Memorandum Opinion for the Deputy Counsel to the President, September 25, 2001. http://www.justice.gov/olc/war powers925.htm.

———. *The Powers of War and Peace*. Chicago: Univ. of Chicago Press, 2005.

Chapter Five: The Courts

Calabresi, Steven G. "A Critical Introduction to the Originalism Debate." *Harvard Journal of Law and Public Policy* 31 (2008), 875.

Carey, George. *In Defense of the Constitution*. Indianapolis: Liberty Fund, 1995.

Chayes, Abram. "The Role of the Judge in Public Law Litigation." *Harvard Law Review* 89 (1976), 1281.

Dow, David. *America's Prophets: How Judicial Activism Makes America Great*. Westport, CT: Praeger, 2009.

Graglia, Lino A. *Disaster by Decree: The Supreme Court Decisions on Race and the Schools*. Ithaca, NY: Cornell Univ. Press, 1976.

Powell, H. Jefferson. "The Original Understanding of Original Intent." *Harvard Law Review* 98 (1985), 885.

Quirk, William J., and R. Randall Bridwell. *Judicial Dictatorship*. New Brunswick, NJ: Transaction Publishers, 1995.

Singer, Peter. *Practical Ethics*. 2nd ed. Cambridge, UK: Cambridge Univ. Press, 1993. See also Peter Singer FAQ, www.princeton .edu/~psinger/faq.html.

Wolfe, Christopher. *How to Read the Constitution: Originalism, Constitutional Interpretation, and Judicial Power*. Lanham, MD: Rowman & Littlefield, 1996.

Chapter Six: Freedom of Speech

Bader, Hans. "Free Speech and Hostile Environment 'Harrassment.'" *Federalist Society, Free Speech & Election Law Practice Group Newsletter* 1 (2) (July 1, 1997).

Koontz, Daniel. "Hostile Public Accommodations Laws and the First Amendment." *New York Univ. Journal of Law and Liberty* 3 (2008), 197.

MacKinnon, Catharine A. *Sexual Harassment of Working Women.* New Haven, CT: Yale University Press, 1979.

Madison, James. *Virginia Report of 1799.* www.constitution.org/rf/vr_1799.htm.

McNamee, Mike. "Will Fahrenheit 9/11 Singe Bush?" *Businessweek,* July 12, 2004.

Rucker, Philip. "Citizens United Used 'Hillary: The Movie' to Take on McCain-Feingold." *Washington Post,* January 22, 2010.

Smolla, Rodney. "Rethinking First Amendment Assumptions About Racist and Sexist Speech." *Washington and Lee Law Review* 47 (1990), 171.

Spakovsky, Hans. "Citizens United and the Restoration of the First Amendment." Legal Memorandum No. 50. Heritage Foundation: February 17, 2010.

———. "Leaked: Obama Executive Order Intends to Implement Portions of DISCLOSE Act." PJ Media, April 19, 2011. www.pjmedia.com/blog.

Volokh, Eugene. "What Speech Does 'Hostile Work Environment' Harrassment Law Restrict?" *Georgetown Law Review* 85 (1997), 627.

Chapter Seven: Religion

Bailey, Maureen K. "Contraceptive Insurance Mandates and *Catholic*

Charities v. Superior Court of Sacramento: Towards a New Understanding of Women's Health." *Texas Review of Law and Politics* 9 (2005), 367.

Carter, Stephen L. "The Free Exercise Thereof." *William and Mary Law Review* 38 (1997), 1627.

Corwin, Edward. "The Supreme Court as National School Board." *Law and Contemporary Problems* 14 (1949), 3.

Dreisbach, Daniel L. "The Mythical 'Wall of Separation': How a Misused Metaphor Changed Church-State Law, Policy, and Discourse." Heritage Foundation: First Principles Series, No. 6, June 23, 2006.

Feldman, Noah. "The Intellectual Origins of the Establishment Clause." *New York Univ. Law Review* 77 (2002), 346.

Gallagher, Maggie. "Banned in Boston." *Weekly Standard* (May 15, 2006).

Hall, Mark. "Jeffersonian Walls and Madisonian Lines." *Oregon Law Review* 85 (2006), 563.

Hamburger, Philip. *Separation of Church and State*. Cambridge: Harvard Univ. Press, 2002.

Knicely, James. "First Principles and the Misplacement of the 'Wall of Separation': Too Late in the Day for a Cure?" *Drake Univ. Law Review* 52 (2004), 171.

McConnell, Michael W. "Free Exercise Revisionism and the Smith Decision." *Univ. of Chicago Law Review* 57 (1990), 1109.

Natelson, Robert. "The Original Meaning of the Establishment Clause." *William and Mary Bill of Rights Journal* 14 (2005–6), 73.

Rienzi, Mark L. "The Constitutional Right to Refuse: Roe, Casey, and the Fourteenth Amendment Rights of Healthcare Providers." *Notre Dame Law Review* 87 (2011), 1.

Story, Joseph. *Commentaries on the Constitution*. Boston, 1833. http://constitution.org/js/js_000.htm.

Chapter Eight: To Keep and Bear Arms

Barnett, Randy. "Was the Right to Keep and Bear Arms Conditioned on Service in an Organized Militia?" Review of *The Militia and the Right to Arms, or, How the Second Amendment Fell Silent*, by H. Richard Uviller and William G. Merkel. *Texas Law Review* 83 (2004–5), 237.

Cooley, Thomas. *A Treatise on the Constitutional Limitations which Rest upon the Legislative Power of the States of the American Union*. Boston: Little, Brown and Co.,1868.

Kopel, Dave. "Cooking Up a Collective Right." September 2011. http://davekopel.org/2A/Mags/Collective-Right.html.

Malcolm, Joyce Lee. *To Keep and Bear Arms: The Origins of an Anglo-American Right*. Cambridge, MA: Harvard Univ. Press, 1994.

Mehr, Tina, and Adam Winkler. "The Standardless Second Amendment." American Constitution Society Issue Brief, October 2010.

Somin, Ilya. "Locked Liberties." *Legal Times*, July 28, 2008.

Volokh, Eugene. "Implementing the Right to Keep and Bear Arms for Self-Defense: An Analytical Framework and a Research Agenda." *UCLA Law Review* 56 (2009), 1443.

———. "The Commonplace Second Amendment." *New York Univ. Law Review* 73 (1998), 793.

Wills, Garry. "To Keep and Bear Arms." *New York Review of Books*, September 21, 1995. http://www.nybooks.com/articles/archives/1995/sep/21/to-keep-and-bear-arms.

Chapter Nine: Life, Liberty, and That Other Thing

Claeys, Eric R. "Takings, Regulations, and Natural Property Rights." *Cornell Law Review* 88 (2003), 1549.

Dinan, Stephen. "Feds Shut Down Amish Farm for Selling Fresh Milk." *Washington Times*, February 13, 2012.

Epstein, Richard. "The 'Necessary' History of Property and Liberty." *Chapman Law Review* 6 (2003), 1.

Freddoso, David. *Gangster Government: Barack Obama and the New Washington Thugocracy*. Washington, DC: Regnery, 2011.

Golda, Andrew. "Regulatory Takings and Original Intent: The Direct, Physical Takings Thesis 'Goes Too Far.'" *American Univ. Law Review* 49 (1999), 181.

Harrington, Matthew. "Regulatory Takings and the Original Understanding of the Takings Clause." *Maryland Law Review* 45 (2004), 2053.

Liu, Goodwin. "Rethinking Constitutional Welfare Rights." *Stanford Law Review* 61 (2008), 203.

Pilon, Roger. "The Constitutional Protection of Property Rights: America and Europe." Economic Education Bulletin. American Institute for Economic Research, June 2008. http://www.cato.org/property-rights.

Rogers, James Steven. "The Impairment of Secured Creditors' Rights in Reorganization: A Study of the Relationship between the Fifth Amendment and the Bankruptcy Clause." *Harvard Law Review* 96 (1983), 973.

Sandefur, Timothy. *The Right to Earn a Living: Economic Freedom and the Law*. Washington, DC: Cato Institute, 2010.

Shankman, Kimberly, and Roger Pilon. "Reviving the Privileges and Immunities Clause to Redress the Balance Among States, Individuals, and the Federal Government." Cato Institute Policy Analysis No. 326. November 23, 1998.

Shattuck, Charles E. "The True Meaning of the Term 'Liberty' in those Clauses in the Federal and State Constitutions Which Protect 'Life, Liberty, and Property.'" *Harvard Law Review* 4 (1891), 365.

Siegan, Bernard H. *Economic Liberties and the Constitution*. 2nd ed. New Brunswick, NJ: Transaction Publishers, 2006.

Sunstein, Cass. *The Second Bill of Rights: FDR's Unfinished Revolution and Why We Need It More Than Ever.* New York: Basic Books, 2004.

Warren, Charles. "The New 'Liberty' Under the Fourteenth Amendment." *Harvard Law Review* 39 (1926), 431.

Chapter Ten: Cruel and Unusual

Abramson, Jeffrey. "Death-Is-Different Jurisprudence and the Role of the Capital Jury." *Ohio State Journal of Criminal Law* 2 (2004), 117.

Bowling, Brian. "Prisoner Lawsuits on the Rise as Inmate Population Increases." *Pittsburgh Tribune-Review*, February 15, 2010.

Chipman, Nelson. "The Indiana Death Penalty: An Exercise in Constitutional Futility." *Valparaiso Univ. Law Review* 15 (1981), 409.

Goldberg, Arthur J., and Alan M. Dershowitz. "Declaring the Death Penalty Unconstitutional." *Harvard Law Review* 83 (1969–70), 1773.

Granucci, Anthony F. "'Nor Cruel and Unusual Punishments Inflicted': The Original Meaning." *California Law Review* 57 (1969), 839.

Scalia, Antonin. "Originalism: The Lesser Evil." *Univ. of Cincinnati Law Review* 57 (1989), 849.

———. "Outsourcing American Law: Foreign Law in Constitutional Interpretation." American Enterprise Institute, Working Paper No. 152 (2009). www.aei.org/paper/100034.

Schlanger, Margo. "Inmate Litigation." *Harvard Law Review* 116 (2003), 1557.

Smith, Douglas. "How Cruel and Unusual?" *American Spectator*, June 7, 2010.

Stinneford, John F. "The Original Meaning of 'Unusual': The Eighth

Amendment as a Bar to Cruel Innovation." *Northwestern Univ. Law Review* 102 (2008), 1.

Sullivan, Larry. *The Prison Reform Movement: Forlorn Hope*. Boston: Twayne, 1990.

Chapter Eleven: Federalism

Adler, Jonathan. "Swamp Rules: The End of Federal Wetland Regulation?" *Regulation* 22 (1999), 11.

Carpenter, Amanda. "Sanctuary Cities Embrace Illegal Immigrants." *Human Events*, May 4, 2007. http://www.humanevents.com/article.php?id=20547.

Cox, Archibald. "Federalism and Individual Rights Under the Berger Court." *Northwestern Univ. Law Review* 73 (1978), 1.

Kincaid, John. "State-Federal Relations: Cooperative Coercion." In *The Book of the States 2010*. Lexington, KY: Council of State Governments, 2010.

McAffee, Thomas B., Jay S. Bybee, and Christopher Bryant. *Powers Reserved for the People and the States: A History of the Ninth and Tenth Amendments*. Westport, CT: Praeger, 2006.

Somin, Ilya. "Closing the Pandora's Box of Federalism: The Case for Judicial Restriction of Federal Subsidies to State Governments." *Georgetown Law Journal* 90 (2002), 461.

———. "A False Dawn for Federalism: Clear Statement Rules after *Gonzales v. Raich*." *Cato Supreme Court Review* (2005–6), 113.

Walsh, James H. "Sanctuary Cities, States Undermining the American Republic." *Social Contract* 15 (Spring 2005), 192.

Zywicki, Todd, and Ilya Somin. "Federalism and Separation of Powers: Ramifications of Repealing the 17th Amendment." *Engage* 12 (September 2011), 88.

Chapter Twelve: Come the Revolution

Caplan, Russell L. *Constitutional Brinksmanship: Amending the Constitution by National Convention*. New York: Oxford Univ. Press, 1988.

Lessig, Lawrence. *Republic, Lost: How Money Corrupts Congress—and a Plan to Stop It*. New York: Twelve, 2011.

Natelson, Robert G. "Amending the Constitution by Convention." Goldwater Institute Policy Report. Three-part series. September 16, 2010. http://goldwaterinstitute.org/article/amending-constitution-convention-complete-view-founders-plan-part-1-series.

Reynolds, Glenn Harlan. "Divine Operating System?" *Tennessee Law Review* 78 (2011), 651.

Rogers, James Kenneth. "The Other Way to Amend the Constitution." *Harvard Journal of Law and Public Policy* 30 (2007), 1005.

Swindler, William F. "The Current Challenge to Federalism: The Confederating Proposals." *Georgetown Law Journal* 52 (1963–64), 1.

Van Sickle, Bruce M., and Lynn M. Broughey. "A Lawful and Peaceful Revolution: Article V and Congress' Present Duty to Call a Convention for Proposing Amendments." *Hamline Law Review* 14 (1990), 1.

INDEX

ABOUT THE AUTHOR

ADAM FREEDMAN, one of America's leading commentators on law, holds degrees from Yale, Oxford, and the University of Chicago. A former columnist for the *New York Law Journal*, he covers legal affairs for Ricochet.com and hosts a regular podcast devoted to legal and constitutional issues. He lives in Brooklyn, New York, with his wife and two daughters.